# VICTORIOUS
## IN
# DEFEAT

*wallace brown*

# VICTORIOUS IN DEFEAT

*Not drooping like poor fugitives they came*
*In exodus to our Canadian wilds,*
*But full of heart and hope, with heads erect*
*And fearless eyes, victorious in defeat.*

*william kirby*

*hereward senior*

# The Loyalists in Canada

 *methuen*

*toronto  new york  london  sydney  auckland*

**Canadian Cataloguing in Publication Data**

Brown, Wallace, 1933–
    Victorious in defeat : the Loyalists in Canada

ISBN 0-458-96850-1

1. United Empire Loyalists.*   2. Canada – History –
1763–1867.   I. Senior, Hereward.   II. Title.

FC423.B76 1984      971.02′4      C84-099019-7
E277.B76 1984

Printed and bound in the U.S.A.

1 2 3 4   84   88 87 86 85

# contents

preface    vii

a note on terminology    ix

1 | Neighbour against neighbour: loyalists and the American Revolution    1

2 | No longer alien: the great migration    21

3 | A spot to call our own: land distribution    53

4 | An uncultivated country: land development    69

5 | Foundations laid: loyalist culture    93

6 | Unfinished business: external relations    113

7 | Cursed republican spirit: politics    131

8 | The promised land: black loyalists    169

9 | The loyalist indians: Shaganosh    191

10 | The loyalists in history: epilogue    205

bibliography    213

index    221

"When a man poses before the world—even the Canadian world—in the role of an author, he is expected to step up to the footlights, and explain his purpose in presenting himself before the public in that capacity."

Canniff Haight, 1885.

# *preface*

IN THE BOOK *The Good Americans* Wallace Brown, co-author of this book, attempted to tell the story of the Loyalists—those Americans who opposed independence—from about 1760 until the end of the war in 1783. The present work is a partial sequel since it deals with the history of the exiled Loyalists in their most important haven, Canada. While the first chapter describes the origin of the Loyalists during the Revolution and the last suggests their long-term importance, the heart of the book deals with their arrival and settlement in Canada, from 1783 until the War of 1812.

Like the Loyalists, we regret the Revolution. We are less certain that a victory of the Crown forces would have been for the best. Looking at the past with Ireland in mind, Edmund Burke wrote, at the beginning of the war, "Victory would only vary the mode of our ruin." It could, indeed, have left behind a legacy of hate and bitterness. Yet a glance at conciliatory gestures made during the war and at British policy after 1783 suggests a happier alternative. George Washington might well have been made viceroy of a British American Federation with Jefferson as his prime minister.

One of the Loyalists' complaints was that Britain was more generous to her enemies than to her friends. As it was, those Loyalists—the majority—who remained in the United States made their peace with the Republican regime. Those who fled abroad created new societies in New Brunswick, Ontario, the Bahamas, and Sierra Leone, and made significant contributions to many older ones including Britain, Nova Scotia, Prince Edward Island, and the British West Indies. Traditionally in American history the Loyalists are "losers," but in exile their history is much more constructive, and, as the English-speaking founding fathers, they are second only to the French in the development of Canada. Yet they have rarely received credit, partly because of exaggerated claims by their descendants and an unfair linking of them with the Family Compacts and other aristocratic traditions, not to mention the antipathy of later immigrants and widespread Canadian sympathy for the American Revolution.

With a few exceptions, such as Wolfe's defeat of Montcalm on the Plains of Abraham in 1759, Canadian history lacks the climactic, symbolic events, such as the signing of the Declaration of Independence in 1776 or the surrender at Appomattox Courthouse in 1865, that have punctuated the history of the United States. The achievement of Canadian independence, for example, stretches from the eighteenth century to the present. The Loyalist epic is also diffuse—both Spring and Autumn fleets arrived in Nova Scotia in 1783, New Brunswick was created in 1784 and Ontario in 1791, and the Battle of Queenston Heights was in 1812. It is typically Canadian that no single anniversary date can be assigned to the Loyalists. Yet their history is no less important for that.

Our intention is to examine the role of the Loyalists in Canadian history without falling under the spell of the Loyalist myth or Loyalist-phobia. Their story is a crucial part of Canada's relevant past in its "search for identity."

Quotations have been left as in the originals and *sic* has not been used. Oddities and misspellings should not be attributed to faulty proofreading.

We offer our particular thanks to Paula Brown, Darrell Butler, Robert Elliott, Jean Kyte, Jock Lees, Diana Moore, Graeme D. Ross, and Elinor Senior for all their help.

Wallace Brown, Sharon, Connecticut, June 1984
Hereward Senior, McGill University, Montreal, June 1984

# a note on terminology

FOR THE READERS' convenience it is necessary to give some definitions.

*Loyalists:* Inhabitants of the thirteen colonies who opposed the American Revolution and remained loyal to George III. They were also known as "friends of government" and "the King's friends." Their enemies dubbed them *Tories*, a pejorative term, unfairly linking them with the British Tory tradition of support for the royal prerogative and opposition to the Revolution of 1688. Many other colonists, in such places as Nova Scotia, Quebec, and Jamaica, were also loyal, but, despite the arguments of some historians, they were not known (and are not known) as Loyalists. Those Loyalists who fled the United States were called *provincials*, if they were demobilized members of provincial regiments, and *refugees*, if they were civilians; but the distinction was not always precise, and "refugee" was often a synonym for Loyalist. Another contemporary generic term, *royalist*, was often used by government officials.

*Patriots:* Americans who supported the Revolution. They also called themselves *Whigs*, a deliberate linking with British Whigs who traditionally opposed the royal prerogative. To the British and Loyalists they were *rebels* and *banditti*.

*Canada and Canadians:* Terms used to designate the present Dominion of Canada and its inhabitants, or any part thereof. Strictly speaking, this usage is anachronistic before Confederation took place in 1867. Before that, *British North America* consisted of the following colonies: *Nova Scotia*, from which *New Brunswick* was split in 1784; *Prince Edward Island*, known as *Isle St. Jean* until 1799; *Quebec* (known as Canada during the Revolutionary period), the ancient colony of *New France* which had been extended westward by the Quebec Act of 1774 to include the Great Lakes Region, and which was divided in 1791 into *Upper Canada (Ontario)* and *Lower Canada (Quebec)*, the modern terms becoming current in 1867. *Cape Breton* was detached from Nova Scotia as a separate province from

1784 until it rejoined in 1821. The *Maritimes* or the *Maritime Provinces* comprise Nova Scotia, New Brunswick, and Prince Edward Island.

*United Empire Loyalist:* Lord Dorchester's Order in Council, Quebec, November 9, 1789, bestowed "a Mark of Honor" on "Families who had adhered to the Unity of the Empire, and joined the Royal Standard in America before the Treaty of Separation in the year 1783." These people "and all their children and their Descendants of either sex" were to be "distinguished" by "U.E." "affixed to their names.... Alluding to their great principle the Unity of the Empire." Very quickly the term "U.E. Loyalist" became current in Upper Canada, partly as a means of distinguishing Loyalists from later American immigrants. It would seem that, strictly speaking, the designation applies only to Ontario, yet it is argued that because Dorchester was titular governor general of all of British North America the title is implied for Maritime Loyalists as well. Certainly qualified Maritimers have a strong moral claim to the title.

# NEIGHBOUR AGAINST NEIGHBOUR

## LOYALISTS AND THE AMERICAN REVOLUTION

*"I never had an idea of subduing the Americans; I meant to assist the good Americans subdue the bad."*

*Gen. James Robertson*

THEIR ENEMIES variously defined them as "the timid," those of "weak parts," "Rottin' sheep," even scatologically as the "ordure of 5,000 years." Many agreed that the first Loyalist was Cain, and that, "A Tory is a thing whose head is in England, and its body in America, and its neck ought to be stretched." The Loyalists themselves usually described each other as men of honour, devotedly loyal to the British constitution, particularly as practised in the colonies, and to good, orderly government, genuine freedom, and evolutionary reform. To this day they remain an enigmatic group, widely interpreted, but little understood.

As in any large group of people, everyone from the most noble to the most base can be found. Clearly, a common-sense definition of a Loyalist is one who opposed independence and the war necessary to maintain it. But many difficulties arise. What of those colonists who changed sides, sometimes more than once, as a result of pressures such as the fortunes of war? What of those who joined the king opportunely, overawed by seemingly invincible power, or attracted by salaries and supplies?—"able body'd beef devourers ... eating up the ... Royal Bounty," as one official complained. Frequently a colonist was branded a Loyalist simply because he traded with the British army for strictly non-ideological cash, and became permanently compromised. What of the numerous Americans who hated the Revolution but, fearing reprisals, never expressed their sentiments outside their circle of intimates? Defining a Loyalist is analogous to defining an English "gentleman": There isn't any, but if you are thought to be one, you are one.


BUT IN THE beginning there were no Loyalists. Or rather, everybody was loyal. Most writers treat loyalism as an aberration, but rebellion was the aberration. In 1763 virtually all Americans, like George III, gloried in the name of Briton, and independence was not mentioned outside of lunatic asylums; until he lost his mind in 1771 the Massachusetts firebrand, James Otis, sincerely protested his loyalty, and even in 1775 independence was a daring and, for most Americans, a frightening prospect. Less than a year before he wrote the immortal, if inaccurate, Declaration of Independence, Thomas Jefferson considered it the last resort: "I would rather be in dependence on Great Britain, properly limited, than on any nation upon earth, or on no nation."

Although British policies between 1763 and 1775—"too much history in too short a time"—triggered the American Revolution, it was the remarkable maturity and sophistication of American society that enabled it to succeed so well. The American Revolution was the coming of age of a colonial dependency, the first example in modern history of a process that became commonplace in the nineteenth and twentieth centuries. This seemingly inevitable trend, plus the rapid progress of the United States, have overshadowed the Loyalists' role in the Revolution, consigning them to history's dust-bin.

Since their beginnings in the seventeenth century, the American colonies had enjoyed internal self-government, bowing to London only in matters of foreign affairs and commercial regulation. At the end of the Seven Years' War (1756–63), beset by debt, various British ministries embarked on reform programs that in ten short years turned Americans' attitudes from contentment to open rebellion. Primarily, the confrontation resulted from British attempts at taxation, which in turn challenged the sovereignty of the thirteen popularly elected assemblies. The lines were drawn during the Stamp Act crisis of 1765–6. Here the British tried for the first time to tax the colonists directly. This power was utterly denied and opposition, taking the form of economic boycott, was so fierce that the act was repealed. At the same time, the Declaratory Act asserted Parliament's right to legislate for the colonies "in all cases whatsoever," obviously including taxes.

Both sides backed off, but the clash of principle went unresolved. In 1767 the Townshend Acts contained another attempt at taxation. Again there was a crisis, again the colonists resorted to economic boycott, again the British eventually backed down. Meanwhile the spearheads of the American opposition, "the Sons of Liberty," were becoming very well organized, especially in Massachusetts, under the skilled leadership of Samuel Adams. He coordinated Committees of Correspondence that brought together an inter-colonial, radical (ultimately revolutionary) network of patriots.

The final crisis began with the Tea Act of 1773 (a blunder rather than a British plot) which undercut colonial tea merchants. Because tea carried an import duty, the act was viewed as yet another direct tax. Protests erupted, notably the famous Boston Tea Party at which Whig vigilantes dumped barrels of tea into the harbour. Massachusetts was punished by having its government emasculated and Boston by having its trade halted, actions that helped to spark the meeting of representatives of twelve of the colonies at the First Continental Congress in Philadelphia in the fall of 1774. The Congress strongly opposed British policies, adopted the Continental Association that pledged the colonies to another economic boycott, and set up committees to enforce it.

In April, 1775, fighting broke out at Lexington and Concord. The War of Independence had begun, although the Second Continental Congress did not declare independence until July, 1776. Battling continued until the British were defeated at Yorktown, Virginia, in 1781. The Peace Treaty of 1783 recognized the sovereignty of the United States; five years later the Revolution was completed by the adoption of the federal constitution and the election of George Washington, who had commanded the army throughout the war, as the first president of the new Republic.

Most future Loyalists, like future rebels, opposed British reform measures from the Stamp Act onward. William Smith, chief justice of New York and later Quebec, took the lead in that opposition. Jonathan Odell, the foremost Loyalist poet and future secretary of New Brunswick, wrote of the Stamp Act:

> Suppose the right in Britain to be clear,
> Britain was mad to exercise it here.

Egerton Ryerson, the famous, Loyalist-descended Ontario Methodist, writing in 1880, mirrored the views of the Loyalists he was describing when he equally "abhorred the despotic conduct of George III and his corrupt ministers" and the War of Independence which resulted. Before the "calamity" of "blackest rebellion ..., the horrors of unnatural civil war" and "the ill-shapen, diminutive brat, INDEPENDENCY," to quote a contemporary pamphleteer, Loyalists disagreed with patriots only on the *mode* of opposition, preferring constitutional, or at least peaceful, protest to the inherent anarchy of violence and mobs. But looking back, some of the more conservative Loyalists criticized their activist brethren who "first set the building on Fire and then ran away."

There was, for example, the Allens, one of Philadelphia's most distinguished families. William Allen was the chief justice of Pennsylvania until his death in 1780 and, though a government official, was so moderate that another Loyalist accused him of being "a great Enemy" of England. His son Andrew sat in the First Continental Congress before backing the Loyalist cause. At the end of the war a British functionary remarked, with raised eyebrow: "He makes no scruple to avow that his Sentiment was ever opposed to the Idea of unlimited Taxation." Another son James, who led the Philadelphia mob in the Stamp Act riots, left one of the most interesting Loyalist diaries. It shows how fear of social conflict edged many rich conservatives from the Whig into the Loyalist camp. In May, 1772, he wrote:

> I am at present much engaged in prosecutions for breaches of the
> laws of Trade and have libelled four or five Vessels and Cargoes
> for Captain Talbot of the Lively Man of War. I am doing as a
> Lawyer what I would not do as a politician; being fully persuaded
> of the oppressive nature of those laws.

Three years later in July, 1775, he wrote:

> The Eyes of Europe are upon us; if we fall, Liberty no longer
> continues an inhabitant of this Globe: for England is running fast
> to slavery. The King is as despotic as any prince in Europe; the
> only difference is the mode; and a venal parliament are as bad as
> a standing army.

By October, 1775, he was cautiously drilling with the American militia. "My inducement principally to join them is; that a man is suspected who does not; and I chuse to have a Musket on my shoulders, to be on a par with them, and I believe discreet people mixing with them, may Keep them in Order." The same day he complained that "the most insignificant now lord it with impunity and without discretion over the most respectable characters."

Five months later, in March, 1776, he wrote:

> The plot thickens; peace is scarcely thought of—Independency
> predominant. Thinking people uneasy, irresolute and inactive.
> The Mobility triumphant.... I love the Cause of liberty; but
> cannot heartily join in the prosecution of measures totally foreign
> to the original plan of Resistance. The madness of the multitude
> is but one degree better than submission to the Tea-Act.

The next month, he wrote:

> A Convention chosen by the people, will consist of the most fiery
> Independants; they will have the whole Executive and legislative
> authority in their hands.... I am determined to oppose them
> vehemently in Assembly, for if they prevail there; all may bid
> adieu to our old happy constitution and peace.

The similarity between Whigs and Tories is upheld by the work of modern scholars and by the behaviour of Americans at the time. Consider the razor's edge that separated Peter Van Schaack, a reluctant Loyalist, from his close friend John Jay, a reluctant rebel.

Jay and Van Schaack were remarkably alike—both graduates of King's College (renamed Columbia by the rebels), both prosperous lawyers, both of non-English ancestry (Huguenot and Dutch respectively), both native-born, thoroughly good, conservative Americans, both opponents of British reforms beginning with the Stamp Act, both members of the Committee of Fifty-One formed in New York City in 1774 to combat the Boston Port Act (one of the "coercive acts" that followed the Tea Party), both trying to avoid what Van Schaack called "two extremes,... absolute *dependence* and *independence*." Yet in 1778 Jay was part of a committee that exiled his friend as a traitor. Jay had supported the Continental Association and accepted the Declaration of Independence and war; Van Schaack had also supported the Association but could not accept the War of Independence, although he tried in vain to maintain a personal independence by refusing on the one hand to take the oath of allegiance to the New York Provincial Congress (the rebel government) and on the other hand by refusing to help the British war effort. The two men's friendship survived the Revolution. Van Schaack returned to obscurity in his native land; Jay became the first chief justice of the United States.

Daniel Leonard was elected to the Massachusetts House of Representatives in 1769 where he voted with the Whigs and served on committees with the likes of Samuel Adams, John Hancock, and Joseph Warren, finally joining the Committee of Correspondence in 1773. His good friend and fellow lawyer John Adams testified that Leonard "made the most ardent speeches that were delivered in the House against Great Britain in favour of the colonies." It was only when the Boston Tea Party revealed Samuel Adams' more-than-constitutional protests that Leonard parted company with the Whigs. In 1774 and 1775, writing as "Massachusettensis," he accused the radicals of self-interest, demagoguery, and unsound constitutional history, arguing that independence would lead to what we would call Balkanization. He was answered by John Adams, writing as "Novanglus." The Adams-Leonard friendship also survived the Revolution and, in 1799, Leonard wrote from exile in London to the second president of the United States: "My heart recognizes all its former friendship, and I flatter myself you sometimes recollect with pleasure our professional intimacy."

In New York, Isaac Low was a member of the First Continental Congress and supported the Continental Association; John Alsop sat in the Second Continental Congress. Both of these prominent merchants became Loyalists. Conversely, in Pennsylvania, Robert Morris, who became the great financial genius of the Revolution, voted against independence; John Dickinson, "the Penman of the Revolution," also opposed the move though he went on to become president of revolutionary Delaware. Many conservative rebels, notably Alexander Hamilton, supported the return of exiled Loyalists at the end of the war and, like George Washington, John Adams, and numerous rebel leaders, Hamilton shared many of the Loyalists' views.

Virtually all sufficiently educated Americans, rebel or Loyalist, shared the views of John Locke, the seventeenth-century English Whig philosopher, whose themes of natural rights, government as a contract between governors and governed, and the right of revolution if the contract were broken, underlay the Declaration of Independence. Again, the quarrel centred on how to apply the theory rather than on the theory itself. However, this is not to suggest that there were no differences between Loyalists and Whigs. Already the Loyalists' dislike of violence and their rock-bottom faith in the traditional British empire are apparent. Further differences will become clear in later chapters dealing with the Canadian experience. But at this point their rationale should be examined.

The Loyalists offered a valid critique of the Revolution and indeed an alternative to it, a middle way, as Van Schaack put it, between dependence and independence. Among the alternatives were Joseph Galloway's famous Plan of Union—calling for a federal colonial government with a veto over British measures affecting America—defeated by only one vote in the First Continental Congress, and William Smith's largely private plan for an American parliament. The Loyalists' anticipation of Confederation and the ideal of a federated empire or even the modern British Commonwealth, and their devotion to the constitutional efficacy of monarchy and the "Unity of Empire" are not ignoble. The Loyalists and their descendents kept alive the concept of the family of English-speaking people that attained popularity during and after the Second World War. As L.F.S. Upton has written, William Smith "showed an early and keen appreciation that New York was but one part of a great empire. This was an unusual quality among colonial politicians who lived in societies as egocentric as those of Greek city states."

The Loyalists deserve admiration for being less parochial and more cosmopolitan than the patriots. They looked beyond Republican ideology to a pluralistic society and produced "the first significant justification of partisanship in American political thought." The Loyalists were more modern than their opponents, who sought a harmonious, corporate society reminiscent of the seventeenth-century Puritan ideal, but which had unfortunate tendencies toward moral absolutism—for example, the abolitionist and prohibitionist crusades, McCarthy-ite witch-hunts, and the crusading zeal during the idealistic entry into World War I have been as common in American history as they are rare in Canadian history.

The Loyalists can be credited with pointing out that the Revolution was not one of unalloyed righteousness, and with foreseeing the dangers of American lawlessness and what Tocqueville later called "the tyranny of the majority." As the Reverend Samuel Seabury stated, "If I must be devoured, let me be devoured by the jaws of a lion: and not gnawed to death by rats and vermin." The Reverend Jacob Bailey's "The Factious Demagogue" argued:

> That right and wrong, that good and ill,
> Were nothing but the rabble's will:
>
> . . .
>
> That men from all restraints are free,
> At liberty to cut our throats;
> 'Tis sanctified by major votes;
>
> . . .
>
> To set up *Hancock* for a *God*;
> Yea, they have pow'r to godify;
> An onion, turnip, or a fly:

The Loyalist critique of the Revolution is well illustrated by returning to John Jay and Peter Van Schaack. Reflecting on the great events, Jay wrote to Van Schaack:

> No one can serve two masters: either Britain was right and
> America wrong; or America was right and Britain wrong. They
> who thought Britain right were bound to support her; and
> America had a just claim to the services of those who approved
> her cause. Hence, it became our duty to take one side or the
> other.

In his reply Van Schaack absolutely denied Jay's almost totalitarian stance. Because he could not deem either side completely right or wrong he decided "as ever in a doubtful case, I would rather be the patient sufferer than run the risk of being the active aggressor." Van Schaack added a sentiment ultimately shared by many Loyalists: "If America is happier for the Revolution, I declare solemnly that I shall rejoice that the side I was on was the unsuccessful one." American historian Carl Becker, commenting on the Jay-Van Schaack rift, said that in reality the issue was deeper than America or Britain, it "was an aspect of the venerable quarrel between the 'One and the Many'. In the end he [Van Schaack] was exiled ... because he refused to place allegiance to the State above allegiance to his own conscience."

Not only were settlers of the Western Hemisphere divided, but so too were inhabitants of the British Isles. Loyalists who crossed the Atlantic were shocked to discover a widespread antipathy toward themselves and a sympathy for the American Whigs, which was shared by most of the Irish (who had similar grievances to the rebels), large sections of the British lower classes, English radicals and non-conformists, the followers of Chatham and Wilkes, and even several Tories, such as James Boswell. Many recent immigrants to America were prominent on the rebel side, including the following: Thomas Paine, who arrived from England in 1774 and in 1776 wrote *Common Sense*, one of the most influential pamphlets of all time; Gen. Richard Montgomery, a recent immigrant Irishman and former British officer, killed during the assault on Quebec in 1775; and John Paul Jones who arrived from Scotland in 1773 and soon became the great, flamboyant naval hero of the war.

WHO WERE THE Loyalists? The whole gamut of society: from ex-slaves like David George of Georgia, who became a Baptist missionary in Nova Scotia and Sierra Leone, and indentured servants like John Hennesy, who came from Ireland to Charleston, South Carolina, where he lived as a drayman, to the richest in the land like Oliver De Lancey, the great Hudson Valley landlord; from the first immigrants, Indians like Mohawk chief Joseph Brant, to scions of ancient families like William Byrd III of Virginia, to recent arrivals like Flora MacDonald of North Carolina, formerly Bonnie Prince Charlie's accomplice. There is a popular misconception, fed by pride and snobbery, particularly in the Maritime provinces, that the Loyalists were usually aristocrats and college graduates. In fact, statistically, the typical Loyalist was a yeoman farmer (as were most Americans of that time) or a modest artisan. Nevertheless it is true that the rich, the urban, the official, the conservative, the immigrant all contributed proportionally more than other segments of the population.

The Whig ranks were more glittering, but the loyal exodus from Massachusetts has been aptly likened to the Huguenot migration from France, and everywhere the loss was considerable. To name only one exile from each colony: Benjamin Thompson of New Hampshire, a scientist of international renown, second only to Benjamin Franklin; John Singleton Copley of Massachusetts, the greatest American painter of the age; Peter Harrison of Rhode Island, the finest colonial architect; Benedict Arnold of Connecticut, a skilled general for both sides; William Smith of New York, an outstanding jurist there and in Quebec; Jonathan Odell of New Jersey and later New Brunswick, possibly the best American poet of the era; Joseph Galloway of Pennsylvania, distinguished politician and prolific pamphleteer; Thomas Robinson of Delaware and later Nova Scotia, merchant, landowner, and the most prominent citizen of his native colony; Jonathan Boucher of Maryland, Anglican cleric, writer, and social reformer; John Saunders of Virginia, later chief justice of New Brunswick; David Fanning of North Carolina, ferocious soldier and later lieutenant-governor of Prince Edward Island; Dr. Alexander Garden of South Carolina, a leading naturalist (*viz.* gardenias) and later vice-president of the Royal Society; John J. Zubly of Georgia, a Presbyterian cleric and a skilled pamphleteer, albeit on the Whig side until 1776.

The question of Loyalist numbers will never be completely resolved. However, estimates can be made. If the notion, attributed to John Adams, that America, like Gaul, was divided into thirds (Whig, Tory, and neutral) is discredited, we must also dismiss the myth of patriot unanimity. The best educated guess is that active Loyalists probably numbered one-fifth (half a million) of the white population during the revolutionary years. The Loyalists were probably stronger than the Whigs in no colony, but they posed a serious threat in Georgia, New York and, to a degree, Pennsylvania. They were also quite powerful in South Carolina, New Jersey, and Massachusetts. In absolute numbers, New York, though seventh out of thirteen in population, contained up to four times more Loyalists than any other colony. In descending order, South Carolina, New Jersey, and Pennsylvania made up the other areas of numerical strength. Certain towns had high proportions of Loyalists; in descending order of proportional strength they were Savannah, Charleston, Boston, Norfolk, Annapolis, New York, Baltimore, Portsmouth (New Hampshire), Newport (Rhode Island), and Philadelphia. Rural strength was notable in New York and South Carolina. Between sixty and eighty thousand Loyalists went into permanent exile: in proportion to the American population, at least five times as many as fled the French Revolution and more than fled Castro's revolution.

There were certainly more active rebels than Loyalists, but the largest segment of all was the grey middle, including quietist Loyalists, apathetic Whigs, and various neutrals, pre-eminently religious pacificists like Quakers. John Adams called them "insipids" and "mongrels." In his poem, "The Birds, the Beasts, and the Bat," Francis Hopkinson likened the "trimmer" to the bat, "always ready to proclaim himself as all bird when the birds were in luck, and as all beast when the beasts seemed likely to win."

Neutrality and trimming were the order of the day. Samuel Miles, a Connecticut farmer, echoed a common sentiment when he said he "kept as much out of the way as possible," as did the Long Island innkeeper who, when asked which side he was on, replied, "I was for peace." (Shades of the English farmer who, asked during the seventeenth-century civil war whether he was for king or Parliament, replied, "What, be they two at it again?") For cageyness, there is Matthew Lymburner of Penobscot who "affected to be neutral in political disputes ... but in private was a Loyalist." For deviousness, there are Francis Pemart of Peekskill, who served as a rebel forage master but with "an intention of serving the Loyalists" and Vermonter Thomas Johnson, deemed "a rebel among rebels, a loyalist among loyalists." A case of expediency is afforded by Benjamin Towne whose *Pennsylvania Evening Post* was a Whig paper until late 1777, when the arrival in Philadelphia of the British army was hailed as "the dawn of returning Liberty." With the departure of the army, King George again became the "British tyrant," and Towne reverted to his Whig stance "as though nothing had happened."

The classic example of America's less-than-total dedication to the Revolution is the plight of Washington's army at Valley Forge contrasted with the easy circumstances of British general William Howe's, well supplied with funds, at Philadelphia. Even the very Whiggish Rhode Islanders rushed to trade with British forces in 1775. At one point, Washington complained that lack of public support was "infinitely more to be dreaded than the whole [British] force." Perhaps half the rebel militia and one-third of the Continental line deserted during the war. Many Loyalists were pardoned by Whig regimes on condition that they joined the rebel militia—thus, even military service was no guarantee of sincere commitment.

A close connection between allegiance and military success is shown by the way large areas of the South appeared restored to loyalty when the British swept northward in 1780, only to return to rebellion as the patriot army followed behind. In Vicar of Bray fashion, one Loyalist wrote disarmingly, in 1775, "we are at present all whigs until the arrival of the King's troops." The nineteenth-century historian Jared Sparks told an amusing story: In June, 1775, the provincial congress of New York was alarmed to learn that George Washington, rebel commander-in-chief, and William Tryon, royal commander-in-chief, were expected in New York City on the same day. The congress dispatched a force prepared to welcome "either the General, or Governor Tryon, whichever should first arrive, and wait on both sides as well as circumstances would allow."

Many Americans took a position reluctantly, as a result of coercion. It is unlikely that Georgia would have joined the Revolution without the coercion of

South Carolina. The efficient work of Whig committees with recalcitrants is notorious and took on aspects of terrorism. This force usually produced "patriots," but not always. James Moody, a native-born "happy farmer" of New Jersey, politically uninvolved, tried to remain "silent" and "not to give offence." However, he was "harrassed" by Whig committees, even shot at, and finally, his dander up, fled to the British with seventy-three neighbours and became a daring soldier and spy. Although Jacob Bailey, Anglican minister of Pownalborough, Massachusetts, could not in conscience violate his oath of allegiance to the king, he tried to be neutral but was assailed by the Whigs. "And pray, Gentlemen, what have I done to injure the American cause?" he asked his accusers. He had neither taken up arms nor attended meetings to aid England. He added, "I sincerely wish to see the Prosperity of my country and am willing to submit to the Authority of the present government." But he was forced out of his homeland and became a dedicated frontier missionary in Nova Scotia. Tench Coxe disliked both British legislation and the violent opposition to it. He became a victim of a patriot witch-hunt and was forced to flee Philadelphia in December, 1776. His *cri de coeur*, "I am (if permitted) likely to become a good American," was to be answered when he lived down his equivocal past and eventually became a prominent government official in the 1790s.

As lines hardened from 1774 onward, neutrality became increasingly difficult. James Allen of Philadelphia complained that, though neutral, he was branded a Tory "under which name is included every one disinclined to Independence tho' ever so warm a friend to constitutional liberty and the old cause." Nathaniel Whitaker wrote, "those who are not for us, must be against" us. An open press disappeared and, in Whig-controlled areas, all but the most courageous Loyalists and neutralists laid low.

After the war the equivocal nature of American allegiance continued to be demonstrated, as later chapters will show. The distinguished Canadian historian W.S. MacNutt has reminded us of the "commercial character" of the migration of "scores of traders from New York to Kennebec [who] slipped their moorings and sailed north for Nova Scotia" in the autumn of 1783, following the news that the Navigation Acts, excluding foreigners from the West Indian trade, would apply to the United States.* There was the ease with which many Loyalist émigrés were

---

*The Navigation Acts, which had ruled the British Empire for a hundred years, confined much of the empire's trade to British and British-colonial traders and vessels. The former thirteen colonies had been very active in trade with the British West Indies, and there was hope that this trade could continue after the Revolution. Great Britain refused. Hence, so-called Loyalists emigrated simply to enjoy the West Indian trade.

able to return to the young Republic. There was the alacrity with which thousands of American speculators and frontiersmen, so-called "late Loyalists," deserted their homeland in response to offers of Crown land in Upper Canada in the 1790s.

Of course, not all Americans were without principle, and not all Loyalists were motivated by fear of British power or love of British gold. Many stuck to their cause for intellectual and constitutional reasons, despite material loss, persecution, and rebel bribes. Religion was not usually the key, although loyalism had an Anglican tinge in New Jersey, New York, and especially New England, where Anglicans were a beleaguered minority. (Everywhere, the Loyalist elite was largely Anglican.) Immigrants were somewhat more likely to be loyal than the native-born, because they had not become Americanized. Scottish Highlanders, many of them ex-Jacobites, were grateful for government land grants. Naturally, those such as royal officials, whose livelihood or well-being depended on the British government, were the most automatically loyal.

Two groups, blacks and Indians, had a special relationship with government. British offers of freedom to rebels' slaves who would join the lines were taken up by several hundred blacks for one obvious reason: the Whigs, committed to slavery, would not match the offer. Indians also tended to be Loyalists because they were accustomed to dealing with the imperial authorities, whom they much preferred to the rapacious frontiersmen who were a threat to their lands. The Indians' role in the war has created a mythology regarding their so-called atrocities, partly a result of sour grapes because the patriots tried, but failed, to attract them to their side. In the South, the famous McGillivray family kept the Creeks loyal, as John Stuart, the Superintendent of Indians, did the Cherokees. In the North, the celebrated Johnson family, headed by Sir John Johnson (who later became the most prominent Loyalist exile in Quebec), played a similar part with the Six Nations. At the end of the war, Joseph Brant, the great Mohawk chief, led many Iroquois into Western Canada.

An interesting key to Loyalist motivation, argued by William H. Nelson, is that most Loyalists belonged to a "cultural minority." Some examples have already been given and others abound: the Scottish tobacco factors disliked by the planter society of Chesapeake Bay as rapacious agents of British tobacco companies; the Huguenots of New Rochelle, New York, the only ones still speaking French; New England Baptists persecuted by the established Whig Congregational church; Carolina back-country farmers, alienated from the dominating Whig seaboard society; Georgians in general, threatened by the Spanish and their Indian allies. Nelson adds, as a corollary, the tendency of Loyalists to come from peripheral areas threatened economically and politically by richer neighbours: thus, in Rhode Island, declining Newport was loyal while rising Providence was aggressively Whig.

But when all the intellectual generalizations have been made, there are enough exceptions to remind the historian of the often personal, sometimes irrational, nature of motivation. Families, friendships, businesses, faculties and students, churches, legal partnerships, even marriages were split. Benjamin Franklin's son, William, the last royal governor of New Jersey, cursed with an open mind—no equipment for a patriot—was Whiggish, admitting the reality of American grievances. But he believed more strongly in the legitimacy of the empire and legal opposition over riot and war. In contrast to his estranged father, who became the Grand Old Man of the Revolution, William died a forgotten man in British exile, distrusted by both sides because he understood both sides. Benjamin Faneuil was the Loyalist nephew of the Whig, Peter Faneuil, who built the Boston hall that has his name, dubbed the "cradle of liberty, in which the Revolution was rocked." Samuel Quincy, Harvard class of 1754, was a brilliant lawyer who prosecuted Captain Preston after the "Boston Massacre," but became a rather reluctant Loyalist, supporting royal, constitutional government because he was unconvinced that mankind was virtuous enough for a republic. His father, brother, and wife were rebels! Like Franklin, he went on to exile and obscurity. Dr. Isaac Wilkins, a rich Westchester Loyalist, married Isabella Morris, sister of Gouverneur and Lewis Morris, both prominent Whigs, the latter a signer of the Declaration of Independence. A third brother, Staats Morris, was a Loyalist who became a British general and member of Parliament.

Given their considerable strength and their alliance with Britain, then the strongest power on earth, the Loyalists' failure seems surprising. One reason for that failure was that the Loyalists lost the propaganda war. It was much easier to popularize the easily understood, simple proposition of independence from a "tyrant" king than the more subtle, less obviously attractive concept of subordination within the empire. As Daniel Leonard put it, "the Tories' plan supposed a degree of subordination, which is rather a humiliating idea." Even regardless of such disadvantages, Loyalist propagandists and leaders were far less talented than the Whigs. They were also poorly organized and fragmented in contrast to superb, coordinated Whig efficiency sufficient to excite the envy of Lenin, Mussolini, Chairman Mao, and the IRA.

The rebels were skilled in "dirty tricks." The distinguished Canadian historian A.R.M. Lower has compared the Revolution to the 1948 Communist coup in Czechoslovakia, and his statement does contain a grain of truth. The not-so-friendly persuasion of the Whig committees ranged from mild social pressure to murder, and continued throughout the war. Although there was nothing to compare to the guillotine of the French Revolution, there was an American "Terror," as tarring-and-feathering and rail-riding became major spectator-sports. Riding on a rail was especially gruesome. It consisted of jogging the victim roughly along on "a sharp rail" between his legs. The painful effect of these "grand Toory Rides," as a contemporary called them, can readily be imagined. Seth Seely, a Connecticut farmer who later fled to New Brunswick, was brought before the local committee in 1776 and, as punishment for signing a declaration to support the king's laws, was "put on a Rail carried on mens Sholders thro the Street, then put into the Stocks and besmeared with Eggs and was robbed of money for the Entertainment of the Company." Appropriately, the term "lynch law" originated to describe the treatment of Loyalists in Virginia.* At a more legal level, the various states disfranchised, imprisoned, banished, and fined obnoxious Loyalists, and confiscated vast quantities of their property.

This persecution offers a parallel with the fate of Japanese Americans after Pearl Harbor. To quote Alexander Hamilton:

> I am more hurt at ... [their persecution] because it appears to me unmixed with pure and patriotic motives. In some few it is a spirit of blind revenge and resentment but in more it is the most sordid interest. One wishes to possess the house of some wretched Tory, another fears him as a rival in his trade or commerce and a fourth [sic] wishes to get clear of his debts by shaking off his creditor or to reduce the cost of living by depopulating the town.

For many years a controversy has raged among historians as to whether the Revolution was a *real* revolution. The persecuted Loyalists would find the question laughable if it were not so tragic. Consider, for example, the pathetic case of Filer Dibblee, a native-born Connecticut lawyer, and his family. In August, 1776, they fled from Stamford to Long Island, but a few months later the rebels

---

*The term "lynch law" owes its origin to the activities of Judge Lynch, a colonel of the Virginia Militia, who held an informal court in his parlour where he imposed fines and imprisonment on suspect Loyalists, and ordered many to be beaten until they shouted "Long Live Liberty." Lynch did not impose the death penalty, but, as he acted without the authorization of any constituted authority, the state of Virginia passed an act of indemnity after the war "to secure him against prosecution." Henceforth, "lynch law" became a kind of shorthand for informal law enforcement.

turned Dibblee's wife and five children "naked into the Streets," having stolen the very clothes from their backs as well as having plundered the house. The family fled to New York City where Dibblee obtained sufficient credit to settle at Oyster Bay, Long Island. But in 1778 the rebels plundered the family a second time, and carried Dibblee as prisoner to Connecticut, where he remained imprisoned for six months, until exchanged. With further credit, the family established themselves at Westhills, Long Island, where they were "plundered and stripped" a third time. Then came a move to Hempstead, Long Island, and in 1780 a fourth ravaging. Dibblee now, for the first time, applied for relief from the commander-in-chief and received about one hundred dollars. In 1783 the whole family moved to Saint John, New Brunswick, where they managed to survive a rough winter in a log cabin, but Dibblee's "fortitude gave way" at the prospect of imprisonment for his considerable indebtedness and of the fate his family would suffer as a consequence. The result was that he "grew Melancholy, which soon deprived him of his Reason, and for months could not be left by himself." Finally in March, 1784, "whilst the Famely were at Tea, Mr. Dibblee walked back and forth in the Room, seemingly much composed: but unobserved he took a Razor from the Closet, threw himself on the bed, drew the Curtains, and cut his own throat." Shortly afterward, the Dibblee house was accidentally burned to the ground. It was then rebuilt by the heroic widow, only to be accidentally razed again the same year by an Indian servant girl.

THE WAR OF Independence divides into two major campaigns, one northern, one southern, both of which ended in disaster for the British and the Loyalists.

In the autumn of 1776 British forces secured New York City and by the beginning of 1777 had driven Washington's army across New Jersey. Later that year a knock-out blow was attempted which would rally the New York rural Loyalists, erroneously believed to be a vast majority, and isolate New England, correctly believed to be the centre of the rebellion. General John Burgoyne moved down from Canada via Lake Champlain to the Hudson River. General Sir William Howe, commander-in-chief, was supposed to advance north and effect a meeting. Howe never got beyond capturing Philadelphia (September, 1777). In October Burgoyne's army of regulars, Loyalists, and Indians was forced to surrender to the Americans at Saratoga, a defeat that electrified the rebels and persuaded France to make an alliance with them. Without French aid it is doubtful whether the rebellion would have succeeded. In the spring of 1778 Howe was replaced by Sir Henry Clinton who, because of the French threat, evacuated

Philadelphia and moved back to New York City, which remained the great British stronghold throughout the rest of the war. Major fighting in the North had ended.

In May, 1780, with the capture of Charleston, South Carolina, the British southern campaign began. Again, both regular and Loyalist regiments were involved. The strategy was to sweep northward, rallying the supposed majority of grateful Loyalists. Superficially all went quite well, though after Cornwallis' armies moved on, many so-called Loyalists welcomed the returning rebel troops. By the autumn of 1780 Cornwallis had successfully advanced through Virginia to the Yorktown peninsula where a temporary, unexpected control of the sea by the French admiral de Grasse resulted in a humiliating surrender to French and American forces. Britain decided to cut its losses and substantial fighting ended, though the peace was not formally signed for another two years.

Because they convinced the authorities that they were the majority, the Loyalists were partly responsible for the faulty strategy of the two campaigns. The British tended to view Loyalist soldiers as incompetent amateurs, and alienated many civilians by treating them as rebels. Although the British rarely used them effectively, the Loyalists were very important militarily. They prolonged the war. It is claimed that in 1780 roughly eight thousand Americans were fighting for George Brunswick when only nine thousand were fighting for George Washington. Eventually about nineteen thousand Loyalists, forming some fifty provincial regiments, armed, supplied, and paid by the British, formally took up arms.

Examples among many outstanding Loyalist regiments include the following: Sir John Johnson's Royal Yorkers, who fought the vicious battle of Oriskany in the Mohawk Valley during Burgoyne's expedition; the Queen's Loyal Rangers, almost wiped out at the battle of Bennington during the same campaign; the Queen's Rangers and the New Jersey Volunteers, who saw much action both North and South; the British Legion and the Royal North Carolina Regiment which gained a victory at the battle of Camden, South Carolina, in August, 1780.

Unlike the rebels, Loyalist regiments were usually subordinated to British policy, and the many able Loyalist officers, such as Col. David Fanning of North Carolina or Col. Thomas Browne of Georgia, could not attain the highest commands. In addition to full-time units, Loyalists were widely employed as militia, guerrillas, propagandists, counterfeiters, spies, guides, foragers, pilots, pioneers, and other civil aides.

The most important point about the Loyalists' part in the War of Independence was that this made it a more genuinely civil war than *the* Civil War a century later, which, in a sense, was a war between two nationalities, North and

South. The Loyalists were distributed right across the board by religion, nativity, occupation, and status. As a contemporary put it, "Nabour was against Nabour." Particularly nasty internecine fighting occurred in upstate New York, the vicinity of New York City, and in the Carolina back country.

Guerrilla warfare raged over the "neutral ground" of Westchester County where James De Lancey's Westchester Refugees (many of whom later settled in Nova Scotia and New Brunswick) were known to their enemies as "cowboys" and "cattle rustlers." The rebel irregulars were called "skinners" by the Loyalists because they skinned their victims of all their possessions. In the back parts of New York and Pennsylvania, Col. John Butler's Rangers made valiant, effective raids.

Perhaps the worst fighting of this sort occurred in South Carolina, involving such Loyalist corps as the South Carolina Regiment and the South Carolina Royalists, many of whom later sailed for Halifax, Nova Scotia. But pre-eminent in the South were the American Riflemen and the Legion, led respectively by two British officers, Patrick Ferguson and Banastre Tarleton. The horrors of civil war were well illustrated by the engagement at King's Mountain on the border between the Carolinas, October 7, 1780, in which all the combatants except Major Ferguson were Americans. Prominent Loyalist regiments involved were the King's American Regiment, the Loyal American Regiment, and the American Volunteers.

After the rebels gained the Loyalist stronghold on the spur of the Blue Ridge range that gave the battle its name, a desperate mêlée ensued in which Ferguson was killed. The failing Loyalists asked for quarter, only to receive the chilling answer, "Tarleton's quarter!"—that is, no quarter, in acknowledgment of Tarleton's massacre of patriot troops at the battle of Waxhaws, North Carolina, earlier in the year. Before patriot officers could restore order, the day's toll of dead and wounded stood at well over two hundred Loyalists compared to a mere ninety rebels.

Although the Stamp Act was opposed from Quebec to the Leeward Islands, when war came, most of the inhabitants of Quebec, Nova Scotia, the Floridas, Bermuda, the Bahamas, and the West Indies (a majority of the British Colonies in the Western Hemisphere) remained loyal or at least neutral or quiet. Many provincial troops who fought for Britain were enlisted in Quebec, Nova Scotia, and the Floridas. Even the French Canadians contributed at least one hundred. A few Canadians, however, actively supported the Revolution, including some Quebec habitants tempted to the rebel lines during the invasion of 1775 (led by the generals Benedict Arnold and Richard Montgomery), and a handful of transplanted New Englanders, living at Maugerville in the Saint John Valley, who aided Col. Jonathan Eddy's abortive expedition on behalf of "the United Colonies of America" against Nova Scotia in 1776. More important, if largely forgotten, were some hundreds of Nova Scotians and Quebeckers who fought for the Continental Congress, mainly as members of the Canadian Regiment. At war's end some returned home, while others were eventually granted land in Ohio and upstate New York.

After the war, the majority of Loyalists remained in the United States and, with rare exceptions, discarded their previous politics. Avowed Loyalists became as hard to find as Nazis in post-war Germany. Over time they were lost to public memory. At first, in the manner of ex-colonial peoples today, Americans set about founding a myth of unanimity. Part of the process involved removal of reminders of the past, not only royalist (for example, the Queen's Head Tavern in New York City was renamed Fraunces Tavern) but also Loyalist (for example, Hutchinson Street in Boston was renamed Pearl Street). Thomas Hutchinson, one of the most important men in the history of his native Massachusetts, virtually disappeared from the Commonwealth's tradition and was even ignored by professional historians until very recently.

Hutchinson is an example of the way Loyalists became non-persons, rather like enemies of the state in communist countries today. The poet Jonathan Odell is not commemorated in any way by Princeton, his *alma mater*; similarly, Yale neglects the Reverend Thomas Bradbury Chandler, an outstanding Anglican pamphleteer. A few Loyalists are remembered, such as Robert Rogers, a hero of the Seven Years' War, but conveniently the Loyalist parts of their careers are forgotten. One rare exception is Benedict Arnold, but he is the kind that gives Loyalists a bad name. Another is Benjamin Thompson (Count Rumford), but he left all his money to Harvard!

Like American Whigs in the United States, American Loyalists in Canada began their own myth. The rest of this book is devoted to that myth and the reality behind it.

# 2 NO LONGER ALIEN

## THE GREAT MIGRATION

*... the dispossessed, strangers and pilgrims*
*traveling down the Oswego River\* to Sackett's*
   *Harbour*
*or sailing rat-infested ships to the Maritimes*
*in simple desperation*
*to belong somewhere*
*no longer alien*
*and outlawed from the land of their birth.*

                                              *Al Purdy*

\* Poetic licence—the Black River was the route to Sacket's Harbor, the Oswego River led to Oswego, another Loyalist gathering-place.

THE AMERICAN REVOLUTION resulted in a great migration of thousands of Loyalists and their families from the land of their birth or adoption. It was a significant folk-movement, particularly in the colonization of North America. It stretched to the limit the resources of the Crown and the fortitude of the exiles, but both emerged meritoriously. The vindictiveness of the victorious American rebels toward the Loyalists, while understandable, is less praiseworthy. After the abject failures of the war and the peace treaty, the migration began a striking success story that belies the tradition (mainly American, but shared by the English and even to a degree by Canadians) of the Loyalists as "losers." The great migration begat secondary migrations as the Loyalists moved within colonies, between colonies, and sometimes back to the United States—always firmly in the North American tradition of movement for betterment. In this, the Loyalists were no different from the seventeenth-century Puritans, the eighteenth-century pacifists, the nineteenth-century gold-seekers, or the twentieth-century Okies.

On October 19, 1781, the British army, commanded by Gen. Charles Cornwallis, formally surrendered at Yorktown, Virginia, to Generals Washington and Rochambeau. As the troops marched out to lay down their arms, the band played "The World Turned Upside Down." The aptness of the title, signifying the victory of a bunch of upstart peasants over the greatest power on earth, was rubbed in when the Marquis de Lafayette called for "Yankee Doodle," the rebel theme song. Ironically, "Yankee Doodle" began as a British putdown, foreshadowing Loyalist satire, of the crude colonial who imagined a feather in his hat equalled the fashionable macaroni wig, and "The World Turned Upside Down" was originally the British ballad, "When the King Shall Enjoy His Own Again." Benjamin Franklin claimed, "the infant Hercules ... has now strangled his second Serpent," but in fact the asphyxiation was performed primarily by French troops, who outnumbered the Continentals two to one, and by the French fleet, under Admiral de Grasse, which secured a temporary domination at sea. The world was not yet upside down; France had merely taken an important trick in its perennial power game with Britain.

The Loyalists' disillusionment with British policies had been deepening as the war progressed, yet, as Thomas Hutchinson, Jr. said, "the unhappy...news ...stunned" them. Worse was what William Franklin, Ben's Loyalist son, termed the "great uneasiness and apprehensions" engendered by the bad tidings that Cornwallis had failed, in Article 10 of the Capitulation, to secure amnesty for his Loyalist troops. Young Franklin considered the Loyalist prisoners no better than "Runaway Slaves restored to their former Masters," while John Wesley, ever a Loyalist supporter, complained in verse that Cornwallis protected "his tools of war,/But left the Loyalists to feel/the mercy of those Fiends from Hell."

The Loyalists, who correctly saw that Yorktown was a military setback, not a mortal blow, continued for a time to believe the war could be won. Those who fought the guerrilla campaigns in the back country of New York and Pennsylvania and in the vicinity of New York City understandably considered themselves to be on a winning side. As always, their fate was determined by others. On hearing the news from Virginia, Lord North, the British prime minister, exclaimed, "Oh, God! It is all over." He was right. The ruling class lost the will to continue the war.

In March, 1782, the House of Commons voted in favour of peace negotiations, whereupon North resigned and George III contemplated abdication. North was succeeded by Lord Rockingham who was succeeded on his death that July by Lord Shelburne. Meanwhile, in early May, Sir Guy Carleton arrived in New York to replace Sir Henry Clinton as commander-in-chief with orders to be conciliatory, and a month earlier government official Richard Oswald was dispatched to Paris to begin peace talks with Benjamin Franklin. Now the Loyalists had to reconcile themselves to the unthinkable—victory for the despised rebels and independence for the United States. Satirical "for sale" adverts appeared in the Loyalist New York *Gazette*, for a "map of the British Empire in America on a very small scale," and thirteen volumes on the same area "abridged by a royal hand to a single pocket duodecimo." The Loyalists' hopes, pinned on favourable terms from the peace treaty, were to be gravely disappointed and the apprehensions created by Article 10, confirmed—one reason why few Loyalists were Anglophiles. Those in exile in Britain were jolted by that country's corruption, extremes of wealth and poverty, and widespread pro-rebel sentiment. Those remaining in the colonies were shocked by the disdain of the British and German troops who frequently harassed and robbed them. The Loyalists brought to the birth of English-speaking Canada an almost equal suspicion of the United States and Great Britain, misgivings that history periodically confirmed.

Although it did not become definitive until September 3, 1783, the preliminary treaty, signed on November 30, 1782, was the blueprint for the Loyalists' future. They had been the thorniest issue faced by the negotiators. The British wanted them entirely restored to their rights and property; the Americans wanted them entirely excluded from the treaty. Not surprisingly, the final document contained ambiguities in excess of diplomatic norms. There was, for example, a tortured attempt to discriminate between British-born and American-born, and between those who had and had not borne arms. However, the ambiguities, and indeed everything regarding the Loyalists, were largely academic because under the Articles of Confederation, then the American Constitution, Congress had no powers of compulsion over the thirteen states and could only "earnestly recommend." These recommendations included the granting of twelve months during which the Loyalists could endeavour "unmolested" to recover their confiscated property (but only for "the *bona fide* price" paid to the new owners), and a revising of the anti-Loyalist laws in a "spirit of conciliation ... justice and equity" (both in the infamous Article V). Article VI added that there should be no future "confiscations" or "prosecutions" of Loyalists. In fact, confiscations and prosecutions continued; Loyalists returning from exile were frequently molested and sometimes even murdered, and chances of recovering property were slim. Permanent exile was to be the ultimate price paid by many for loyalty to the Crown.

The knowledge of victory that the peace treaty clinched removed a moderating influence from the patriots—the fear of British reprisals. Cavalier Jouet said that while a prisoner in New Jersey he was well treated until the news of the peace arrived, when "a number of fellows came about me with sticks and whips" and he was threatened with execution. The prevailing attitude to the Loyalists was epitomized in 1782 by Henry Laurens, recently released from the Tower of London, who asked rhetorically how a Tory could say to the Congress, "I am a Loyalist, I used my utmost Endeavors to get you all hanged and to confiscate your Estates and beggar your Wives and Children: Pray make a Provision for me or let me enjoy my Estate." Typically, the New York legislature saw no reason to restore Loyalist property if Britain were not going to pay for damages inflicted on the patriots; a public meeting at Worcester, Massachusetts, May 12, 1782, resolved that the "parricides" should not return and that the restoration of property would be "unreasonable, cruel, and unjust"; a similar meeting the same month in Dutchess County, New York, declared that the prospect of the return of those who have "covered our land in blood; and whose principles are utterly repugnant to our free government ... fills us with indignation"—they deserved nothing "but detestation and Chastizement." George Clinton, governor of New York, bluntly asserted that he would "rather roast in hell to all eternity than ... show mercy to a damned Tory."

The vindictive treatment of the Loyalists was out of step with contemporary civilized practice by which civil wars were ended by "generous acts of amnesty and restitution." (It also contrasted with the treatment of the South after the American Civil War.) As the nineteenth-century historian W.E.H. Lecky showed long ago, European precedents were broken: the Treaty of Antwerp, 1609, ending the revolt of the Netherlands, treated the refugees well, as did Charles II's Act of Amnesty and Oblivion in Restoration England. To quote recent historian L.F.S. Upton, "The new era of mass emotional involvement, irresistible in war and vindictive in peace, had arrived." But the question remains: would the Loyalists, in victory, have treated the rebels any better? Many military Loyalists would have been harsh, but they would have been restrained by the Crown. The tone of most Loyalist writing was more of sorrow than anger, perhaps an indication that their approach would have been a moderate one.

The boundary settlement was of great concern to the Loyalists. There were demands that the thirteen colonies be partitioned, using the analogy that only seven of the seventeen Dutch provinces had gained independence from Spain in the seventeenth century. But the Republic retained not only all the states, but a great deal more. By the treaty, the United States was bounded on the west by the Mississippi River and on the east by the St. Croix River. In between, the line generally followed its present way along the watershed between the St. Lawrence and the Atlantic until it joined the river near present-day Cornwall, thence along the middle of the river and the Great Lakes to the Lake of the Woods and finally to the Mississippi. Partly because the map used by the negotiators was inaccurate, several problems arose during the following year, which will be discussed in a later chapter.

The Loyalists found the boundary settlement, like the rest of the treaty, incredibly generous to their enemies. Why, they asked, was independence conceded at the outset, rather than being used as a bargaining factor? In the East, the choice of the St. Croix rather than the much more westerly Penobscot dashed the hopes of the Maine Loyalists; in the West, Britain's abandonment of much of the Great Lakes country, part of Quebec since 1774, was a particular blow to the Iroquois who lost most of their traditional lands, over which they did not acknowledge the king's sovereignty—"it was not his own to give."

It could have been worse. Although the British did not take Franklin's demand for all of the rest of British North America seriously, they were considering ceding all of Southern Ontario, before the successful defence of Gibraltar strengthened their hand. But it also could have been better. France, anxious to keep its infant ally down in size, was outmanoeuvred by American negotiating skill and British accommodation. Neither Detroit nor Niagara had been cap-tured, yet they were ceded. (Along with a few other Western posts, they were not actually handed over until 1796. The British hung on to them in order to placate their Indian allies and because of American failure to honour the peace provisions regarding the Loyalists and payment of debts to British merchants.) Similarly, there was no military necessity to surrender the Ohio Valley. As it was, the treaty confined Canada to the northwest. The Montreal fur-traders would have to follow the northern water-routes that eventually led to dominion north of the forty-ninth parallel, all the way to the Pacific.

Generous treatment of the United States was the policy of the forward-thinking Lord Shelburne, "the friend of America," who, influenced by the free-trade theories of Adam Smith, looked to the Republic to develop the American interior as a market for British manufactures and investment. He even envisaged a sort of Atlantic alliance, including both economic union and a common foreign policy. The ministry's attitude is illustrated by the retort of a British delegate to a Frenchman who remarked at a party, after the signing of the preliminary treaty, that the United States would become "the greatest empire in the world"—"Yes, sir, and they will *all* speak English, every one of 'em."

Shelburne's name became anathema to the Loyalists. They had been like children keeping a vigil at the bedside of a seriously ill parent. Finally, they could only hope for a decent funeral and good news in the will. News of the treaty left them, they declared, in a mood "little short of actual rebellion." But some welcomed the peace, and even exile, as an end to uncertainty. Ward Chipman, a future New Brunswick judge, wrote in December, 1782: "I am heartily tired of the war," adding that he looked forward to "prospects for future life without the continued apprehensions of having them all deranged." What a relief it must have been for the likes of the wife and family of Benjamin Ingraham, a provincial sergeant. For four years, while they eked out a living near Albany as tenants on their own confiscated farm, they had no news, not knowing if he were alive or dead. After the peace he appeared without warning, and within a few days the reunited family was en route to New York and, shortly after, a new life in New Brunswick.

The British ministry appreciated the plight of what George III termed "the American sufferers," but Shelburne pleaded "the unhappy *necessity* of public affairs"—a "*part* must be wounded, that the *whole* empire may not perish." Shelburne's policies were not only attacked by the Loyalists, but also by his political enemies in Britain, who brought down his ministry by fulminating against "this base Treatment," this "lasting monument of national disgrace."

Apart from the boundaries, however, what else could have been done? There were the undeniable realities of America's political system and the state of its public opinion. As Shelburne said, the alternative was "*either to accept the terms proposed, or continue the war.*" The friendliness of his government and the general lack of rancour in Britain was even shared by George III, who told ambassador John Adams: "I was the last man in England to consent to ... independence. Now that you have got it ... I shall be the last man to disturb it."

Asked by some Britons, "How are the Refugees to be provided for?" Henry Laurens, a member of the commission congress sent to negotiate, replied, "They are yours, maintain them...." The British government was indeed compelled to take on the resettlement of thousands of Loyalists who, by choice or necessity, were exiled from the United States. This demanded a change of attitude toward Canada. Throughout the eighteenth century, different British ministries had essentially shared Voltaire's low opinion of Canada as "*quelques arpents de neige*" (a few acres of snow). In May, 1783, James Monk, the attorney general of Quebec, wrote regarding the treaty and Canada's desirability as a Loyalist refuge: "Canada is a worm that may prey on the Extremities & even reach the body but does not sting eno[ugh] to rec[eive] a Consideration while more important Animals engross attention." Nevertheless, despite little conscious effort to found a second British Empire, the northern lands were retained partly to serve as a haven for the Loyalists. In October, 1782, Richard Oswald was instructed to gain a better boundary between Massachusetts (until 1820 Maine was part of Massachusetts) and Nova Scotia than the previously accepted Saint John River because it was accurately suspected that that valley would prove useful to the refugees.

Before considering the immigration to Canada in detail, aspects of the entire Loyalist migration must be sketched. The British looked around their remaining empire for locations—even the newly established penal colony of New South Wales was briefly but seriously considered. Australia's attraction was available land, but closer at hand were the Bahamas and the British West Indies, favoured by Southern Loyalists for the climate and slavery, and British North America, favoured by Northerners. Great Britain, devoid of free land, attracted the well-to-do, office seekers, pensioners, and those with well-placed friends. However, rich and poor, Northerner and Southerner, penetrated all the Loyalist havens to some degree.

The life of many a Loyalist became a veritable odyssey at the end of the Revolution. Stephen De Lancey, for example, left his native New York for England, lived in Quebec and Nova Scotia for a time, became chief justice of the Bahamas and eventually governor of Tobago. The Reverend Mather Byles of

Massachusetts complained from New Brunswick to his daughter in Halifax: "My Family is now breaking up, wandring like Gypsies & playing Puss-in-the-Corner about the Globe. You and I seem to be the only stationary Beings." He added, half-jokingly, that he soon expected to hear that her husband had "gone to live like a Gentleman at Sierra-Leone."

Only a small minority of the Loyalist émigrés were legally banished by the state legislatures, even fewer permanently. Many more were in practice banished by continuing hostility and the ineffectiveness of the peace treaty. One Loyalist declared that "the peace years" were "worse than the time of fighting" and though she hated to leave the land of her birth, the Mohawk Valley, at least "I shall hear no more the words 'Tory' and 'Parricide.'" That "the violence and malice of the Rebel Government against the Loyalists" left them with "no other resource ... but to submit to the tyranny of exulting enemies or settle a new country," as the Winslows put it, became a Loyalist chorus. On August 17, 1783, General Carleton wrote to Elias Boudinot, president of the American Congress, pointing out that the evacuation was being slowed by increased "violence" against the Loyalists so "that almost all within these lines conceive the safety, both of their property and of their lives, depend upon their being removed by me."

Many Loyalists would not stay even if they could, holding that "animosities" had "been so heightened" by bloodshed "that the Parties can never be reconciled." As Vermonter Justus Sherwood wrote, "no Loyalist of principle and spirit can ever endure the thought of going back to live under the imperious laws of a Washington and his minions." Col. John Butler added that the Loyalists "would rather go to Japan than go among the Americans where they could never live in peace."

Some left more easily than others, quitting "this damned country with pleasure." But more typical was James De Lancey who said goodbye to his native New York in April, 1783, to embark for Annapolis, Nova Scotia. A friend commented: "Nature soon obtained the mastery and he burst into tears." Recent immigrants, such as Scottish Highlanders, including many Jacobites who arrived in New York and the Carolinas on the eve of the Revolution, found it less difficult to abandon the United States than those with deeper roots. Members of fighting regiments (including the Highlanders) shared a justified fear of an automatically deepened American antagonism and were inclined to follow their officers out of the country.

As usual with migration, there were attracting as well as expelling forces. The authorities promised free land, provisions, tools, and supplies in most areas. This tempted not only Loyalists. For example, the executioner of the British officer

Major André (condemned for his role in Benedict Arnold's defection), occupied land at Kingston, Ontario, for a short time, before he was discovered and whipped out of town. For the elite, there was the promise, or hope, of government posts. In August, 1783, the announcement that the Navigation Acts would apply against the United States inspired a wave of late, commercially minded immigrants. It is not only "late Loyalists" whose motives may be questioned. Few could have escaped at least an echo of a Whig parody.

> "To go—or not to go"—is that the question?
> Whether 'tis best to trust the inclement sky,
> That frowns indignant o'er the dreary Bay
> Of Fundy,... — or stay among the Rebels!
> And, by our stay, rouse up their keenest rage,
> ...
> Hard choice ...!

THE LOYAL Hamlets' dilemma was resolved by mass exodus: the evacuations of Savannah and Charleston in 1782, of New York in 1783, and of East Florida in 1783–5. But it must be remembered that emigration, beginning as early as the Stamp Act crisis in 1765, took place throughout the revolutionary period and even beyond. It must also be remembered that only a minority of the estimated total of five hundred thousand Loyalists actually left the United States. For example, the provincial regiments, which made up about one-half of the immigrants to New Brunswick, had declined through desertion to about one-quarter of their original strength before the evacuation of New York. The story of the Loyalists who stayed remains to be told.

TRADITIONALLY IN the Maritimes, especially New Brunswick (where "Squire John" is the Loyalist symbol) the typical Loyalist has been considered wealthy, educated (a Harvard graduate), aristocratic, and likely to hail from New England, especially Massachusetts. While such creatures are easy enough to find, and there were certainly more of them than in a normal American colonial cross-section, modern research has demolished the stereotype. A thorough analysis of the New Brunswickers reveals that 70 per cent came from the Middle Colonies (40 per cent from New York, 22 per cent from New Jersey) and only about 22 per cent from New England (13 per cent from Connecticut, 6 per cent from Massachusetts); the

Southern Colonies supplied a mere 7 per cent. All but 10 per cent of the total were American-born and about half were ex-members of provincial regiments and their dependents. Very few New Brunswick Loyalists were "gentlemen" (defined as men who did not work with their hands—professionals, officeholders, large landowners, and merchants). The majority were modest farmers, with the next largest category being craftsmen and artisans—carpenters, masons, coopers, shoemakers, and the like.

The Nova Scotia profile is similar except there were more European-born and fewer provincials, more Southerners (about 30 per cent) and fewer from the Middle Colonies (about 50 per cent). The Quebec Loyalists were never part of the myth of gentility and certainly comprised fewer wealthy and educated persons than those in the Maritimes. The vast majority were modest, backwoods farmers from New York and, to a much lesser extent, Vermont, New Hampshire, New Jersey, and Pennsylvania. There was a hefty portion of the European-born, mainly Scots and Germans, plus Indians. As in New Brunswick the white population was equally divided between provincials and civilians.

Upper Canada, Britain's first "inland colony," isolated and indefensible by the Royal Navy, seemed destined for a much more modest future than that of the favoured Maritimes. The Upper Canadian Loyalist was, therefore, less likely to be disappointed, less likely to be shocked by the wilderness. While the humble origin of so many Canadian Loyalists may disappoint modern snobs, their character was best fitted to the main task at hand.

Traditionally, the number of exiles has been put at a hundred thousand, but this is certainly too high. British North America received up to forty-six thousand, Bermuda no more than a hundred, the Bahamas about two thousand, and the British West Indies at least four thousand (over three thousand in Jamaica, about four hundred and fifty in Dominica, and a smattering scattered throughout various other islands). East and West Florida were the temporary homes of quite large numbers, but only a handful stayed on after the provinces were returned to Spain in 1783. In Central America a few settled the Mosquito Shore (in present Belize and Honduras). The British Isles received up to ten thousand and a small number headed to Europe, mainly Germans returning to the Rhine Valley. The total is in the neighbourhood of sixty-three thousand. To these may be added some of the six thousand black Loyalists (who ended up in the Maritimes, Sierra Leone, the Bahamas, and the West Indies, but were not counted), as well as some of the two thousand Indians, mainly Iroquois in Upper Canada, but also a few Creeks in New Providence, the Bahamas. Also, thousands of American slaves accompanied the Loyalists, mainly to the southern islands, but a few thousand went to British North America. Allowing for some whites lost to the records, the grand total would be a maximum of seventy thousand. Only if the thousands of "late Loyalists" who flooded into Upper Canada after 1791 are mistakenly included, would the traditional hundred thousand be accurate.

It could be argued that the approximately eight thousand free blacks and Indians were not really Loyalists and, of the whites left, some were not Loyalists at all, while others were marginal. The non-Loyalists were disbanded regular British and German troops and their dependents, who numbered well over five thousand in the Maritimes alone (about 20 per cent of the total in Nova Scotia, 5 per cent in New Brunswick), plus a much smaller number in Quebec. Also, non-Americans served in the provincial regiments, mainly as officers. The marginal Loyalists were those like the Highlanders already mentioned, who arrived in the colonies very shortly before the war broke out. Finally, a clear, but unknown, number must be subtracted from the total to account for those Loyalists who sooner or later returned permanently to the United States.

The quantifier of the Loyalists is further hindered because governments at that time were unable to keep accurate statistics. Existing figures are partial and sometimes contradictory, and, to add to the confusion, the Loyalists moved about frequently, especially in the early years. Even with more research, numbers will remain partly intelligent guesses. What is clear is that the young Republic lost a lot of people, that it lost a lot of talented people, and that these "transplants" enriched the host-countries. In some places, particularly Canada, they began a new era.

The migration of over forty thousand Loyalists to Canada is a significant chapter in the history of the colonization of North America. It compares in importance to the Great Migration of twenty thousand Englishmen to New England between 1630 and 1640. It created three new colonies and many new settlements and towns.

Above all was New Brunswick, split from Nova Scotia in 1784, which, before the arrival of the Loyalists, was largely wilderness, apart from the scattered habitations of some three thousand pre-Loyalists—Acadians, New Englanders and British, plus the hunting grounds of a few Micmac and Malecite Indians. The most important location was the lower and middle valley of the Saint John River (including the capital, Fredericton, and the city of Saint John), a settlement that formed a major link in the land communication between Halifax and Quebec City.

Next was Upper Canada (the future Ontario and ultimately the richest Canadian province), split from Quebec in 1791, and like New Brunswick virtually a wilderness, apart from the presence of a few fur-traders and Mississauga Indians. "The Front," that is, the northern shore of the St. Lawrence and Lake Ontario, was the most important settlement area and New Johnstown (Cornwall) and Cataraqui (Kingston) the most important towns. In the long run the occupation of Upper Canada led to western expansion to the Pacific.

Finally, Cape Breton, little developed since taken from France in 1763, was split from Nova Scotia in 1784 as a separate colony because of the Loyalist influx. The population of Prince Edward Island was substantially increased and the town of Summerside, second only to Charlottetown, was founded. The twelve thousand pre-Loyalist population of old Nova Scotia was more than doubled, settlement vastly expanded, and the development of the colony "accelerated ... by two generations." In old Quebec the Loyalists were largely lost, often assimilated into the mass of French Canadians, but they pioneered the settlement of parts of the Gaspé and the Eastern Townships.

The Loyalists came to Canada in two ways: by ship from New York and overland from the back country. Nova Scotia was largely settled the first way, Quebec the second. There were exceptions. Examples of Loyalists who did not come from New York to the Maritimes include: 500 evacuees from Charleston who arrived in November, 1782; the Penobscot Loyalists who crossed Passamaquoddy Bay from Maine after the British evacuation in 1783 and founded the town of St. Andrews; a shipment of destitutes direct from London to Halifax in 1784; evacuees from East Florida during 1784 and 1785; and 140 settlers from Quebec City to Cape Breton in October, 1784. Conversely, about thirteen hundred Loyalists sailed to Quebec with the evacuation of New York in 1783, and in 1792 over three hundred were shipped from London to Upper Canada.

ON HIS ARRIVAL in New York on May 9, 1782, Commander-In-Chief Sir Guy Carleton (who as governor of Quebec had repulsed the American invasion of 1775) began "perhaps the happiest period" of his career, despite the complicated situation he faced. New York City had remained a British garrison and a Loyalist haven since its capture in September, 1776. During 1782, as it became clear that the war was lost and that the rebels remained antagonistic, refugees flooded in to camps set up on Long Island, Staten Island, and the Jersey Shore. Carleton was faced with many more than he expected, a total of perhaps thirty thousand. What's more, Savannah and Charleston, as well as New York, had to be evacuated (the evacuees included not only Loyalists but also German mercenaries and regular British troops); shipping was insufficient; and the Americans demanded the return of escaped slaves and a speedy withdrawal as laid down in the peace treaty.

Carleton refused to abandon blacks who had joined the flag before the treaty, and the last British ships, under Admiral Digby, did not leave until December 4, 1783, when all the Loyalists had been evacuated, with great skill and at government expense, to the destinations of their choice, whether Great Britain, the Bahamas, the Floridas, the West Indies, or, above all, British North America. British North America took on the sort of appeal that Canada and the United States have had for Jews, Hungarians, Poles, Vietnamese, and other refugees of our own time. "I have turned myself out of doors for your sakes," wrote William Fraser from New York to his sons at Sorel, Quebec: "For God's sake, don't neglect us but do your best to get us into Canada." A few years later, in 1798, even French refugees from the "Terror" were granted lands in Upper Canada.

Carleton's instructions from London commended the Loyalists to his "tenderest ... care," and commanded him to give them "every assistance and prudent assurance of attention in whatever parts of America ... they chuse to settle." If Shelburne was "the friend of America," Carleton was the friend of the Loyalists. Not long after his arrival Loyalists began to hold meetings with an eye to settling in Nova Scotia. They asked for ships, provisions, supplies, and land. Without real guidance from the British government, which still vainly hoped for a fair deal from the United States, Carleton requested the cooperation of the acting governor of Nova Scotia, Sir Andrew Snape Hammond. Later, in the autumn of 1783, Carleton dispatched thousands of disbanded Loyalist troops to the fine lands of the Saint John River, despite Whitehall's orders to send them to Halifax.

The first fleet of nine transports and two frigates arrived from New York at Annapolis on October 19, 1782, with a few hundred immigrants. The Spring Fleet of over thirty transports left Sandy Hook at the end of April, 1783, with some seven thousand settlers bound for Halifax, Port Roseway, and the Bay of Fundy, including almost three thousand who went to the mouth of the Saint John River. Disembarkation there began on May 18, a date now revered in New Brunswick as the Loyalist landing day anniversary. The June or Summer Fleet of eighteen transports which left in mid-June brought about twenty-five hundred more to Annapolis, Port Roseway, Fort Cumberland, and the Saint John River. By July, the ships of the Spring Fleet had returned and began to sail back north intermittently. These irregular sailings—unremarkable, often unrecorded—increased in August when Carleton, pressured by numbers, decided to hire private vessels, including many belonging to patriots. The voyages continued until November. The final large-scale sailing was the Fall Fleet, the main body of which left on September 15 with about twenty-two hundred and fifty disbanded provincial soldiers and dependents bound for the Saint John River and an additional seven hundred for Halifax. On September 9, several ships had left for the Saint John River, Annapolis, and Port Roseway and, on September 24, several more ships sailed for the latter area. A total of about thirty-four hundred arrived at the mouth of the Saint John during the fall of 1783, and perhaps ten thousand added to the whole of Nova Scotia. The comment of August 21, 1783, by Maj. Joshua Upham, a future New Brunswick judge, that "everybody, all the world moves on to Nova Scotia" from New York, was borne out.

An analysis of a sample of over seventy-five hundred Loyalists in the New York area reveals that almost 90 per cent wanted to emigrate north. Of these 18 per cent chose Quebec, almost 2 per cent Prince Edward Island, and the remaining 80 per cent Nova Scotia where the Saint John River, Port Roseway, and Annapolis were, in descending order of importance, the favourite locations. Though it was Hobson's choice for many, the popularity of Nova Scotia is no mystery. It had a natural attraction for inhabitants of the Northern Colonies, particularly New Englanders who had regarded it as their "outpost" for over a century and a half. Its climate and terrain were familiar, and its fish, large tracts of empty land, and potential trade with the West Indies well known. After 1759, thousands of New England settlers, "the neutral Yankees" of the Revolution, were attracted by British offers of land, partly as replacements for the Acadians deported a few years earlier as security risks.

The immigration of New England Loyalists to Nova Scotia and their support at public expense began in early 1775. The next year Halifax received the first large group of Loyalist exiles—some eleven hundred who fled with the British forces evacuated from Boston, though most soon moved on to Britain. Throughout the war there were occasional arrivals of New Englanders to the infant Warden of the North and, in 1780, the British government had looked favourably on a scheme to set up New Ireland, a Loyalist colony in the Penobscot area of Northern Maine. The plan was rejected on a legal technicality, but it provided "a measure of inspiration" for northern settlement. So the migration of 1783 was not new in theory or practice. The novelty lay in the huge number.

It is likely that Brook Watson, the able, experienced commissary general who helped oversee the evacuation of New York, favoured Nova Scotia, where he had lived and had business interests. Certainly, by early fall, 1782, Carleton was publicizing the region's advantages as a Loyalist haven. At the same time the refugees themselves were taking an interest. Before the end of 1782 the Port Roseway Association, with Joseph Pynchon as president, had been formed from over one hundred and twenty families keen to settle an area suggested by Hammond and designated by Col. John Parr, the newly arrived governor, as highly suitable.

The fleet that reached Annapolis in October, 1782, was accompanied by three scouts sent by a Loyalist organization called the Board of Agents: Amos Botsford represented Lloyd's Neck, Long Island; Samuel Cummings represented Queens County, Long Island; Frederick Hauser represented Bergen County, New Jersey. Their report, presented January 14, 1783, was important in popularizing Nova Scotia, especially when the depressing news of the peace negotiations filtered into New York during the following months. The coast from Annapolis to St. Mary's Bay and the Annapolis Valley were commended but it was the Saint John Valley, which they penetrated as far as Oromocto, that received the most attention. The river, deemed comparable to the Hudson or the Connecticut, had an excellent ice-free harbour and was navigable to ocean-going vessels for eighty miles; above all, the interval land, enriched by annual spring floods, possessed "a most fertile soil" which "produces crops of all kinds with little labour." Fine prospects for cattle and wheat on "the up lands" and cod-fishing in the Bay of Fundy were also noted. A trip up the tributary Kennebecasis revealed "a large tract of interval and up land, which has never been granted."

The Loyalists usually left New York in groups, either the structured remnants of the provincial regiments, or "companies" formed by the authorities, each with an appointed captain. Sometimes the groups were self-generated. Walter Bates, who later became the respected sheriff of Kings County, New Brunswick, recalled that in April, 1783, the Reverend John Sayre came to Eaton's Neck, Long Island, and told his fellow Connecticut Loyalists living there about the British offer of land and provisions in Nova Scotia. A meeting was held and they resolved to go as a group of over two hundred "to enjoy the comforts of a church and school in the wilderness," which they later accomplished at Kingston, New Brunswick.

Bates and friends began embarkation on the *Union*, April 11, sailed a few days later to the town of New York, and did not leave Sandy Hook, New Jersey, with the convoy for the actual journey until April 26. These preliminaries could take longer and be more trying than the voyage itself. On May 25, 1783, Sarah Frost and her family (like Walter Bates, they were natives of Stamford, Connecticut, and future New Brunswickers) boarded the *Two Sisters* at Oyster Bay, Long Island, but it was three weeks later before the June Fleet was assembled and ready to depart. Meanwhile the heat made them sleepless, rough weather caused sea-sickness, crying children drove her "crazy," and the 250 passengers "thronged on board" (six families shared her cabin) made it "comfortable for nobody." As the transports took one passenger per one-and-a-half tons, the 287-ton *Union* was indeed overcrowded. However, only 164 passengers actually sailed to Nova Scotia—one person per 1.75 tons. In an age when emigrants commonly journeyed to the New World at one person per ton, and slaves at five per two tons and even higher, the Loyalists' accommodation, though rough by modern standards, was adequate.

The Loyalists en route to new homes must have experienced a turmoil of emotions: sorrow at leaving their homes, relief at escaping the belligerent Republic, doubts about the wilderness for which they were headed, but hopes for new lives. As Nancy Cameron sadly prepared to leave her beloved home on the Upper Mohawk to make her way to the unfamiliar wilderness north of the St. Lawrence, she wrote to her cousin in Scotland of her despair. Her one consolation was that her ears would no longer ring with the hateful taunt of "tories."

The voyage from New York to Halifax or the mouth of the Saint John usually took from a week to a fortnight depending on the weather and the navigator's skill. After the exultation of being "*Off at last!*" and the initial exhilaration of the fresh sea-breezes, tedium soon set in. The army-style rations of bread or flour, salt beef and pork, butter, peas, and oatmeal were filling but dull, and no rum was issued. For Mrs. Frost, the boredom was broken by the occasional diversion: she saw "something floating on the water," maybe a wreck, maybe a dead whale; the captain fired a warning shot at a "rebel brig" which had refused to "lie to"; otherwise there were always "games of crib." The weather could bring less welcome variety: "The wind blows so high ... I am afraid to go to bed for fear of rolling out." Then fog set in and the ship was becalmed for three days.

Edward Winslow, Sr., the father of the great New Brunswick Loyalist of the same name, reported a "disagreeable" fourteen days. His daughter Sarah added that there was "not one hour good weather" during the whole voyage. Everyone was sick and frightened except the old gentleman who "was neither sick nor afraid of anything, except that he should get victuals enough to eat—which was rather an unnecessary concern, for no others of the party had any inclination to partake of his delicacies."

Crowded passengers were always prone to disease and many arrived "sickly." The *Two Sisters*, for example, suffered a measles epidemic. Smallpox could also be a problem. The greatest danger, however, was shipwreck, particularly in the stormy Bay of Fundy. Surprisingly, only one disaster was reported. In September, 1783, the *Martha* struck rocks off Cape Sable Island near the entrance to the Bay of Fundy "and in the course of a few hours wrecked in a thousand pieces," with the loss of 115 men, women, and children from two provincial regiments—the

Maryland Loyalists, and the 2ⁿᵈ De Lanceys of New York. Some fifty survivors were rescued by fishing boats. Another six floated on a piece of wreckage for a couple of days before two died of exposure. Eventually the remaining four reached an island where they lived for a week on "a few raspberries and snails" before they were found.

The captain of the *Martha* was accused of incompetence and cowardice, but generally there was high praise for the captains of the transports. Mrs. Frost called Captain Brown "as kind a captain as ever need to live," and the passengers of the *Sovereign*, a late summer arrival, offered Captain Stewart their "unfeigned thanks" for his "generosity, kindness and attention."

Arrival in the north was a mixed experience. On June 26, 1783, Mrs. Frost wrote that she was "tired of being on board ship" (and doubtless tired of wandering) and longed to see Nova Scotia, "though a strange land." Two days later they anchored off Fort Howe, at the mouth of the Saint John, where some of the men went ashore and brought back gooseberries. Mr. Frost did rather better with "a fine salmon." The next morning she observed that "it looks very pleasant on shore," but when she landed with her children, what a shock: "the roughest land I ever saw ... this is to be *the city* they say!"

The poignancy of the twenty-eight-year-old Mrs. Frost's story is increased by the knowledge that, at her departure, she had said farewell to her parents, who were staunch rebels, and five weeks after she arrived, she gave birth to a daughter, Hannah. (It was not uncommon for babies to be born during the voyage.) Another Loyalist recalled her arrival the same year at the same place: "I climbed to the top of Chipman's Hill and watched the sails disappearing in the distance, and such a feeling of loneliness came over me that, although I had not shed a single tear through all the war, I sat down on the damp moss with my baby in my lap and cried." That lady became the grandmother of Sir Leonard Tilley, New Brunswick's Father of Confederation.

Discounting three or four thousand transients, the common estimate for the total number of Loyalists in the Maritimes in the early years is about thirty-five thousand: twenty thousand in peninsular Nova Scotia; fifteen thousand in what became New Brunswick in 1784; four hundred in Cape Breton; and eight hundred in Prince Edward Island. In addition, a very few families settled in Newfoundland. Although the provincials were found everywhere, they were concentrated in the Townships of Upper Canada and in the Saint John River Valley. The great concentration of civilian Loyalists was at Shelburne. These were the three major Loyalist settlements in North America. The first two were largely successful, the third an almost complete failure.

Generally, the Nova Scotia Loyalists, who in fact probably numbered only sixteen thousand, were given land in unsettled areas. Some were found in every modern Nova Scotia county, but the largest and most bizarre early settlement anywhere, containing for a time about one-quarter of all the Loyalists in Canada, was at Port Roseway on the South Shore. The location was suggested by Sir Andrew Snape Hammond in 1782, and by the autumn of that year the Port Roseway Associates had been formed in New York with a view to settling there. Strongly encouraged by Governor Parr, about four thousand arrived in May, 1783, to find Benjamin Marston, a Massachusetts Loyalist, already at work surveying. When Parr paid an official visit at the end of July and named the place Shelburne, after his patron, the population had reached five thousand and spectacular progress had been made. Land had been cleared, a chequerboard street plan laid out, and wooden houses built. Parr was entertained with full vice-regal ceremony, including a grand dinner and ball.

By 1784 the population had probably reached ten thousand, making Shelburne the largest town in British North America and one of the largest on the entire American seaboard. It was confidently expected to outstrip Halifax in economic importance, with high hopes for fishing, whaling, shipbuilding, and trade, particularly with the West Indies. The royal imprimatur was bestowed by the visit of Prince William Henry (the future William IV) in 1785. In an astonishingly short time Shelburne boasted the amenities of a major city: fine houses, taverns, a jeweller, a dancing instructor, a hairdresser, churches, schools, three newspapers, sawmills, and shipyards.

The decline of Shelburne was almost as dramatic as its mushroom growth. People began to leave as early as 1786, after a bad storm and the end of food distribution. Two years later, 360 houses were reported empty and a drastic decline continued into the 1790s. By 1815 the population was a mere six hundred. The reason was partly the inexperienced and imprudent settlers, but more important was the poor site. Shelburne had a magnificent harbour (which froze) but little else. The hinterland was weak, soil and timber poor, inland communications primitive, whaling and the fisheries disappointing. Nova Scotia could support only one metropolis and Halifax had a head start at a much superior location.

Other important settlements were Digby and Annapolis (and the Valley) on the Bay of Fundy; Halifax and northward to Windsor and Truro; Dartmouth (and nearby Preston) and along the Eastern Shore, particularly Guysborough and the Chedebucto Bay area; Cumberland County, especially Parrsboro; the North Shore including Antigonish, Pictou, Ramsheg, and the Cobequid Road. On

Cape Breton Island the Loyalists settled mainly in the Sydney area, but also in Baddeck and St. Peter's, with a few at Port Hood, Margaree, and Port Hawkesbury.

Prince Edward Island is inadequately researched but the main settlement was the isthmus between Malpeque and Bedeque Bays where Summerside, the Island's second town, was founded in 1784. Other areas were Pownal, Vernon River and the upper reaches of Orwell Bay, and Montague where some Rhode Islanders settled. About six hundred of the eight hundred who arrived stayed.

In New Brunswick the great core of settlement—probably ten thousand people—was the Saint John Valley which began at Saint John (incorporated 1785) and proceeded up the river (and several of its tributaries) to Fredericton, another Loyalist town. Upstream from Fredericton, blocks were surveyed for the disbanded provincials who moved in, mainly in 1784, as far as Woodstock. The British government, in the interests of cohesion and defence, was anxious to settle the various regiments together. The second most important location was Passamaquoddy Bay (particularly St. Andrews) and the St. Croix estuary (particularly St. Stephen). Less important settlements were along the Bay of Fundy, the Petitcodiac River, Sackville, the Vale of Sussex, the Miramichi, and Baie de Chaleur.

Whereas most Loyalists first arrived by ship in the Maritimes after the evacuation of New York, immigrants to Quebec trickled in from 1774, throughout the war, and beyond, by a variety of more difficult routes and methods. Of course within the colony itself there was the great highway of the St. Lawrence and Lake Ontario. Although a couple of groups led by Capt. Michael Grass and Capt. Peter Van Alstine arrived by sea in 1783, Quebec was usually reached from the back country of New York via various rivers, lakes, and portages.

The classic route, or rather warpath, between the thirteen colonies and Quebec was up the Hudson to the Richelieu River via Lakes George and Champlain, and down to the confluence with the St. Lawrence at Sorel. During the war this was the most common route and many Loyalists were found at Ile aux Noix, St. Jean (St. Johns), Chambly, St. Ours and Sorel, and at Machiche (now Yamachiche) across Lac St. Pierre near Trois Rivières (Three Rivers) where a camp for soldiers' dependents was set up. Others branched off to Montreal and neighbouring Lachine and Pointe Claire.

At the end of the war Loyalists were more likely to take the Mohawk River and a branch called Wood Creek to Lake Oneida, thence down the Oswego River to the British fort of the same name, a route that required a total of thirty miles of portage. A variation was another Mohawk waterway that led to the mouth of the Black River at Sacket's Harbor. Yet another method was up the Hudson and across the Mohegan mountains to the Moose and then the Black River. From Fort Oswego and Sacket's Harbor, lake ships took the migrants north to the Bay of Quinte or west along the southern shore to Niagara. The same journeys could also be made by land. Some avoided Lake Ontario and proceeded to the Upper St. Lawrence by following the Oswegatchie to modern Ogdensburg; taking Long Lake and the Raquette River to modern Cornwall; arriving at the same place via Lake Champlain, Plattsburg, and overland; or, as Sir John Johnson did in 1776, along the Sacondaga and St. Regis Rivers. A daunting journey was undertaken by a few frontiersmen who arrived at Detroit from Florida via the Mississippi, Wabash, and Maumee Rivers. Later, numbers of discontented Maritime Loyalists ascended the Saint John River, reached the Lower St. Lawrence via Lac Témiscouata and the Grand Portage, and then sailed to Upper Canada.

Such journeys were filled with hardships. Travellers banded together whenever possible, cooperation easing such problems as portaging. "Through the forests we must trust to Indian guides," remarked one refugee. Pack horses, hand and horse carts, and simple Shanks' pony were used. On the water, canoes, bateaux, skiffs, and lake boats had to be brought, made, bought, or hired.

Almost no first-hand accounts of these journeys are known. An exception is "A Journey to Canada" (Albany to Montreal) written by Richard Cartwright around 1779, just after his trek. Cartwright later became a leading merchant and member of the Legislative Council of Upper Canada. The twenty-year-old set out on horseback from his native Albany under a rebel pass on October 27. Though sorry to leave his parents and friends he was glad to escape the "Caprice" and "Anarchy" of "usurped Authority" which also made bearable the "Wet and Dirt,... the Badness of the Roads, and the various Difficulties of so long a Journey at this late season of the Year...." The size of his party is not mentioned but it contained his nine-year-old niece Hannah, servants, and wagons.

On October 31 they reached Fort George at the southern tip of Lake George. They had spent the nights and all of one day (when heavy rain prevented progress) at houses along the way, one of which "had an obliging Lanlady ... good Company, and plenty of excellent Victuals and Drink." The "once agreeable and delightful" land around Stillwater "now displayed a most shocking Picture of Havock and wild Desolation," the result of "the Rage of War"—the campaigns of 1777. Fort George itself was in ashes but the party "fortunately met with a Boat" that took them five miles up the lake to Diamond Island, "a barren Rock," where they spent a cold night in a tent alongside some British soldiers.

The next morning, November 1, they left on a barge that had come to evacuate the post. "A brisk southerly Breeze" brought them by nightfall to

Ticonderoga Landing at the southern end of Lake Champlain where they were welcomed by the army and spent the night "much crowded." The next morning Cartwright proceeded to Fort Ticonderoga where he "spent most of the Day in visiting" old friends "who had fled from the Persecution of the Times." That evening at dusk, "having with some Difficulty procured a boat and got our Baggage round to the Fort," they sailed a few miles up the lake, landed, lighted a fire, and spent a comfortable night in their tent. On the morning of November 3, they had to row until another "brisk southerly Breeze" took them to Split Rock, about forty miles up from Ticonderoga on the western shore, where they boarded the *Liberty*, a former rebel schooner. They sailed through the night, and next morning reached Point au Faire. There they boarded their boat once more and sailed on the Richelieu to St. Jean that evening. They were obliged, because they could not get any "Carriages," to stay in St. Jean for two days in living quarters that "were not extra-ordinary."

On November 7 they loaded their baggage onto some rented "Carts," one of which carried his niece, while he and the servants walked along "18 miles of the worst Road I ever saw" and arrived by evening at La Prairie, about nine miles from Montreal. The carters would not go any further to the ferry at "Long-Isle" and no boat could be found, so they spent the night there. Next day Cartwright, accompanied against his wishes by Hannah, walked to the ferry through a snowstorm and arrived in Montreal in the late afternoon, the girl "much fatigued and both not a little dirty."

Cartwright's was a rather easy journey, entirely via settled areas or army posts. Today's outdoor adventurers might even consider it a vacation. His worst moment came when he had to rescue Hannah who had "tumbled headlong into the Lake,... but dry Cloaths and a good Fire prevented us receiving any Detriment." The thirteen-day length was much shorter than expected—"many who left Albany before or together with us did not arrive till many Days after." Those Loyalists who took other routes, which had awkward portages and lacked the opportunities for speed on the open water of Lake Champlain, were in for up to two or three months of "long and hard" slogging, a far cry from the comparative luxury of a two-week sail from New York to Halifax.

Apart from the hardships of the overland route, the Loyalists who took refuge in the province of Quebec found themselves in an area of continuous military operations. Those who came in the summer of 1775 entered a province threatened by invasion. The majority of the French Canadians were prepared to remain neutral, but an active minority of both French and English cooperated with the invaders.

The first Loyalists to arrive were a party of eighty Highlanders brought from the Mohawk Valley by recruiting parties for service in the Loyal Highland Emigrants Regiment. The composition of this unique corps, which is classed as a Loyalist unit, illustrates the difficulty of identifying true Loyalists. It consisted of Fraser Highlanders disbanded from Wolfe's army in Canada; contingents from emigrant ships intercepted on their way to New York; and others from besieged Boston, and from Halifax and Newfoundland. To these were later added prisoners of war taken during the siege of Quebec in 1775-6. This unit became the 84th Regiment of the line and, at the close of the revolutionary war, some of its men were settled on the north bank of the Ottawa River. Ironically, then, former rebels who had attacked Quebec City now had their names placed on the United Empire Loyalist lists.

The second substantial group of Loyalists to arrive in Quebec was also drawn from the Mohawk Valley. Led by Col. Guy Johnson, a relative of the famous Sir William Johnson, along with Indian agent Col. Christian Daniel Claus, the great landowner John Butler, and the Mohawk chief Joseph Brant, this group included two hundred wives and children and some three hundred Mohawk warriors and their families—in all about fifteen hundred.

These Loyalists had barely settled in around Montreal when their place of refuge was invaded by the Continental forces which occupied Montreal during the winter of 1775-6 and besieged Quebec City. Those French and English Canadians who opposed the invaders, temporarily found themselves in much the same position as the Loyalists in the old colonies. Some were arrested and sent to prison camps in the revolting colonies.

This was the first occasion in which Loyalists and Canadians fought side by side. The relative weight of the Loyalists in this campaign can be measured by a roll call of the defenders of Quebec City: Royal Highland Emigrants (about half Loyalist), 186; French militia, 300; English, 200. The remainder of the 1,200-man garrison was made up of regulars and ships' companies from the Royal Navy and merchant marine.

Parties of French Canadians, Indians, and Loyalists on the Upper St. Lawrence harassed the rear of the invading forces, and were the first to re-enter Montreal on the heels of the retreating Continental army in June of 1776. With the departing American forces went a handful of Canadians—French and English—who had worked too openly with the occupying forces. Most of these joined the Continental army and, at the end of the war, were given land grants by the American government and resettled in the United States.

With the defeat of the invading forces, neutralism in Quebec gave way to support of the war effort. As refugees continued to flood into the province the obvious course was to organize the able-bodied into military units. By this means strength was added to the Crown forces while the families of those serving were put on the military budget, without resorting to charity.

Serious recruiting among Loyalists began in the summer of 1776 when Sir John Johnson, son of Sir William Johnson, escaped along with two hundred tenants to the Indian village of St. Regis opposite present-day Cornwall, after a gruelling nineteen-day trek through the wilds of upper New York. Johnson and other prominent Loyalists with military reputations or aspirations, men such as Edward Jessup and Robert Leake, were given commissions to raise regiments. Few were able to recruit anything larger than companies, and the smaller corps were later incorporated into Johnson's King's Royal Regiment of New York.

Throughout the long war Loyalists continued to pour into Quebec, their numbers swollen by a wave of refugees that came in the wake of Burgoyne's defeat in 1777. Many more came by way of raids that Sir John Johnson launched into New York to rescue families of Loyalist volunteers who had been left behind. By the end of the war some seventeen hundred Loyalists were receiving relief, and the several thousand in Loyalist corps, when disbanded, would be in need of it.

The responsibility for their welfare rested with Sir Frederick Haldimand, the Swiss Protestant who had replaced Carleton as governor in 1778. Haldimand had been attentive to Loyalist needs during the war, but opposed their permanent settlement in the province on the grounds that lands west of the Ottawa were Indian territory and the eastern half of the province the patrimony of the French Canadians, although he was prepared to allow the handful of Loyalists at Niagara and Detroit to remain there. The provincial surveyor, Maj. Samuel Holland, was sent to survey the western lands, but Haldimand insisted that the Loyalists in the heart of the province must go to the Maritimes.

Meanwhile, Carleton in New York feared that Nova Scotia could not absorb all the Loyalists. When he learned that there was good land in the Cataraqui area of present-day Kingston, he sent a Loyalist contingent by sea. This group managed to go as far as Sorel in 1784, thus adding to Haldimand's burdens.

Happily, the governor had discovered by this time that the western Indians would welcome Loyalist settlers in the West as a guarantee of the continued British presence in the interior of the continent. It was then that Haldimand decided to resettle Loyalists west of the Ottawa, a decision that was unpopular with the Loyalists along the Richelieu Valley who hoped to settle in the Missis-quoi Bay area. The Hawley family had settled there as early as 1776 and by the end of the war some sixty families had squatted on the Caldwell and Christie seignieuries, farming and marketing their excess produce at St. Jean. As an alternative to a move west and to help settle a seigneury he owned, Haldimand sent 315 Loyalists to the Gaspé, where they founded New Carlisle, the birthplace of Quebec Premier René Levesque.

A new dimension to the pattern of settlement was added when it was decided to found a settlement of disbanded soldiers at Sorel, because of its strategic importance at the mouth of the Richelieu River. Some 316 Loyalists were settled there, later joined by disbanded regulars. Isaac Weld, in 1795, reported that Sorel was the only town between Montreal and Quebec where "the English language is dominant" and the inhabitants "largely Loyalists from the United States."

Other Loyalists not living on government land or receiving assistance are difficult to identify because they rarely appear in government records as Loyalists. They must have numbered several hundred at least, and most of them were in Montreal. At the start of the war, this was a walled city of about six thousand which, apart from the garrison, included about one hundred English families. During the course of the war, its population increased by about two thousand Loyalists and by a garrison that reached its height in 1777 with the presence of Burgoyne's forces. As many Loyalists moved west in 1784, it is unlikely that those who remained in Montreal exceeded three hundred in number. The testimony of Isaac Weld, who visited the city in 1795, indicates that very few of the French spoke English, while most of the English inhabitants were well acquainted with French. Yet the Loyalist names of Johnson, Platt, Richardson, Logan, and others, which appear among the Montreal elite, testify to the continuing influence of Loyalist families in Montreal.

Although Quebec City was never a refugee area, it became the centre for Loyalist civil servants. These were headed by Chief Justice William Smith and his son-in-law, Solicitor General Jonathan Sewell. At Trois Rivières there was a cluster of Loyalists including schoolteacher William Nelson, whose two doctor sons were prominent in the rebel ranks in 1837–8. Other small groups of Loyalists could be found at Chambly and St. Jean. In the Ottawa Valley Loyalists such as the Albrights, Jones, Hydes, and LeRoys were at St. Andrews East, the Van Kleeks at Van Kleek Hill, and the Cushings at Lachute. Beauharnois was not an area of Loyalist settlement, although the seigneury was acquired by the Ellice family who had been driven from their estates in the Mohawk Valley.

Haldimand could not force self-sufficient Loyalists westward from Montreal, but he was determined to move the sixty or so squatter families from Missisquoi

Bay. As a move in this direction he cut off their relief and ordered them to leave, but as Haldimand left the province late in 1784, his successors did not interfere with the squatters and even restored their rations.

Like the Loyalists who remained in French Canada, those already settled in the West had no occasion to move. Detroit was their most distant settlement. This had been, by turns, a French and British military post, and continued to be a centre of the fur trade. By 1787, some 115 Loyalists—mainly Butler's Rangers—had taken up grants in the new western settlements, now Colchester and Gosfield Townships. However, by 1794 their numbers had dwindled down to about twenty-three. A few Loyalists settled at Sandwich, now part of Windsor, and at Amherstburg, frequently as tenants and labourers. When Detroit was finally evacuated by British troops in 1796, a number of its settlers crossed the river into Canada.

Less remote than Detroit but far from the main Loyalist settlements was Niagara, which remained in British hands throughout the war. In the winter of 1778 Col. John Butler had built barracks for his Rangers on the site of Niagara-on-the-Lake, and Haldimand encouraged a civilian settlement there as a source of supply for the garrison. This civilian settlement began in 1780 with just a few families, who might be called the Pilgrim Fathers of Upper Canada. By 1782 seventeen Loyalist families enjoyed a modest agricultural prosperity and, in exchange for giving their surplus crops to the troops, they were issued provisions, tools, and seed.

In June, 1784, the Rangers, some regulars, and most of the Indian Department were disbanded. Those who wished it received transportation to the Bay of Quinte and the Upper St. Lawrence. However, six hundred remained at Niagara, and its remote location led to acute logistical problems, slow surveying, and generally rather chaotic conditions for a number of years.

For nearly all Loyalists in the heart of Quebec their settlement meant a move up the St. Lawrence to lands already found suitable for farming. The journey was less hazardous than the move from their homes in the old colonies, but more difficult than a sea journey from New York to Halifax.

The embarkation point for Loyalists bound for the Upper St. Lawrence and the Bay of Quinte was Lachine, near Montreal. The route was navigable, but only with difficulty. From Lake Ontario to Montreal the river drops 225 feet in 190 miles, creating 120 miles of rapids, chiefly the Long Sault, the Galop, and the Beauharnois. The Long Sault rapids, now tamed by the Long Sault dam near Cornwall, were the most formidable, dropping 45 feet in 9 miles.

Passengers boarded Lachine-built bateaux, boats specially constructed for the rapid-strewn river, each manned by experienced crews of four or five French Canadians, one of whom steered. This type of bateau, weighing two tons, was strongly built, 24 to 40 feet long, 5 to 7 feet in the beam, pointed at both ends, flat-bottomed for a shallow draft of 3 or 4 feet, and equipped with oars, poles, and a sail. Four or five families and their modest belongings might be accommodated on each vessel. "Brigades" of ten or twelve bateaux, the passengers often members of a single provincial regiment proceeding to their assigned township, travelled together under the command of a "conductor." The combined manpower was useful for difficult water and portages. At the rapids, passengers alighted with their valuables and the bateaux were poled and dragged by men (including Loyalists) with lines, both on shore and in the water; horses and oxen were also used if available and in some places windlasses. Sometimes on open water both oars and sail were used. Progress could average eighteen miles a day, hence the trip from Montreal to Cataraqui (Kingston) could be done in ten days, but it might stretch into a month. At night the company usually went ashore and slept in tents made of canvas tarpaulins hung over branches and poles. Sometimes there was hospitality from French Canadians (they were "very kind to strangers") and Loyalists already settled on shore. Always the journey could become unpleasant or dangerous from plagues of insects, rough accommodation, bad weather, and hazardous water.

Loyalist descriptions of the journey westward are as rare as those of the journey from the New York back country, but again there is at least one exception. In 1789 Miss Anne Powell, originally of Massachusetts, accompanied her brother, William Dummer Powell, a prominent Upper Canadian, from Montreal to Detroit where he had been appointed "First Judge." Miss Powell travelled in style, with servants, but her journal recorded experiences that even the humblest Loyalist must have shared.

There was a convoy of boats, one of which was "well filled" with the Powells and sixteen other passengers. There was "an awning to protect us from the weather" and not much room which "was of no consequence" because it was so "cold on the water" that "we were glad to sit close." She found the travel from Montreal "very tedious." The first night they stayed at the house of an "Habitan" who gave them his best room "where we spread our beds and slept in peace." The next day they unloaded while the boats were taken through one of the locks that bypassed the rapids near Montreal. That night they stayed at an inn or "Public House" but were so "tormented with Fleas and Dirt" that they resolved never to use another if any other accommodation could be had. This proved no problem because by 1789 there were lots of houses of disbanded soldiers. The Powells "went from a Coll to a Captn, from a Captn to a Major" spending pleasant nights in "good houses." Evening diversions, apart from chatting with their hosts, included walks along the beautiful river bank, perhaps to observe the Indians fishing with harpoons by firelight. Each night they "always drest a dinner [a picnic] for the next day, so when we were disposed to eat it the cloth was laid in the boat and the table served with as much decency as could be expected." The sailors, however, "went on shore and boiled their pot, smoked their Pipes, etc." One night a bonfire was lighted, which spread through the dry leaves for over half a mile, creating "the most beautiful illumination and a feeling of joy." Miss Powell commented revealingly: "We had heard, just before we left Montreal, of his Majesty's recovery, so, if you please, you may set down all this rejoicing on that account, tho' I doubt whether it once occurr'd to our minds, yet we are very loyal people." That same night "the weather was so fine that we ventured to sleep out" in tents made of boat sails and blankets. She liked it so much that she "regretted we had ever gone into a house. It is the pleasantest vagabond life you can imagine."

On the tenth day they reached Kingston, already a small town, stayed three days, then boarded a Lake Ontario boat for the four-day passage to Niagara. Fifteen people were squeezed into "a small Cabin where there were only 4 b'rths," the males divided from the females by "a Blanket partition." After a sojourn at Niagara they sailed Lake Erie to Detroit in five days, "better accommodated" because "the weather was so fine that the gentn all slept upon deck."

Strangely enough, if there are very few Loyalist accounts of the trip up the St. Lawrence we do have a picture, possibly somewhat idealized, of a Loyalist camp at Johnstown on the banks of the river in June, 1784. This painting by a surveyor, Lieut. James Peachey, is the earliest depiction of the Loyalists in Canada.* These Loyalists, judging by what looks like a more permanent wooden structure to the right of the large tree, may have already reached their destination and were waiting to proceed to their lands since Johnstown was a base camp for the townships that stretched westward. Nevertheless, by examining it closely one can gain an impression of life in an overnight camp and the activities of the day. The refugees are washing clothes, carrying water, cooking, fishing, and sharpening knives on a grindstone. An axeman rests from the labour of chopping up a newly felled tree. The party seems to be regimented: more than one person is wearing a

---

*"Encampment of the Loyalist's at Johnston, a New Settlement, on the Banks of the River St. Lawrence in Canada, taken June 6ᵗʰ 1784." Watercolour and pen and ink over pencil; [166mm × 365 mm]; PAC/ACP [C-2001]. See book cover for illustration.

uniform (probably of the King's Royal Regiment). The man in the left foreground could be the officer in command. The bateaux which probably brought them are beached at the head of the inlet in the middleground. Their oars seem to be among the tents on the left.

Life in such tent cities was a common Loyalist experience. Two items stand out: nature's bounty in the form of wood, fish, and game (three birds appear to be roasting on spits over the fire on the right); and government's bounty in the form of tents, axes, kettles, and possibly even the cows. A second tent settlement is shown to the right on the far bank. Further to the left, on the inlet, a large tent with several adjoining smaller ones suggests a headquarters, perhaps of the surveyors. Above, the presence of fencing and the log cabins on the left middleground indicate the growing permanency of what became the town of Cornwall.

The main Loyalist settlements were divided into the Royal Townships, eight in number, beginning at Coteau-du-Lac and ending just beyond the present site of Brockville. Here a stretch of rocky ground separated them from the Cataraqui Townships which ran from Kingston to the Bay of Quinte. By mid-June of 1784, Loyalists had taken up land in the eight Royal Townships along the northern bank of the St. Lawrence. Sir John Johnson's 1ˢᵗ battalion of the King's Royal Regiment of New York settled the first five; Maj. Edward Jessup's Loyal Rangers settled the next three. Progress was slower in the eight Cataraqui Townships that stretched westward from the head of Lake Ontario, yet by the end of 1784 Capt. Michael Grass' New York party of "associated Loyalists" was ensconced in number one; part of Jessup's Rangers in number two; Maj. James Rogers' King's Rangers in number three; and the 2ⁿᵈ battalion of Johnson's regiment in number four. Number five contained mainly British and German regulars. The three other townships were not settled until later; Belleville, in number eight, for example, was founded in 1790.

As in New Brunswick, the British government wanted the Loyalists settled as far as possible by regiment, for reasons of cohesion and defence, and Haldimand's arrangements accomplished this. The Loyalists themselves asked to be divided by race and religion. Thus, in the first five Royal Townships, Catholic Highlanders, Scottish Presbyterians, German Calvinists, German Lutherans, and Anglicans were settled roughly in that order.

In 1790 the government bought part of the Thames River area from the Indians, and this would become the prime agricultural land of Southern Ontario. Here a few scattered settlements developed, including some by evacuees from Detroit in 1790. The peninsula at Long Point on Lake Erie was purchased from the Mississaugas in 1784, but it remained unoccupied for some time since Governor Simcoe had aborted plans for a naval base there. Finally, in 1793, Loyalists began to move into this area from Niagara as well as from faraway New Brunswick. These were joined by "late Loyalists" from the United States, among whom the most important was Capt. Sam Ryerse (or Ryerson), formerly of the New Jersey Volunteers. Ryerse founded and built mills at Port Ryerse which boasted a population of 160, by 1796.

The old province of Quebec sheltered about eight thousand Loyalists, exclusive of the Indians. Of these about six thousand were in the area of present-day Ontario. A government report of 1786 shows their distribution as: New Johnstown (Cornwall), 2,047; New Oswegatchie (the Prescott area), 759; Cataraqui (Kingston), 1,853; Niagara, 946; Fort Erie, 147; Detroit, 6. As for the Indians, there were about eighteen hundred settled along the Grand River.

In estimating the number of Loyalists east of the Ottawa, we must rely on guesswork. At least 375 were sent to the Gaspé; another 315 were at Sorel. Petitions signed by 380 came from Missisquoi Bay in 1786, and, as previously suggested, 300 is a reasonable estimate for Loyalists remaining in Montreal. As others in the province could not have numbered more than a few hundred, the total Loyalists in French Canada must have amounted to about two thousand.


OVERALL, THE migration of the Loyalists had two major results. First, their number and affiliation with Britain enabled Quebec to escape conquest by the United States, inspired in the nineteenth century by the concept of Manifest Destiny. The British Empire, unlike the American, allowed the French to keep their way of life. Second, as L.F.S. Upton has pointed out, when British emigration got underway "in the 1820's there was a British America for it to go to. The Loyalists performed a vital holding operation...." Without the thin blue line from Detroit to Newfoundland, modern Canada would not exist.

However, even in areas of greatest Loyalist strength, direct political domination was more or less ephemeral, either because of Loyalist defections, or post-Loyalist immigration, or both. The Loyalist population fluctuated for many years. The great exception was in New Brunswick, where 85 per cent of the Loyalists remained and where little new immigration took place until after the War of 1812. The Loyalists were powerful here until Confederation. In Cape Breton the Loyalists were overwhelmed by massive Scottish immigration beginning in 1802, but they remained socially and politically dominant until the colony rejoined Nova Scotia in 1821. The Nova Scotia Loyalists entered an established society and, far from dominating, ceased to exist as a separate group within a very few years. Also, Nova Scotia lost more Loyalists than any other colony. By 1787 Roger Viets, the Loyalist Anglican clergyman at Annapolis, was reporting "the great Emigration" from economic disappointment (partly because the old inhabitants had laid claim to the best sites), encouraged that year by the ending of government provisions and the new portability of military pensions and half-pay. The population of Annapolis dropped from 1,900 in 1784 to 40 families in 1787; more dramatically, Shelburne declined from perhaps 10,000 people to a mere 1,600 by 1795. Almost everywhere the figures show the same trend. Some, like the inhabitants of Port Mouton on the South Shore who transferred to Guysborough, moved to other parts of the province. Some (like 600 Shelburners attracted to Prince Edward Island by Lieut.-Gov. Walter Patterson) moved to other parts of the Maritimes, some went to Upper Canada, particularly the London area, and a few went to Great Britain, Jamaica, and the Bahamas. The vast majority, however, seem to have returned to the United States. Nova Scotia, in fact, may have lost two-thirds of its Loyalists immigrants! The classic nineteenth-century migration of Maritimers to the "Boston States" actually began at this point, in the late eighteenth century.

The modern trend of "goin' down the road" to Ontario dates back in a similar way. An unknown number of New Brunswick Loyalists—probably several hundred plus a few pre-Loyalists—settled on the marginal lands of the Miramichi, the Penniac (a tributary of the Nashwaak), and Grand Lake. Here they caught "Niagara Fever"—tempting offers of free, fertile land from John G. Simcoe, the first lieutenant-governor of Upper Canada, who took office in 1791. Thus, Upper Canada gained rather than lost Loyalists, though a few did return to the United States. Much more often the movement was in the opposite direction as hordes of American frontiersmen caught the same fever.

By 1794, as Carleton University Professor Sydney Wise states, "all pretence that persons being granted lands ... were Loyalists had disappeared." By 1812, the population of Upper Canada was 100,000 but probably only one-fifth were Loyalists or their children. The remainder, the "late-Loyalists," included some "lukewarm" and even some committed Loyalists, but were mainly American frontiersmen who, at best, were apolitical. A similar phenomenon, involving much smaller numbers, occurred in Quebec's Eastern Townships.

The true émigré Loyalists, "displaced persons" or political refugees, are an early example of what has become increasingly familiar in our own time. Although a sad portent of things to come, they were by no means the first. They have often been compared to the Huguenots who fled from seventeenth-century

France, and in the Maritimes, they sometimes moved to the lands vacated by some six thousand Acadians expelled in the mid-1750s when, like the Loyalists, they could not transfer their allegiance to a new régime. The Reverend Jacob Bailey, who had fled from Massachusetts, noted a further irony:

> Some of those very persons who in their younger years were employed to transport them from Nova Scotia to New England are now compelled to take refuge here and to receive offers of hospitality and neighborhood from those people they had formerly so injured and ruined.

For the authorities having to deal with the waves of refugees, the problems of peace were, as always, more complex than those of war. Maintaining the Loyalists in provincial regiments and refugee camps or shipping them off to the Bay of Fundy was much easier than settling them on their new lands.

# 3 | A SPOT TO CALL OUR OWN

## LAND DISTRIBUTION

*"Sir, we have served all the war, your honour is witness how faithfully. We were promised land; we expected you had obtained it for us. We like the country—only let us have a spot to call our own."*

*—from an address by provincial sergeants to Edward Winslow, October, 1783*

HISTORY'S GREAT divide is the Industrial Revolution. But the Loyalists were barely touched by the changes that created the modern world. Stirrings were evident enough, however: Dr. John Jeffries of Massachusetts made the first flight across the English Channel, by balloon, in 1785; Joseph Eve of South Carolina invented a cotton gin in the Bahamas in 1793; Benjamin Thompson of New Hampshire, at war's end, began an international scientific career that included important heat experiments. Some Loyalists lived long enough to glimpse the industrial age. James Segee, born about 1772 on the New York frontier, arrived in New Brunswick on the Fall Fleet with his parents, and in 1816 became captain of the first steamboat running between Fredericton and Saint John.

But 90 per cent lived on the land, planting, harvesting, and tending animals, sometimes hunting and fishing, sometimes lumbering, largely self-sufficient, and little dependent on manufactured goods, except those they made for themselves. Land was life, independence, wealth, investment, and status. Thus, the paramount aim of the refugees was to gain their land and the paramount objective of the British was to help them gain it.

Wherever the Loyalists went the archive shelves groan under the mass of land papers—regulations, reports, registers of disputes, petitions, patents, and cadastral maps—which far exceed any other documentation. The details are complex, even tedious, and not fully researched. Only the themes are important.

The British government prescribed a general scale of land allotment to Loyalists which in broad outline approximated what actually happened: 100 acres per head of family and 50 acres for each member. Disbanded soldiers above the rank of private got more: NCOs, 200 acres; subalterns, 500; captains, 700; field officers, 1,000. The land was given free, with the costs of survey being borne by the Crown.

There were Crown lands galore in Canada (and still are). But the obstacle lay in the inevitable red tape that had to precede their settlement. The Loyalists met with exasperating delays and their temporary quarters were far from pleasant. During the first year or two, although some groups and individuals set down randomly near their projected lands or simply where they fancied, most Loyalists were crammed into various centres, frequently with inadequate food and supplies. Older towns like Halifax and Annapolis were so overcrowded that even when all public and private buildings, including churches, had been pressed into service, the majority of the settlers had to make do with boats, makeshift huts or, more likely, tents which were banked with snow and spruce boughs against winter. Tent cities sprang up—indeed at the mouth of the Saint John, at St. Anne's (the future Fredericton), Shelburne, Johnstown, New Oswegatchie, and Cataraqui, little else was available. The two largest groups were at Shelburne and the mouth of the Saint John. The Shelburners were at least in the vicinity of their lands and could start building, but the Saint Johners huddled in a ghetto that endured a winter of discontent: quarrels, drunkenness, malnutrition, bitter cold, exposure, and even death.

Meanwhile a small army fanned out across the Canadian wilds on the gigantic task of survey: marking, mapping, sketching; and recording the condition of the land, rivers, lakes, and ponds, the quality of soil, timber, and minerals. The job took years, even decades, as later immigrants and the children of Loyalists had also to be supplied. Supervision fell to the surveyor general of each colony: Charles Morris in Nova Scotia, George Sproule in New Brunswick, Samuel Holland in Quebec. The New England township system was followed because it was practical and, as Quebec's Gov. Frederick Haldimand said, the Loyalists were "most used to it."

Most of the work in the field was performed by deputy surveyors, the majority of whom, like Holland and Sproule, were Loyalists with army surveying experience. Some had formal training, some did not. Benjamin Marston, a former Marblehead, Massachusetts, merchant, who surveyed in both Nova Scotia and New Brunswick, probably had no formal training, though he was more competent than many who had. In an age when land was all important, a knowledge of surveying was commonly picked up by ambitious Americans—George Washington is a classic example.

Despite Marston's statement, the "job is a hard service & tho I make good wages, 'tis all earned," at ten shillings a day the surveyors were not well paid and often had other jobs. Sproule appealed to one deputy's sense of duty: "Indeed, this can be your only inducement for little or no profit can attend it." Early in 1784 Lord Sydney ordered the Treasury to rush replacements for twenty-four sets of surveying instruments sunk en route to Nova Scotia, but generally the British were notoriously stingy with their loyal workers. The surveyors obtained essentials only with difficulty, and both Sproule and Morris on occasion used their own money.

All three were competent and exceedingly hard-working. Simcoe reported in April, 1792, that Samuel Holland "is worn out, though in full possession of his intellect," adding that his deputy, John Collins, now "possesses neither strength nor intellect." Many other deputies were equally conscientious. Marston's diary proves that he slaved seven days a week, dawn to dusk, with no time for his own affairs. "My head is so full of Triangles, Squares, Parallelograms, Trapezias, & Rhomboidses that the corners do sometimes almost put my eyes out."

Sometimes guided by local settlers or agents of a regiment or association, each deputy was accompanied by an axeman and two chain-bearers. These aides cleared away trees and bush to establish lines of sight, carried the two and four pole chain-links (a pole equals five and a half yards) used for measuring, and generally expedited the job of the surveyor, who worked with compasses, theodolites (fitted with spirit levels), and telescopes. The surveyors laid out farm lots primarily but also had to mark off town and garden lots, roads, public landings, and government reserves for defence, religion, and education. They might also have had to check old surveys and vet petitions and memorials to the governors.

Many problems beset them: geographic ignorance, complicated by the lack of adequate maps, or, in the case of Upper Canada, their entire absence; confusion caused by dense forest, snow, and magnetic error; poor or non-existent equipment; bad weather; "multitudes" of insects; attacks by bears; difficult terrain; and lack of cooperation, including the occasional refusal of an established settler to permit access. In 1785, the Nova Scotia government threatened the Loyalists with loss of their lots if they did not help by providing axe and chain-men. The same year Patrick McNiff, a deputy surveyor in Upper Canada, appealed to applicants to supply axemen and chain-men and appealed to each township to help cut the roads, a plea that became official policy in 1792.

Even when the surveyors were competent and adequately equipped, it is not surprising that delays and troubles arose. There is a hint of desperation in one of Marston's diary entries: his provisions almost finished, "one of our two axes broke and one of my best men having broke his snowshoes to pieces, I gave over the survey...." The deputies were too few. In New Brunswick twenty-seven were recruited but only six surveyed regularly, and, in some outlying areas, the settlers themselves were licensed to do their own surveys. Surveys had to start largely from scratch. The few extant were usually inaccurate. George Sproule found the New Brunswick survey "in a very perplexed state."

The new ones, however, often turned out to be equally "perplexed"—hasty and inaccurate—causing many problems. Joseph Laird, for example, a Carolina Loyalist, received land in Prince Edward Island in 1786, but after nine years' work had to leave when it was discovered that through a surveyor's error he was on someone else's land. He received no payment for his improvements and moved to Vernon river where he built up another small but prosperous farm, only to find himself in 1803 facing ejection again because of a similar error.

The world of modern transportation easily forgets the importance of water. In eighteenth-century Canada, with roads few and poor and horses and carriages expensive, water was the major way to move people and goods conveniently. Craft ranged from large ocean- and lake-going ships down through the hefty bateaux and Durham boats of the rivers to the modest punts and canoes of the humble settlers. Travel was slow by our standards but remarkably effective. The Bay of Fundy, for example, plied by innumerable boats, was much less a barrier than it is today. In winter most inland water froze, creating ice-roads and bridges ideal for sleighs drawn by hand or horse. Falling water provided the chief source of pre-industrial power for driving saw and grist mills.

The early Loyalist lots were oblong in shape, stretching back from river, lake, bay, or ocean in a pattern reminiscent of the feudal grants in old Quebec. Typically, in the Cataraqui Townships, four 200-acre farms were found per mile: about 440 yards of frontage, with the "concession" stretching back 2,200 yards. Competition was fiercest, and lots narrowest and smallest, in densely populated places like Saint John, Shelburne, and Kingston. Generally the desirability of water frontage for ease of transportation discouraged the early growth of villages and encouraged dispersed settlement. Inland survey came afterward.

Charles Morris and his over-burdened staff began the survey of New Brunswick by laying out lots on the site of Saint John and roughing out the blocks for the disbanded regiments, but it was not until the creation of the new province in June, 1784, that the job of matching families to farms went into high gear. Even then there was some initial delay. Governor Carleton and his officials arrived in November, but Surveyor General George Sproule did not appear until six months later. This generated friction for a time between him and Jonathan Odell, the provincial secretary, who had been handling land matters in the interim. A trickle of land granted eventually swelled in the two peak years of 1786 and 1787 to about 200,000 acres and 185,000 acres respectively.

On April 21, 1783, Charles Morris engaged Benjamin Marston as surveyor at Shelburne. He arrived on May 2 and, by May 23, the first settlers were on their town lots. By mid-July, the town was laid out and the standard draw had begun for farm lots. All proceeded well, but the influx of thousands more refugees in the Fall Fleet meant that many spent the winter without land. Marston carried on surveying until the riots of late July, 1784 (*see* Chapter 8), forced him to leave; but his assistants remained and, by autumn, over 3,000 homes, store, and wharf lots, plus 800 country lots were occupied. Throughout Nova Scotia, as in New Brunswick, many blocks of land were simply granted to regiments and similar associations, and the subdivision was left to them to complete.

In late 1783, John Collins arrived at Cataraqui and, by November, had surveyed the township of Kingston. About the same time Justus Sherwood was active along the St. Lawrence and Bay of Quinte. Although thirty deputies began a "crash" survey in March, 1784, when the Loyalists arrived in June the Royal townships were merely "sketched" and few lots laid out. But by mid-September all settlers were on their land.

Progress was less rapid in the Cataraqui Townships. It was July before survey of the 3rd township began, and, when the surveyors departed in October, 1784, not everyone had been positioned. Yet by the end of 1784 almost four thousand were settled in the two sets of townships, mostly on good land. In the remote Niagara, Detroit, and other western regions, surveying took much longer and conditions were rather chaotic compared to the east, especially around Detroit where large tracts were coopted by a few Loyalist officers who, in a rare instance, succeeded with an illegal Indian treaty.

Survey and allotment were similar throughout British North America. At first in Nova Scotia the procedure was as follows. A Loyalist petitioned the governor for land, sometimes a specific plot, sometimes merely the prescribed acreage. The governor and sometimes the executive council initialled the petition and sent a warrant to survey to the surveyor general who, in due course, sent a survey report and description to the governor and the surveyor general of the king's woods. This latter official, charged with reserving mast trees for the navy, issued a certificate which accompanied the surveyor's material to the provincial secretary, who made out the grant. This grant, when signed by the governor, gave legal title.

In New Brunswick at the beginning of 1785, Carleton and his executive council began to meet "almost daily as a land committee" to decide the validity of land petitions that went first to Sproule and to Secretary Odell who kept a register. Occasionally the land could not be granted for a variety of reasons, but usually "conditional approbation" was given. Grantees were required to advertise in the newspaper for three consecutive weeks to allow any counter-claims to be made. Petitioners who did not request a particular plot were listed and granted land by lot as survey proceeded. Either way, once survey was completed and counter-claims handled, the governor signed a patent. Later problems were handled by the courts. Grants were subject to the completion of certain improvements which varied according to the nature of the land and had to be completed within three years, proof being submitted at the county courts.

All settlers had to take an oath of allegiance to the king which, as Lord North made clear, did not imply acquiescence to taxation by British Parliament. Thus British North America started life exempted from the claims that had caused the American Revolution.

Essentially land grants and issuance of legal title were the responsibility of the governors and their councils with the aid of such officials as the attorneys general and the provincial secretaries. The surveyor's job was primarily surveying and describing the land, although Benjamin Marston did distribute grants, probably in his capacity as a magistrate. The actual assignment of land often fell to local officials: officers of the disbanded regiments, agents of Loyalist associations, country and parish officials and, for a time in Upper Canada, district land boards. At least in New Brunswick, initially only blocks were properly surveyed and, although disbursement was rapid, official survey and grant of legal title was delayed years, decades—sometimes permanently.

"Thursday last the people drew their town lots," Benjamin Marston wrote of Shelburne on May 24, 1783. The approved method of obtaining an actual lot was by public draw. In the Cataraqui Townships pieces of paper, each marked with the number of a lot, were placed in a hat. A Loyalist drew a slip, was given a "location ticket," and the surveyor wrote down his name on a map. Records of allotments were kept by the receiver general. Regarding the process, Marston added, not surprisingly: "Some grumble, some are pleased." More constructive than complaining was swapping and, for the wealthy, buying.

A recruiting handbill for a Loyalist regiment in 1777 read: "Such spirited Fellows, who are willing to engage, will be rewarded at the End of the War,... with 50 Acres of land, where every gallant Hero may retire and enjoy his Bottle and his Lass." The encouragement of discharged soldiers as immigrants dates back to the settlement of Ulster by the earl of Essex during the reign of Elizabeth I. In America, where land was plentiful and money scarce, there was nothing new in granting land for military service. The French had done it in 1665 in Quebec, the British in 1749 in Halifax and elsewhere in Nova Scotia. In the thirteen colonies, fifty acres were given to each enlisted man after the French and Indian War (1756–63). The great novelty of 1783 was the extension of grants to civilians, the precedent for which was set as early as 1775 when Lord Dartmouth instructed the governor of Nova Scotia to make "gratuitous grants" of land to Loyalist refugees. (Military grants continued after the War of Independence in both the United States and British North America. After the War of 1812 the King's New Brunswick Regiment was so rewarded, and British regulars were offered land in both Upper and Lower Canada.)

Sir John Johnson, commander of the Royal New Yorkers, suggested that because his regiment "were the foremost in opposing His Majesty's enemies and first joined his Forces ... they may be indulged with the first choice of lands." Haldimand replied that he would stick by the law. However, it was in fact far from unknown for lands in British North America to be assigned without benefit of the draw to the wealthy and the influential. Johnson, despite Haldimand's orders, allowed his officers to avoid competition by lot with the other ranks, and appropriated large chunks for himself.

Reasons for delay and confusion varied. For example, in 1783–4 it was partly lack of transportation that kept the provincials at the mouth of the Saint John away from their lands upstream. There was some incompetence in high places, notably from Governor Parr of Nova Scotia whose lassitude was compounded by his lack of enthusiasm for promoting the distant area that became the rival province of New Brunswick. Closer to home, notably at Shelburne, Parr quarrelled with the surveyors, denied them adequate supplies, interfered with their work, and behind their backs grabbed land for himself and his cronies. At first there was a serious lack of specific instructions from London, and throughout the Maritimes there was the problem of the overlapping jurisdiction of Sir John Wentworth, surveyor general of the king's woods, whose job it was to protect the Crown lands. In May, 1784, the settlers at St. Andrews at the mouth of the St. Croix River learned that much of their hinterland fell under the king's broad arrow. As a result many never got their full land grants, and St. Andrews' growth was stunted. (The same month Wentworth's visit to Shelburne provoked "angry remonstrances.")

Another complication in Nova Scotia and New Brunswick was the need to escheat, or reclaim, large tracts of land granted in the 1760s. Escheating began at the end of 1782 and by the end of 1788 about 2.5 million acres had been reclaimed for the settlers. In New Brunswick, Carleton craftily bypassed the cumbersome, lengthy escheat process by an order-in-council of November, 1784, that required the registration of old grants within three months to escape immediate forfeiture.

The Loyalists themselves contributed to confusion by their rapid selling and swapping of lots, and by squatting. Wherever possible the government tried to legalize the squatter through official survey and grant. If he had to be moved, his improvements were supposed to be paid for. In Upper Canada much land was claimed by Loyalists and their children, but never occupied. Some Loyalists indulged in outright fraud by claiming minors or servants or for families that had moved on, while others claimed grants in two or more locations. Still others, through influence, grabbed land not assigned to them or procured advantageous sites or extra-large grants. Officers, sometimes with approval of their commanders, put their children on the muster to get land—hence the expression "Major won't take his pap."

Some surveyors could be influenced, some not. In the latter category was Benjamin Marston who noted, August 9, 1783: "A Capt. McLean has this evening sent a green Turtle.... He is to have a house lot, but this will not blind my eyes, he must have the same chance as his neighbours who have no Turtle to send." Three years later, on the Miramichi, Marston was warned that, if a certain Loyalist did not receive a certain lot, his life would be in danger.

Everywhere there were official complaints about Loyalists taking out lots with no intention other than a quick sale. Charles Morris protested in February, 1785, that "People in every District are disposing of their land for much less than it has cost Govt. for laying it out and never meant to settle in the country but to make the most of us." In March, 1788, Governor Parr grumbled that many privates of the Duke of Cumberland's Regiment "sold their lots for a dollar or a pair of Shoes—or a few pounds of Tobacco—but most for a gallon of New England Rum, and quit the Country without taking any residence...." In Upper Canada during the Simcoe years, location tickets (as good as deeds), traded and accepted as currency by local merchants, became speculative items. Simcoe and his successor, Peter Russell, aggravated matters by giving land grants to favoured individuals in an effort to create an aristocracy. In the 1790s, similar grants in the Eastern Townships attracted a few Loyalist settlers, but mainly benefitted speculators.

Land caused the bitterest disputes among Loyalists. In New York in July, 1783, while the evacuation was still in progress, fifty-five "gentlemen, clergy and merchants" petitioned Carleton for huge grants of 5,000 acres in Nova Scotia on the basis of their self-styled superior status. The humbler Loyalists were incensed and, as we will see in a later chapter, the incident was important in the development of class politics in New Brunswick.

Even before much land had been developed the plebeians were in a suspicious mood. Everywhere there was some dissatisfaction, some inequality. Agents of regiments and civilian associations, "sharks preying upon each other," favoured their own. In New Brunswick those able to pay survey costs had their choice of land. First-comers, who naturally took the best land, equally naturally were resented by late-comers. At the mouth to the Saint John, the bulk of the Loyalists who were from the Middle Colonies found most of the land in the hands of the pre-Loyalists and early-arrived New England Loyalists. Tension was such that in April, 1784, Governor Parr had to dispatch Chief Justice Bryan Finucane to investigate complaints.

At Shelburne, where the worst squabbles in Nova Scotia occurred, the acerbic Benjamin Marston lamented that the settlers were "much at variance with one another," adding that those who arrived in the first fleet were attempting "to engross this whole grant" in order to sell land to newcomers. On the other hand the newcomers "murmur and grumble because they can't get located as advantageously as those who have been working hard these four months." Marston had difficulties from the start when the rank and file challenged the town site he and the company captains had chosen.

In addition there was racial antagonism. The "people hired their own surveyor" to discover alleged black encroachments. Marston's opposition to this attempt to dispossess the blacks was a major reason for his unpopularity and ultimate flight, after which the Nova Scotia Executive Council was obliged to set up a special board to handle the disputes. In Upper Canada the McNiff controversy between ex-officers and rankers (*see* Chapter 7 for details), which resulted, in 1787, in Haldimand sending John Collins and William Dummer Powell to investigate, was partly caused by discontent about land distribution.

The land system underwent several changes. In the future Upper Canada, in response to demands for large grants, Lord Dorchester, in June, 1787, authorized an additional 200 acres to every head of family who had improved his original grant. A year later four districts were created: Lunenburg, Mecklenberg, Nassau, and Hesse (later Eastern, Midland, Home, and Western), stretching from the Ottawa River west to Lake St. Clair. Soon afterward a land board was set up in each district. (In 1792 they became county land boards and in 1794 were superceded by the lieutenant-governor-in-council.) In 1788 Dorchester, bowing to understandable complaints, increased the grants to all ex-officers to the level (considerably higher) promised the 84th Regiment, the Royal Highland Emigrants.

In 1789 Dorchester and the council at Quebec decreed the drawing up of a Registry of bona fide Loyalists—those "who ... had joined the Royal Standard in America before the Treaty of Separation in the year 1783." Their sons and daughters, at the age of twenty-one (younger in the case of girls who married under age), would receive 200 acres. In practice the children of all Loyalists received the grants. No such formal action was taken in New Brunswick but children of Loyalists, like immigrants, were eligible for land.

In 1790 Pitt officially ended free land grants in British North America. Little land was available in Nova Scotia, Prince Edward Island, and Quebec, and in Upper Canada Simcoe ignored the order; but in New Brunswick the ban was enforced for seventeen years, which had the effect of stunting growth and causing much squatting and emigration.

Until the Constitutional Act of 1791 the lands of Western Quebec were not, as elsewhere, held in fee simple (normal freehold) because they were within the French seigneurial system with royal and glebe (clergy) lands reserved. The Loyalists were formally "tenants of the King." The fact that demand for an end to the seigneurial system was the prime political aim of the Loyalists (self-government was a distant second) underlines the desperation of the desire for land.

On February 7, 1792, Simcoe issued a proclamation to those "desirous to settle on the Lands of the Crown in the Province of Upper Canada." Townships ten miles square, or nine by twelve if fronting water, were to be surveyed, one-seventh of which was reserved for the support of the Protestant church and another seventh reserved for Crown use. Farm lots of 200 acres were available almost free to virtually anyone who would take an oath of allegiance to the king. The proclamation, which set the course of land policies in Upper Canada, had two momentous results. The late Loyalists swarmed in, and the Crown and Clergy Reserves, which were dispersed throughout each township on the notorious "chequered plan," had a deleterious affect on later development.

In the Maritimes, Prince Edward Island was an exception to the normality of land held in fee simple. Massive grants to absentees in the 1760s began a complicated farrago, not fully resolved until 1875, in which the Loyalists played but a part. Most could not get clear title, some bought new land, many squatted, others moved away.

DESPITE THE Loyalists' deserved reputation as the Founding Fathers of English Canada we must not forget the English-speaking Canadians who preceded them. They are often called "pre-Loyalists," a term some find condescending: "old Loyalist" has been suggested by a modern scholar; contemporaries used "old inhabitant" and "old settler." Nor can we ignore the native Indians, the Canadiens, and the Acadians. (Relationships between these groups will be considered in depth later.)

In peninsular Nova Scotia most of the good land was already settled before the Loyalists arrived. By contrast New Brunswick was wilderness with plenty of good, virgin land, though far from sufficient. Yet even there, some of the most desirable interval land was occupied, notably by a community of ex-New Englanders at Maugerville, just south of Fredericton. (Interval lands were usually treeless stretches enriched with alluvial soil from the annual spring floods.) Many pre-Loyalists were squatters, but wherever possible their holdings were confirmed and, as in the case of Loyalists, government bore the expense of survey and grant. When an old settler had to be moved off land reserved for Loyalists he was paid for any improvements and "given first choice of available land elsewhere."

Another important pre-Loyalist settlement was at the mouth of the Saint John, where at Portland Point and Conway the New England firm of Simmonds, Hazen, and White had been active in the mast and fur trade since the early 1760s. When the Loyalists arrived, the firm was supporting a vigorous community of some 150 people. In addition there were the Royal Fencible Americans, raised in Nova Scotia and commanded by Maj. Gilfred Studholme, who had been sent to build Fort Howe in 1777. It is an exaggeration, then, to call the Loyalists the founders of the city of Saint John.

Although friction was seldom absent, the old inhabitants and the Loyalists were useful to each other. Existing settlers offered supplies and services. Merchants of Liverpool, Nova Scotia, sold timber to Shelburne. Simmonds, Hazen, and White, who had a mill as far upstream as Oromocto, supplied the New Brunswick Loyalists with timber, food, and even land. In Quebec the particular importance of bateaux men has already been noted. The old inhabitants generally benefitted from the influx of the Loyalists and their capital, as the price of land, provisions, and accommodation rose. In September, 1793, one refugee complained that in Halifax, "Everything is intollerably dear and the old Inhabitants are accumulating wealth at a great rate by the exorbitant prices which they extract from Strangers." In Upper Canada three French forts formed the nuclei of Loyalist settlements: Fort Frontenac (1672) at the mouth of the Cataraqui River, Fort Pontchartrain (1701) on the site of Detroit, and Fort Niagara (1726).

Some of the scattered Acadians in New Brunswick sold land and supplies to the Loyalists, but most, by choice or by force, moved away from them. They lacked clear title. Two Cormier brothers complained to Gov. Thomas Carleton that after sixteen years building a farm on the Saint John "a certain Lewis Mitchell obtained an expulsion order against us." However, in November, 1783, Louis Mercure, a prominent Acadian, informed Haldimand "that many of his countrymen" wanted to move north "for the sake of enjoying their religion with more liberty, and less difficulty in procuring priests." The result, encouraged by Haldimand, Parr, and Carleton as a method of strengthening communications between Halifax and Quebec, was the settlement of the fertile Madawaska valley in the region of the Upper Saint John—the so-called Madawaska republic. In 1785 and 1786 more than sixty families, settled on the Saint John above Fredericton, moved to Madawaska. Around 1800, others, unable to obtain title to their land at Minudie, Nova Scotia, near the border on the Cumberland basin, moved into New Brunswick to nearby Cap Pelee and Shemagoue. Other Acadians moved within New Brunswick to the north shore and Memramcook.

The evidence contradicts the notion of the Acadians being hard done by. Generally, Carleton and his council treated them with compassion. They survived, prospered, and enjoy an influence in present New Brunswick that would surprise but not annoy the Loyalists.

Indians have always been important in the white man's colonization of America: positively, they aided his survival in the wilderness; negatively, they were moved to give him room.

During the dreadful New Brunswick winter of 1783–4, Mrs. Lewis Fisher recalled that the Loyalists "all had to live after the Indian fashion," fishing and hunting moose. Walter Bates recalled that the first morning at Kingston he awoke to the disconcerting sight of ten canoes full of Micmacs, but the Indians proved friendly "and furnished us plentifully with moose meat." Similarly John Cole of Adolphustown recalled that "when first we came" the Indians "brought game in abundance." In the Saint John valley the Indians are said to have introduced the settlers to fiddleheads, those edible fern-sprouts that remain a great delicacy. And, just as in 1620 the Pilgrim Fathers were lucky to inherit land cleared by departed Indians, so Loyalist agriculture was flourishing by 1780 on land the Indians had abandoned on the Niagara peninsula. Later other Loyalists took over similarly abandoned land on the St. Lawrence.

But it was Indian weakness that was the greatest help. Edward Winslow, the leading New Brunswick Loyalist, remarked in a tellingly casual way that with the arrival of the Loyalists "the Indians were of course compelled to leave the banks of the rivers (particularly the St. John) and hunt on other grounds."

In the Maritimes, Indian policy was a local matter. The weak Micmacs and even weaker Malecites, both former allies of the French, were deemed unworthy of treaty or even courtship. The Loyalists sought the same river and ocean frontages prized by the nomads. They reportedly threatened, in Nova Scotia, to bring in the ancient Mohawk enemy, and in New Brunswick Winslow mentions "the barbarous claims of the set of savages." He referred to the trial in 1786 of two former Queen's Rangers for the murder of an Indian man, resulting in "the whole Corps of Indians" from the Upper Saint John encamping threateningly on Judge

Isaac Allen's property near Fredericton "clamouring for an instant decision." In due course the Supreme Court convicted the pair, hanged one, and the Indians were satisfied. The next year Governor Carleton arranged for troops to be sent from Quebec because of an Indian threat to the Madawaska settlements, and in 1792 he claimed the Loyalists above Fredericton were about to pull out for the same reason. In truth, the governor used the Indians as an excuse to justify the stationing of regular troops.

Lord Dorchester urged his brother Thomas Carleton to deal kindly with "some compensation to those people, whose land we come to occupy." In fact, the aborigines were unceremoniously thrust aside. The Malecites were at once moved from the Loyalist area of the Saint John and as settlement spread to the Mirimachi and the Richibucto the Micmacs met the same fate. Indians had to petition to retain any of their ancestral land and an *ad hoc* reserve system grew up with the "red man" confined to the periphery of white society. In Nova Scotia they were rapidly "overwhelmed ... for all time," in historian L.F.S. Upton's words.

In Upper Canada the British insisted on a continuation of the wise policy of the Proclamation of 1763 that had enraged the colonists before the Revolution: official treaties must precede settlement. But the treaties were no assurance of justice. The 1,800 Mississaugas, though stronger than the Micmacs, were too few to offer resistance and fared little better. They were easily persuaded to sell large tracts: in 1781 in the Niagara region; in 1783 the land between Cataraqui and the Trent River along Lake Ontario, and also the land between the St. Lawrence and Ottawa Rivers; in 1784 land west of Niagara including the Iroquois Reserve on the Grand River. The result, in contrast to the settlement of the American western frontier, was that the Canadian West began and continued free of Indian wars, although the Indians were just as cheated.

The only strong Indians the British had to deal with were their own allies, the Iroquois, whose story will be told in a later chapter. As already mentioned their ancestral hunting grounds were ceded without their leave at the peace negotiations. They were settled mainly along the Grand River, though the Lower Mohawks, under Capt. John Deseronto, remained at the original settlement on the Bay of Quinte. The Grand River lands were not supposed to be transferred, but many acres were, in fact, sold to settlers and promoters.

As with the evacuation, the difficulties and complaints which dominate the records must not blind us to achievement. Given the circumstances the Loyalists got their land in a remarkably expeditious way. Some problems were easily solved.

A Loyalist who found himself on a swamp when the snows melted could get a new grant. Others could swap, sell, or migrate. The pervading problem in the Maritimes was the lack of sufficient good land, a fact of nature all governments have been powerless to correct. The only advantage was that the area escaped the baleful influence of speculators who plagued Upper Canada. For many a humble Loyalist, exile meant better land than before, or even land for the first time. The majority of all ranks probably agreed with the denizens of the Royal Townships who, John Collins reported in June, 1785, were "extremely well pleased." The British deserve credit for a policy of free land grants that was not matched in the United States until the Homestead Act of 1864.

As usual when government has tried to closely supervise colonization, there was a wide gap between plan and reality; for example, the tidy assignment of regiments to particular blocks of land broke down. Nevertheless the Canadian frontier, and indeed the Canadian way of life, began, as they were to continue, with much more government intervention than in the great Republic to the south.

# 4 | AN UNCULTI-VATED COUNTRY

## LAND DEVELOPMENT

*"That his only two sons died soldiers in His Majesty's Service during the rebellion and he from a state of affluence obliged to struggle in an uncultivated country...."*

—*testimony of Moses Knapp, a New York Loyalist*

BOTH THE BRITISH and the Loyalists were well aware that more would be needed than mere land, which would take time to clear and bear crops. In New York, Sir Guy Carleton assured one group that government would not put them in Nova Scotia and then say "*we will do nothing for you; You may Starve.*" Whenever possible they sailed away with a year's rations, allocated according to an army scale of 1 lb bread and 12 oz pork or 21 oz beef per day per man; women and children got half-rations. In addition, from army stores came cloth, hose, mittens, shoes, blankets, axes, spades, medicine, and tents. On arrival, articles for husbandry and building were disbursed—ploughs, livestock, lumber, shingles, nails, saws, hammers, knives, files, hoes, stoves, and ultimately equipment for saw and grist mills.

Scattered references to Robinson Crusoe suggest a Loyalist identification with the celebrated castaway. "For a time we led a regular Robinson Cruso life"—meaning the improvisational coping with the uncivilized environment; perhaps government supplies were seen as analogous to those Crusoe rescued from his stricken ship.

Once the Loyalists finally won their land, their task was clear. Their needs were like those of most North American agricultural pioneers of the last four centuries, many of whom have been helped by trading companies, railroad companies, and religious groups. But the Loyalists' colonization was unusual because of the extent of government aid.

During the war largesse in the form of money, food, supplies, employment, and transportation, particularly from Sir Guy Carleton and Frederick Haldimand, had been considerable. The sudden arrival of thousands of immigrants in British North America necessitated much broader action. Normal colonization procedures would not suffice. Without increased government aid, as one observer put it, "many of the people must perish." The Loyalists demanded aid as the price of loyalty, and the British prudently agreed.

The exiled Loyalists received free transportation, land, rations, and various supplies. Soldiers kept their arms and accoutrements; provincial officers, in an unprecedented move, received half-pay for life, and payments were continued at a reduced scale to their widows. A few Loyalists received compensation and pensions for losses incurred by the Revolution—commissioners Jeremy Pemberton and Col. Thomas Dundas, sent out from London, conducted public hearings on such matters in Halifax, Shelburne, Saint John, Quebec, Montreal, and Niagara between 1785 and 1788. A small number got provincial government offices, from governors like Sir Thomas Wentworth, at £1,000 a year, down to the chain-bearers "at the lowest Wages they can be hir'd at." A few Anglican clergymen were employed by the British Society for the Propagation of the Gospel.

London paid most of the costs of the colonial administration and the church. London also paid for defense, built roads, gave contracts for masts, lumber, and food, and provided the protective umbrella of the Navigation Acts. The total cost cannot be calculated, but it is estimated that in British North America about eight and a half million pounds were spent on survey, transportation, food, and supplies. In addition a half million pounds went to compensate for the losses of almost thirteen hundred claimants, and over the years some six hundred ex-officers and their widows received close to a million pounds in half-pay. Considering the value of these currencies even now, the size of the expenditure can easily be appreciated. Britain paid a debt of honour but with the added advantage of helping to create a loyal elite with a vested interest in the imperial connection.

Routinely the regular British armed forces helped in settling the Loyalists. The navy, of course, directed their passages to the Maritimes, and during the first winter Admiral Digby ordered his ships to continue with supplies and general support. But more important was the army, often the only arm of government available. The bateaux that took the Loyalists west from Montreal were organized by the Provincial Marine, an army unit. The army facilitated survey and settlement. At Fort Howe, the future Saint John, Maj. Gilfred Studholme welcomed the Loyalists and issued supplies, including boards and shingles. At Fort Frontenac, later Kingston, Maj. John Ross had done a lot of restoration and building, including a hospital and mills, and had stockpiled cut lumber even before the Loyalists arrived. Many of the supplies and provisions given to the Loyalists were dispensed by the army from its war surplus and, at least in Upper Canada, army blacksmiths produced axes, knives, and frows (tools to cut shingles and staves). In turn, Loyalist farmers sold surplus crops to garrisons at Fredericton, Saint John, Montreal, Kingston, Niagara, and Detroit. In Upper Canada, beginning in 1786, government also subsidized the price.

There was "an abundance of distressful stories" about shortages and unfair distribution of supplies which caused everything from inconvenience to starvation. Interior locations could be hard to reach. In Upper Canada, ship's axes with short handles unsuited to forest use were issued, and everywhere ploughs were in short supply. In September, 1785, a supply ship bound for Chedabucto, Nova Scotia, was hijacked by the crew, which caused great distress to the settlers and starvation among some blacks.

Despite these legitimate complaints, the Loyalists could be exasperating. The *cri de coeur* of the somewhat maligned John Parr—"they are a People very difficult to please"—was more than the grumble of a worthy, overburdened, hack governor. In Quebec a lesser official wrote: "The truth is there is no satisfying those people: if you give them provision they would have you put [it] in their mouths."

Like land, disbursement of "the Royal Bounty of Provisions" was abused. For example: the lack of a suitable depository at Fort Howe led to "repeated thefts"; ineligible persons (non-Loyalists and temporary residents) drew rations (though sometimes needy old inhabitants were officially granted rations); in Shelburne a resourceful Loyalist officeholder put the names of his two dogs on the ration list; some Loyalists drew for absentees, others in "double capacities"; some Loyalists on the Saint John River "sold their six months provisions for a trifling sum,... consequently [becoming] persons of Charity"; and some names were fraudulently put on the half-pay list.

The old saying "Loyalist half-pay officers never die," was inspired by Loyalist longevity. In New Brunswick the last survivor, Lieut. John Ward of the Loyal American Regiment, died in 1846 at the age of ninety-three, and in the same year there still were more than sixty officers' widows drawing pensions throughout British North America. Loyalist soldiers claimed that "Old George" would feed them forever; this was true of half-pay, but supplies and rations ended after three years and so a jolt was felt in 1787 which caused many Loyalists to leave Nova Scotia. In the fall of the same year half-pay was made "portable" and some ex-officers left, especially from the Maritimes, sometimes bound for the United States. About the same time the closing of the claims commissioners' hearings increased this exodus, because compensation was also "portable."

Without government aid the Loyalist settlements would not have survived, or at least would have enjoyed a much lower level of prosperity. Compensation and half-pay stimulated the economy. The Reverend Roger Viets of Annapolis said that half-pay keeps "our poor alive by finding Employment for labouring men." Even ensigns, who received a "pittance" of £32 per annum, had some cash with which to improve their farms. Some used their compensation to start businesses, such as taverns or mills. The rich like George Ludlow, the chief justice of New Brunswick, who used part of his £2,720 compensation to build a fine house, were a boon to craftsmen.

Many Loyalists arrived with nothing more than the clothes on their backs. In 1782, Governor Parr reported some five hundred "coming almost naked from the burning sands of South Carolina to the frozen coast of Nova Scotia destitute of almost every necessary of life." But not all were entirely dependent on government aid. Even some who made their way via the backwoods of the state of New York were able to bring livestock and furniture. The rich who sailed from New York City, often accompanied by servants and slaves, brought considerable property—furniture, bedding, livestock, squared timber, and even dismantled houses. Some brought capital; some kept property and trading interests in the United States that could be turned into capital; and some had family and friends there who sent supplies.

"MON PAYS, *c'est de la neige,*" goes the famous Quebec song. For Canada as a whole *'trees'* is more apt than *'snow.'* Today, forests cover 70 per cent of the land of the ten provinces; in 1783 more than 95 per cent of the land was tree-covered. Most of the land the Loyalists settled was enshrouded in primeval forest. Today's second growth gives us only an impression of the luxuriance and extent of the forest which the Loyalists encountered. The white pine, the tallest conifer in Eastern Canada, commonly grew to a height of more than 100 feet with a diameter of four feet, and in favourable locations reached 175 feet and a five-foot diameter. The pines and spruce towered above the rest like "the palms of the tropics,... a forest planted upon another forest," observed a visiting Scottish clergyman. Occasional giant survivors in our forests recall those bygone days.

In the Maritimes' "Acadian Forest Region" red spruce is characteristic, and associated with it are balsam fir, yellow birch, sugar maple, red pine, Eastern white pine, and Eastern hemlock; also beech, white spruce, black spruce, red oak, elm, ash, red maple, white and grey birch, jack pine, and poplars. Upper and Lower Canada, in the "Great Lakes-St. Lawrence Forest Region," boasts a similar mixed forest: Eastern white pine, red pine, Eastern hemlock, and yellow birch are characteristic, but associated with them are sugar and red maple, red oak, basswood, and white elm; also Eastern white cedar, largetooth aspen, beech, white oak, butternut, white ash, red, white, and black spruce, balsam fir, jack pine, white birch, and poplars. In Southwestern Ontario, the "Deciduous Forest Region," is a narrow strip from the Bay of Quinte westward along Lake Ontario, widening along Lake Erie and stretching all the way to Lake Huron, where mixed with the mainly deciduous trees of the Great Lakes-St. Lawrence Region are such species as black walnut, hickory, black oak, and tulip trees.

The prime task of the Loyalists was to adapt to these forest environments. "A Canadian settler hates a tree, regards it as his natural enemy, as something to be destroyed, eradicated, annihilated by all and any means." Although written in 1838 this statement fits the Loyalists, who turned from war against the generals Washington, Sumter, and Greene to war against *Tsuga canadensis* (hemlock), *Picea rubens* (red spruce), and *Pinus strobus* (white pine). The weapons were no longer sword and bullet but axe and fire. One Loyalist commented on an area first settled in Fredericton: "They called it Salamanca after the fight of that name because they had such a hard battle with the trees when they were first clearing the land." (Wellington defeated the French at Salamanca in Spain in 1812.) A few lucky settlers got natural meadowland or cleared land that had been abandoned. But the majority faced "the new world of Trees," "a boundless expanse of living & moving surface," and were forced to "begin the world."

Exultant Republicans joked about the frozen deserts of "Nova Scarcity." Some Southerners, failing to appreciate the joke, quickly fled to the Bahamas or the West Indies, and even the New England Loyalists found the six-month Maritime winters "long and tedious." Back-country New Yorkers did not experience much of a change in Upper Canada, but the first settlers at Adolphustown took a nip of spirits each morning, "on account of the new climate." Then, as now, winter could kill, and some Loyalists did die during the early period before adequate shelter could be built. During the first winter in Fredericton a Loyalist woman recalled: "Many women and children and some men died from cold and exposure." Survivors resorted to each other's body warmth, to all-night shifts to keep fires going, or to the use of heated boards. European visitors found mosquitoes, blackflies, and other bugs a sore trial in summer, and noted the prevalence of ague or malaria in Upper Canada.

On the other hand, the climate, especially bracing winter, was generally regarded as healthy and conducive to longevity. Freeze-up brought easy transportation and much socializing via sleighs or skates. More prosaically, it facilitated the hauling of wood. Snow not only provided insulation, it slowed down wild animals, making them easier to kill, and provided a deep-freeze for meat storage. Another use of cold was to freeze cider to reduce the water content and so increase the alcohol.


A RARE GLIMPSE of the first days recorded by a Loyalist is in the reminiscences of

Hannah Ingraham, related many years later to a friend. Hannah's father, Benjamin, was a farmer from Albany County, New York, who became a sergeant in the King's American Regiment and fled to New Brunswick with his wife, son John (aged ten), and daughter Hannah (aged eleven), in 1783. They arrived at Oromocto by schooner in October and made their way to their lot at St. Anne's (Fredericton) in a hired rowboat. At first they lived in a tent. "We all had rations given us by the Government, flour and butter and pork; and tools were given to the men too," Sometime during the first winter Benjamin Ingraham built "a log house," a one-room hut, with the help of "a neighbour, a single man" who lived with them temporarily. The site was chosen when Mr. Ingraham "found a nice fresh spring of water, he stooped down and pulled away the fallen leaves..., and tasted it, it was very good, so there he built his house." One morning he led his family from their tent up through the thick snow and trees "and, oh, what joy to see our gable end." There was no floor or window or chimney but there was a roof and a fire, around which they ate toast and butter, "and mother said, 'thank God, we are no longer in dread of having shots fired through our house. This is the sweetest meal I have tasted for many a day.'" Soon "father got a good wood floor down of split cedar, and a floor overhead to make a bedroom, and a chimney built of stones, sticks and mud."

In the spring of 1784, they planted wheat, rye, and beans, the seeds of which they had brought with them. The virgin soil produced a thirty-fold yield of wheat which was threshed by hand on boards. The surplus was sold to "the gentry" who also employed Mr. Ingraham at odd jobs. Sometime between 1785 and 1786 the Ingrahams acquired the first cow in Fredericton—for 10 guineas cash at Maugerville—and added butter and cream to their sales. The cow wore a bell because it roamed the woods.

Other vignettes from the reminiscences include the picking of wild raspberries by the children ("we were proud when we got a pint to take to mother"), and the cooking of beef in a dutch oven ("there was no stoves then"), in 1786. The beef was an unusual treat that only occurred because a neighbour's cow was injured and had to be slaughtered.

Although there were some attempts by the elite to form large estates, most Loyalists built single-family farms. The first task was to "boldly commence chopping," as one observer termed it; hence the basic importance of government-supplied grindstones for sharpening purposes. The once-uncannily-silent forest land resounded with the thud of axes where previously woodpeckers alone were heard. First the underwood or brush was chopped, then the large trees which were stripped and cut into eight- or ten-foot lengths. As the sky was revealed it was like raising the blind in a dark room. Eventually the wood was set on fire, and the charred logs were gathered and burned a second time.

From Cape Breton to Detroit the air was heavy with smoke, the Loyalists black as colliers or chimney sweeps. Sometimes large trees were girdled—a one-inch notch was cut around the trunk about four feet from the ground, thus cutting off the sap flow. In one or two years the girdled tree died, gradually decayed, and could be burned or more easily felled. Sometimes, on land not required for immediate use, a process called "slashing" was used: trees were cut down and simply left to rot. On cultivated land the three-foot-high "plaguy stumps" were more an "eyesore," as one Loyalist observed, than an inconvenience, because crops were sown around them. It took from three to ten years for them to decay, and gradually they were removed. Resinous pine and hemlock might take twenty-five years or more, and were sometimes uprooted to make fences.

The dangers of life in the woods were many. One could be lost (a compass was a boon), treed by a bear, wounded by a slipped axe, or injured or killed by a falling limb or trunk (a particular risk from girdled trees). Burning, best done on a calm day, made "a brilliant spectacle," but runaway fires, such as that which devastated the mouth of the Saint John in June, 1784, were an ever-present hazard.

Opinions vary on the rate of forest clearance. Teams of men using oxen to pile the logs were most efficient. Communal "bees," or "frolics" as they were called in New Brunswick, were often held at burnings, which ended in great drunken parties. Progress depended on the nature of the forest and terrain, on the availability of oxen, and on the experience of the woodsmen. Two expert Loyalists could fell a large tree in thirteen minutes and clear an acre in two days; a single man might take from one to two weeks. It took longer, of course, to burn the wood and prepare the land for planting. In New Brunswick it is estimated that the average family was cultivating about two acres after one year and about twelve acres by the year 1800. The rate seems to have been higher in Upper Canada. One acre of corn and 2.2 acres of wheat might keep a family of six self-sufficient.

During clearing, the Loyalist needed a roof over his head. Whether he began with a government tent, a crude lean-to, or a "wigwam of ... boughs" he chose the site with care. Access to water for drinking and transportation was the priority. Some people had to cut down trees simply to make room for a tent, but everyone, including those getting government boards and shingles, needed logs to build a cabin. Very large or very small trees were unsuitable. Once wood was cut, the basic final timber-frame house could be put up in a few days.

The smaller houses, "shanties," perhaps ten feet by eight feet and six feet high, had a roof of a single slope; the larger ones, "log houses," perhaps fifteen feet by twenty feet and nine feet high, sometimes had a peaked roof. Round logs, notched near the ends, or dovetailed squared logs, were piled to form a rectangle, the base logs being supported with rocks. The chinks were caulked with wood chips and moss, and plastered with clay. The roof consisted of poles covered with bark (frequently elm, birch, spruce, or basswood), hollowed basswood laid like tiles, or thatch made from twigs and hay. At first the door might be a blanket or quilt or a couple of rough boards fitted with wooden hinges and locks. One or two tiny windows were covered with government-issued glass, oiled paper, or a sliding board. Sometimes there were no windows—sufficient light entered through various gaps and holes. Floors were at first dirt, then logs split in half. A small hole under some of the loose boards served as a root cellar. A refinement was a stoop that provided protection from rain, snow, and sun.

The fireplace, built on one of the end walls, was the heart of the home—a source of cheer, warmth, and cooking. The hearth, sometimes set on an existing rock in the ground, was built up with stones. The crudest huts allowed smoke to escape through the walls and a hole in the roof; the rest had chimneys of sticks, logs, stones, straw, and mud. Before the days of matches, lighting a fire was not easy; if embers could not be borrowed from a neighbour, sparks could be made with a knife and a flint to ignite dry grass or punk (rotted sawdust or combustible fungus), or sufficient heat could be generated by the friction of two sticks rubbed together. Settlers worked to keep fires going permanently. Firewood, needed at the rate of five or six cords per head per year, was readily available, but very expensive if purchased already cut because of labour and transportation costs.

The fireplaces and wooden buildings were a constant fire hazard not only to the family but to the whole settlement. A burnt-out family was usually resettled by neighbours, but some communities were not so lucky: Port Mouton, Nova Scotia, settled by over two thousand refugees, was destroyed by fire in 1784, and L'Etang, New Brunswick, was wiped out in 1790. Both were abandoned. In 1811, in New Brunswick, a shrewd visitor wrote:

> Hardly any instance has occurred of accidental misfortune by fire or inundation where the loss has not been covered by liberal private subscriptions. Indeed in two cases which have come within my own knowledge the sufferers were placed in a state of affluence they did not enjoy before.

After a fireplace the priority was a bed. These beds were crudely constructed of poles with mattresses of balsam-fir boughs or bed-ticks stuffed with corn-husks, beech leaves, straw, or feathers. Bearskins made excellent blankets. Another necessity was a latrine, which might begin as a hole behind a bush and end up as a solid wooden outhouse. Soon the pioneer built a rough-hewn cupboard, a table (perhaps merely a suitable stump), and a bench or two which, added to a few knives, kettles, and some treasured pewter-ware brought from his former home, completed his humble abode. In time, improvements—a proper door, better windows, an attic, and extra rooms—increased standards.

Adjusting to life in such "King's chateaux," as the French Canadians derisively called these cabins, was the greatest wrench endured by many Loyalists, "a dreary contrast to our former conditions." Overcrowding could be extreme. In 1785 an English visitor encountered a fourteen-by-fourteen-foot cabin at Elizabethtown. In it were a Loyalist and his wife, his father and sister, plus two friends who got board for helping clear the land. The same year, also in Upper Canada, another visitor found eight people sharing two beds in the same sort of home.

The biggest improvement was the construction of a frame house (occasionally a stone or brick one); the cabin would likely be converted into a farm building. As late as 1804, a visitor to Niagara was surprised to find many people still in log cabins which he unsentimentally described as "nurseries of vermin" subject "to speedy decay, gloomy to the sight, offensive to the smell, and, unless continually repaired,... both cold and leaky." The improved houses, which required mortar, stimulated lime-burning, a process that used immense quantities of firewood.

Naturally, and as always, the rich fared better. They brought more of the comforts of life with them, and, from the start, they could hire carpenters and labourers, if available, to build elegant houses and furniture. In established communities such as Halifax, Annapolis, and Montreal, they were able to rent better houses or apartments, but in the wilderness even the seemingly great might have to live in tents temporarily, as did Lady Simcoe at Niagara in an elaborate "canvas house" once owned by Captain Cook.

Benjamin Marston reported that in Shelburne between May, 1783 and February, 1784, 1,127 houses were built, 80 of which were temporary, 231 frame, the rest, "Log-Homes, built of pieces of Timber framed together at the ends ... sometimes clapboarded over; they may be made permanent buildings to endure many years." By August, 1784, another 300 framed houses had been completed, usually quite large and sometimes even "elegant." In 1791, Patrick Campbell, a Scottish visitor, found Saint John "well planned" with two churches and about five hundred houses "well painted.... The shops, stores and wharfs, numerous and commodious."

Bishop Inglis was also impressed by Saint John. "It affords a striking illustration of what industry is capable of doing [where] scarcely five years have elapsed since the spot ... was a forest." In 1801, Lady Hunter found Saint John "a delightful place; everybody looks stout and hale and contented." The province was "flourishing" and "the country about Fredericton is most beautiful, provisions cheap...." Imported clothes and servants were the only expensive items.

Other towns, such as St. Andrews, Cornwall, Kingston, York, and Niagara, made similar progress. But in 1815, with Saint John's population about five thousand, Fredericton's perhaps one thousand, Kingston's rather less than three thousand, and York's less than one thousand, Loyalist Canada remained overwhelmingly rural.

The forest had been an enemy, but it was now also an ally. Loyalist life was based on forest products. The use of wood for houses, shops, barns, churches, inns, schools, furniture, and firewood has already been mentioned. Toys, plates, spoons, and other utensils were carved from such soft woods as poplar and basswood. Basswood or linden (not found in Nova Scotia or Prince Edward Island) was very versatile not only because it was so easily worked—"as soft as a cabbage-stalk"—but also because of its other uses. The fibrous bark made good rope and string, and the early buds were sometimes boiled with edible wild greens. Birch was useful for furniture and the bark, too, had many uses—canoes, "small cups and dishes," and it "burns like pitch; splits into threads which serve for twine; and the filmy part near the outside, may be written upon in pencil, making no bad substitute for paper." Mrs. Simcoe painted on it.

The simplest wooden artifacts were fences, ranging in style from the unsecured zig-zag worm or snake to the post and rail. Next came furniture, varying from rough country benches to stylish Windsor chairs crafted for the rich. Patrick Campbell noted that with some exceptions the wealthy imported mahogany furniture and ignored the excellent local Bird's-eye maple. Outside a cabin door in Upper Canada might be found a primitive corn grinder called a "Hominy Block." The base was a hollowed-out stump, the top was a wooden "plumper" or, in larger editions, a stone or cannonball on a wooden pole or "sweep." Basic wooden devices were used for wells, ploughing, raking, harrowing, chaffing, and threshing. Other wooden products included fishing rods, forks, wagons, buckboards, sleighs, and gunstocks. The tree called hop-hornbeam, appropriately nicknamed "ironwood," was good for tool-handles, pestles, sleigh-runners and any item requiring particular durability. Wooden wheels and axles were lubricated with pine pitch mixed with lard.

As well as a habitat for game and free-ranging domestic pigs and cattle (mast—the fruit of beech, oak, and chestnut—was good animal feed) the forest was a source of food and drink for the settlers, who consumed many varieties of nuts (even acorns at a pinch) and wild fruits, as well as spruce tea, and beer, a handy anti-scurvy potion pioneered by the Indians. (Boiled dulse was used for the same purpose.) The forest was the source of innumerable home-remedies, partly because of a combination of a lack of doctors and a lack of cash, and partly because of its intrinsic merits. Some of these home-remedies were learned from the Indians: cherry bark for the blood, burdock root for the stomach, catnip tea for the chest.

Many were the complaints about the lack of creature comforts. Loyalists begged their friends in the United States to send them apples, hams, and other familiar treats because they had to rely on forest products. Ersatz tea, also brewed from hemlock and a shrub called the Labrador Tea plant, was an invention borrowed from the Indians, but used only through necessity. The most prized of all forest edibles was maple syrup, a staple sweetener and cooking ingredient. During the first year at Fredericton, wild white beans, which may have been a legacy from early French settlers, were discovered, eaten, and planted. Another unusual source of food at the same place were seeds found in the crops of pigeons which produced "excellent green beans." But eating wild things is always dangerous for the inexperienced. At Fredericton poisonous weeds mixed with fiddleheads caused illness and a few deaths.

Wood, as fuel and building material, was essential for all of the Loyalists' industry and trade. A minor use was as charcoal, particularly important to blacksmiths, but a major use was the production of potash, a crude form of potassium carbonate. Potash was easily made by boiling water with hardwood ashes in large cast-iron kettles and straining the lye through a linen cloth. Further refinements produced the purer pearl ash. Kettles were imported and vast quantities of firewood were used to attain the required 1,000° F. Leaching was done in wooden vats, and the finished product packed in wooden casks. Manufacturing began on individual farms, where the ashes of an acre of forest produced a barrel of potash (fireplace ashes were also used).

Domestically, potash was used for soap-making and fertilizer, but in England it was in demand for fertilizer, and glass- and dye-making. Potash was also one of the earliest sources of cash or barter. By the late 1790s in Upper Canada, merchants had begun a major business with it, triggered by the difficulty of exporting timber through the rapids. It lasted for decades. In the Maritimes potash was much less important. In New Brunswick, Capt. Samuel Hallett, a New York Loyalist, did trade in potash, but the commerce had died out by the 1820s.

The history of mills in Loyalist Canada remains to be written, yet mills were the most significant technology of the period. Mills were usually powered by water (mainly dam, occasionally tidal in the Maritimes), but also by wind and some-times by animals. Dams were made of tree trunks, stones, gravel, and hay. Although some buildings were stone, most were made of wood, as were water wheels and the entire mechanism except millstone or saw. The alternate-leaved dogwood, found everywhere the Loyalists settled, was crucial. "The wood's ability to cope with friction made it a premium material for long-life bearings and shaker slides."

Mills were primarily grist or saw: the former for crushing grain, especially wheat, which was extremely difficult to do by hand; the latter, which replaced the expensive and laborious two-man whipsaws, for turning trees into squared logs and boards. As suppliers of what one Loyalist described as "the staf of man's life" and materials of shelter, mills loomed large on the list of Loyalists' demands, and their register of complaints centred on the small number of them or their distance. In 1785, the inhabitants of Ardois Hill, Nova Scotia, complained to the assembly that they had to travel twelve miles "and there wait two or three days ere we can return with Bread to our Wives and Children." In 1787, Joel Stone wrote from Cornwall to Sir John Johnson: "The difficulty we labor under in this Town for want of a mill obliges me once more to trouble you ... respecting corn millstones."

In Upper Canada the British, supplying cash and materials, commissioned Loyalists to build mills, beginning with one at Niagara in 1783. In the Maritimes, mills were privately built, and in both regions a sufficient number was quickly reached. Saw and grist mills frequently operated side by side. Grist mills, much more important in Upper Canada than the Maritimes, where wheat was less prevalent, required more capital and were riskier ventures than sawmills. Much milling was "custom"—that is, the mill owner was paid by a percentage of a settler's grain or wood.

Profitability varied but mills put many Loyalist entrepreneurs on the road to prosperity and also boosted the growth of their localities. An example is the success of Richard Cartwright at Napanee; another is Capt. John Walden Meyers' mill on the Moira River, which led to the development of Belleville.

Sawmills stimulated two more technologies or industries centred on wood: shipbuilding and house- and barn-building. The former was particularly impor-tant in the Maritimes. In New Brunswick, for example, within ten years of the Loyalists' arrival, over ninety square-rigged ships plus over seventy sloops and schooners were launched. Everywhere countless small boats were made, including canoes from birch or hollowed-out pine. The white oak of Upper and Lower Canada was excellent for boatbuilding and, because it is water-tight, for casks and barrels. Cooperage was another wooden technology needed for, among other things, the export of flour from Upper Canada and fish from the Maritimes to the West Indies. The Maritimes also exported boards, masts, and other naval supplies, trade which received a boost during the Napoleonic Wars.

As the discussion of the forest suggests, nature was a close second to the British government as a provider for the Loyalists. Nature demanded no qualifications, other than frontier skills, and imposed no time limit. A visitor to Shelburne remarked: "It is rather amusing to an English ear to hear a housekeeper … give the boy directions to gather a basket of strawberries, raspberries or gooseberries—not from the garden, but from the woods." Also gathered were blueberries, cloudberries, wild rice, wild grapes, fiddleheads, dandelions, and pig-nuts.

Almost everywhere "amazing quantities" of fish were easily caught with nets, weirs, rods, spears, even pitchforks and guns—there were no game laws. Fishing at night by lantern was normal. Surplus fish was salted or smoked for winter. Salmon, bass, and trout were common, and, in Upper Canada, sturgeon and white fish "a yard long and as fat as butter" were prized. Maritimers also enjoyed a profusion of shellfish and lobsters (the shells were used as fertilizer) and sea-fish, including cod, herring, and mackerel. A visitor to Halifax in 1787 raved about the chowder, and found haddock so plentiful that the locals "will scarce eat skate." In Sussex, New Brunswick, another visitor had "miserable" fare at a Loyalist farm with the exception of "excellent" trout and salmon.

One Loyalist wrote: "Hunger look'd every wretch in the face that could not hunt or shoot for his subsistance." If firearms were scarce many animals, such as rabbits, were trapped or snared; even moose could be killed without guns when caught in deep snow. Flocks of pigeons were so thick in Upper Canada they could be netted. Edible birds abounded, including wild turkeys in Upper Canada, "partridges" (actually grouse) in the Maritimes, and everywhere, in season, ducks and geese.

Few Loyalists were denied the opportunity to enjoy the fruits of the chase. To venison, Maritimers added caribou and moose meat, the latter perhaps eaten more for sustenance than gourmet pleasure, although it made "excellent" soup and the nose, called "muffle," was a great delicacy. Other treats were beaver tail—"a delicious morcel"—roasted porcupine and, in Upper Canada only, rattlesnake soup. Rattlesnakes, no longer common in Ontario, remind us that not all animals encountered were salutary. But like rattlesnakes, which were hunted by hogs and whose oil was a prized medicinal, many pests had their uses. Squirrels which damaged crops "if well dressed … compose a dish which prejudice alone could induce one to reject"; raccoons made raids, but also hats and coats; bears, always hazardous and rarely eaten, provided skins for beds and sleighs.

Skin and furs—beaver, mink, and marten—were, after food, the great value of wild animals and often traded by the Indians. While large settlements had professional tanners and cordwainers (shoemakers), individual families made their own moccasins and leather clothes using leather from domestic animals. The Indians taught the Loyalists how to prepare the deerskins "with the brains of some animal." Leather clothes were very durable, and trousers and petticoats, sewn with basswood thread, could last for more than a decade. Wild leather was used for harnesses and all manner of domestic and farm fittings. Animal fat provided candles, soap, and lubricants.

Fish and game populations declined substantially after a few years. In 1791 on the Nashwaak in New Brunswick, Patrick Campbell was told the settlers "destroy most of" the salmon "in the spawning time," and halfway between Saint John and Sussex the owner of "a miserable little hovel" claimed the caribou and moose were "totally banished," though he could get "as many Pheasant and Hare in snow as he chose." These comments on scarcity were exaggerated but indicate the greed, or at least lack of forethought, that severely decreased stocks and ultimately destroyed the caribou. A similar outlook accounts for the reckless exploitation of the forest.

Agriculture, essential to most Loyalists, was the primary land-use. At first the stump-filled fields were not always ploughed. Seed was sown broadcast, perhaps, after the soil was raked by an "A harrow" consisting of two poles fitted with iron teeth dragged with the "V" pointing to the rear. The grain harvest was threshed with a homemade flail made of two pieces of wood joined by a leather thong.

The first crops were such easy-to-grow-and-store, high-yield items as potatoes, turnips, Indian corn, beans, squash, and pumpkins. The virgin soil gave high yields, without fertilizer, of virtually anything for several seasons—say twenty-five bushels for one sown, or between twenty and fifty bushels per acre. When fertilizer was needed, wood-ashes were readily available. Wheat was common but, until the advent of water-powered stone grist mills, the settlers had the problem of grinding it into flour, which was laboriously done by the primitive hominy block or by government-issued hand mills. Orchards were planted and gardens with beets, radishes, carrots, cucumbers, parsnips, and cabbage soon developed where the soil permitted. Much of the harvest was stored in root cellars dug below the frostline. Fruits were made into jams; meat was salted or smoked. Flax was grown for linen. The men pulled the plant up, let it rot in the open air, removed the seeds, and beat out the fibre; the women then combed, spun, and wove it.

Livestock was scarce at first, but soon sheep provided wool for home-spinning. Pigs were popular for their skill at foraging. Oxen were preferred over horses as draught animals because they were hardier and better suited to uprooting stumps. Cows and oxen were every settler's ambition: some brought them with them, some received them from the government, some bought them from old inhabitants or from the United States. Others, despite their best efforts, could only aspire to them—like Moses Knapp who complained that although "he has laboured hard and been frugal as possible he has never been able to purchase a Cow." The enterprising Christianne Merkley fled from Schoharie, New York, to Upper Canada and in 1782 married Jacob Ross, late of the Royal Yorkers. While her husband cleared his land she worked as a servant in Montreal for almost a year to save enough money to buy a cow.

Much of the Loyalists' land was good for agriculture though, in general, Upper Canada was far better than the Maritimes, shown by the exodus from the latter and the popularity with the late Loyalists of the former. There were some serious pests, particularly the Hessian fly which destroyed wheat, and the cutworm which destroyed virtually anything that grew. Pests, along with poor weather, were responsible for a number of periods of starvation of the kind that often afflicted new American settlements.

The classic "hungry year" in Upper Canada was 1789, which began with the bad harvests of 1787 and about which many harrowing tales have been handed down: one family "leaped for joy at one robin being caught, out of which a whole pot of broth was made"; others ate beech leaves and bled their domestic animals, Masai-style. Less well known is the "dreadful famine" of 1791 in parts of Nova Scotia during which some Loyalists sold their clothes for food, some ate cats and dogs, and some died. Also little known is the fact that Governor Carleton spent £2,000 to help groups made destitute by the severe winter of 1786–7 and by the hail storms of 1789 in the Saint John Valley.

There is a chorus of contemporary praise for the Loyalists as hard-working, enterprising farmers (apart from some half-pay officers who would not roll up their sleeves, other ex-soldiers too fond of rum, and some Prince Edward Islanders whose conservatism inclined them to wheat rather than the more suitable oats, potatoes, and cheese). The praise was sometimes at the expense of old inhabitants. For Colonel Dundas in 1786, Loyalist farms in the Grand Pré part of Nova Scotia stood out by their "neatness" from those of the New Englanders; in the early 1790s Patrick Campbell claimed the Loyalists of Upper Canada had cleared more land in eight years than the French had in one hundred!

Accounts of flourishing agriculture begin astonishingly early. In August, 1784, William Chew, a New Jersey Loyalist, informed Gideon White, a founder of Shelburne, that the land at Maugerville, just south of Fredericton, was excellent: "we have a fine crop at this time of wheat, oats, pease, corn and potatoes with every other vegetable as good and in as great variety as any place I ever saw," an opinion shared by Sergeant Major Cobbett about the same time. In August, 1785, Stephen Jones wrote that fifteen months after his arrival 100 miles up the Saint John River, he and his family had "cut down and cut up twenty odd Acres, half of which is fit for immediate Improvement; I raised this Summer two Acres of Wheat and as much of Oats & Potatoes and in a few days shall put into the Ground four Acres of Wheat and Rye."

In the summer of 1785 Robert Hunter, travelling along the St. Lawrence, "saw abundance of wheat, Indian corn, and potatoes wherever you go"; at New Johnstown he "walked over some fine cultivated ground where a Loyalist lives who has neither plow, harrow or cattle. It is astonishing to see to what perfection he has brought this land.... He must have worked like a Negro." Nearby a family was crammed in a small cabin and though "these good people have been here but a short time ... they have some fine wheat, have a pretty good stock of poultry, one cow and some Indian corn, with a few maple trees to make sugar." Rapid progress is well illustrated by the township of Matilda in Upper Canada. In September, 1787, the population was 247 and 439 acres, about 4 per cent of the grant, had been cleared. About 500 bushels of seed had yielded a harvest of 4,500 bushels which, added to livestock holdings of 68 horses, 141 assorted cattle, 5 sheep, and 18 hogs, provided an adequate livelihood.

In 1791 Patrick Campbell described the flourishing state of farming in areas of good soil in New Brunswick. Near Fredericton, Chief Justice Ludlow had "a fine farm" which, although it was not more than six years since the first tree was felled, produced upto eighty tons of hay annually. Campbell claimed that wheat seed would return thirty-fold if left to ripen fully—which it should not, as the weight would cause it to keel over.

In 1804 Lady Hunter, whose husband was commander-in-chief in New Brunswick, travelled up the Saint John to Fredericton. She noted in her diary:

> We passed many little well-cultivated spots on the river, and some with merely the wood burnt and not yet fallen down, some just begun to be cleared; perhaps the settler has not even food for a cow. General Coffin ... has the largest space cleared that we saw on our first day's expedition. The situation is beautiful, and the ground is very rich. He and all his family were making hay as we passed, of which he seemed to have a most plentiful crop. He is a fisherman as well as a farmer, and has houses erected for smoking salmon, of which he catches vast quantities. A little after four

o'clock we arrived at Sealy, about thirty-five miles from St. John's, where we landed to stay all night. We had a basket of cold meat, which indeed was not necessary here, where we found everything excellent, and met with a most hospitable reception from the landlord, an old soldier. You can form no idea of this little queer spot. I should think he has six or seven acres cleared, on which he has Indian corn, wheat, barley, peas, beans, a rich meadow of hay, potatoes, a garden very neatly and well stocked with vegetables, and three cows which range in the woods, with a bell at the neck of the one that guides the others home. The cottage as neat as possible, and very comfortable beds for the whole of us.... We went to bed with daylight, after a most hearty supper of strawberries, raspberries, and cream.

Successful farming was very much a family affair. In 1791 Patrick Campbell met a Highland settler in Upper Canada who had cleared about ten acres and raised ninety bushels of wheat, almost seventy bushels of corn, plus potatoes and a few other things. "'And what assistance had you to all that?' said I; 'None (answered he) but a hoe and axe, and what that woman could give me,' meaning his wife." Husbands and wives were partners. Women's sphere included baking, cooking, preserving, sewing, spinning, milking, butter-making, and looking after infants, but the sexual division of labour had to be loose.

As always in primitive rural societies "children contribute of the riches of parents." As one anonymous commentator put it: "Their use, however, is not according to the Psalmist to enable him 'to meet his enemies at the gate,' but to cut down trees in the wood. In fact as soon as a child can walk, he becomes useful in some shape or other." On being congratulated on the birth of a child, and with it a further grant of 50 acres, a Loyalist replied: "Yes ... a child is better than a calf. It does not run among the corn the first year." Gideon White of Shelburne wrote banteringly to a friend, "the children come almost as fast as the Period, for Drawing their Subsistance, I expect forty yet—help me to Names for them. I have enough to do to get fish & Potatoes which thank God we all have & have enough of them."

Anne Powell, on a journey in Upper Canada in 1789, reported a disbanded soldier and his wife who, in typical Loyalist and frontier fashion, had just swapped their first farm for one "twice its size." Accordingly they and their three children were again living in a "temporary log house." "A large house was on one side, on the other all the necessary utensils for a family, everything perfectly clean." Miss

Powell asked the wife, Nancy, if she were happy. "'Yes, perfectly so;' she worked hard but it was for herself and her children." She looked after the family, her husband looked after the farm. In her spare time she wove cloth "and mended shoes for their neighbours" for which she was well paid, "and every year they expected to do better and better." Patrick Campbell found the secret of success revealed by a Capt. James French of De Lanceys brigade, settled on the Nashwaak, who had the advantage of half-pay. "He himself and son, who is also a half-pay officer, manage and carry on the work without, while his wife and daughter do the dairy, and that within. By laudable attention and industry, he lives in affluence."

The periods of extreme hardship were temporary and never even felt by many Loyalists. Agriculture provided everything from survival to opulence. As late as 1810 Lady Hunter visited the Miramichi in New Brunswick where "salted salmon and potatoes is the only food of the inhabitants; no bread anywhere, their last year's corn had long been done, and this year's they had not yet begun."

But in 1791 Patrick Campbell visited Simon Baxter on the Kennebecasis in New Brunswick. Baxter, formerly a modest yeoman farmer in New Hampshire, had arrived with only $2.00 in his pocket but had got a nice grant of interval land where "he now sits in ease and affluence..., the most successful farmer in raising stock and clearing land" in all New Brunswick.

The keynote of success was self-sufficiency. As late as 1825 a visitor to Loyalist settlements on Prince Edward Island commented: "A division of labour does not answer well in a new country." He added:

> the American Loyalists ... are in general industrious and
> independent..., extremely ingenious, building their own houses,
> doing their own joiner work, mason work, glazing and painting.
> The men make their own shoes, their ploughs, harrows and carts
> as well as sledges and cabriolles; the women spin, knit and weave
> linens and loose woolen cloth for domestic use.

In 1811 in New Brunswick, General Gubbins commented: "The farms, except those who contract for lumber, have almost everything made at home that is required for the use of their families. They are their own weavers, dyers, taylors, shoemakers and carpenters."

Virtually all Loyalists farmed, though many combined it with other pursuits: fishing on the coasts, and lumbering in the woods, where the temptation of the forest was the bane of New Brunswick agriculture. Craftsmen, professionals, and officeholders frequently did double duty as farmers. When Israel Hoyt, a shoemaker who left Connecticut and settled at Kingston, New Brunswick, died in 1803, his will showed that as well as his shoemaking equipment and supplies he died owning a horse, a yoke of oxen, two pigs, six cows, and twenty-four sheep, plus two ploughs, a cart, forks, shovels, two butter tubs, a churn, and two spinning wheels. The diary of the Reverend Frederick Dibblee, another Connecticut Loyalist and rector of Woodstock, New Brunswick, describes him working daily on his farm; clerical duties received scant mention. Dr. Azor Betts, in the early days of New Brunswick, lamented that he had to turn to farming because of the lack of paying patients, and even Beverley Robinson, Jr., son of one of the richest New York families, recounted in 1784 that: "He is now settling a new farm in Nova Scotia by beginning to cut down the first tree and create a loghouse for the shelter of his wife and two small children, and to accomplish that is obliged to labour with *his own* hands." (my italics). We see here the influence of the frontier in a Turnerian way, i.e., reflecting the American historian's view that the frontier had a levelling, egalitarian effect.

Some Loyalists did abandon agriculture altogether. An elite example is John Saunders who tried at the "Barony" north of Fredericton to recreate a large estate similar to the one he had had in Virginia. "The "Barony" remained largely wilderness because he could not find tenants, and his lucrative political and legal work in Fredericton took up all his time. A more modest example is Stephen Milledge who fled from New Jersey to New Brunswick. He drew "a valuable tract of Uncultivated Land, which after a severe trial I found it impossible personally to till, and to hire I could not, and therefore sold it." He spent all his money exploring "the natural productions and Curiosities of the country," then in 1786 he was recommended to the governor and gained two offices—high sheriff and surveyor—which kept him going until 1796. By then he was married with a growing family and "commenced a Country Trade [i.e., store] and have no reason to regret the honest undertaking in support of my family."

There are very few diaries of the Loyalists' first years on the land. An exception was Henry Nase's, a New Yorker, who as a young ex-ensign and bachelor settled near the confluence of the Nerepis and Saint John Rivers in 1783, after a three-month stay at the harbour some nineteen miles to the south. He arrived "with bag and baggage" on October 16 and, "busy hutting himself,... was comfortable in about eight days." On Christmas day he thanked God that, though it was the seventh Christmas since had had been "driven from my native home" and "beloved parents," he was now "comfortable, whereas I daily see those who have neither house nor home, and scarcely nourishment or clothing to guard them against the attacks of this rigorous season of the year." Nase was better off than most; he was also unusual because he received interval land, and there is, therefore, nothing in his diary about burning off the bush until 1794. Nevertheless his diary does furnish an insight into the Loyalist farming experience.

Nase seems to have worked alone (there is no mention of helpers or size of acreage) and to have worked hard—in 1783 Dr. Adino Paddock called him "very industrious." The diary has the usual farmer's obsession with the weather: rain, snow, ice, frost, floods. It was a justified obsession. On June 15, 1794, for example, an early frost "did much damage: killed corn, beans, pumpkins, potatoes, etc." There are a few mentions of visitors, skating, travel on the river, plus a recipe for a rheumatism cure, but the diary mainly records, against the background of the weather, the immemorial routine of ploughing, harrowing, sowing, harvesting, and threshing, although the latter is not specifically mentioned.

The first event was February 16, 1784, when Nase bought a load of hay. On March 13 he went upstream to Maugerville and brought back a yoke of oxen. During the journey he fell though the ice several times, the danger of which was familiar, as the entry for January 11 had noted that Sergeant Young, late of the New Jersey Volunteers, had gone "too near the water's edge, and the ice broke in, and he perished immediately." On April 2 "while cutting down a small sapling I had the misfortune to stick the corner of an axe in my leg which I fear will lay me up for several days." Basically, however, life was relatively sweet—"Never was there better weather in this world, than we experienced this winter."

With spring came the first plantings: May 22 corn, June 25 buckwheat, July 28 turnips. Only the buckwheat harvest on September 20 is actually recorded, then the planting of winter wheat October 10, rye November 2, and clover November 14. In the spring of 1785 corn, buckwheat, and turnips were again planted, but during the second season potatoes, beans, peas, cabbages, and apple seeds were added. In 1786 the only new item was the fodder crop, Timothy grass. Evidently his livestock was increasing—the entry for August 1 notes cryptically "was put in the possession of the mill, oxen etc," and that for September 1 "Finished mowing." The sawmill was held in partnership with his friend and patron Maj. John Coffin who lived at nearby Alwington Manor, but Nase did all the work. Another innovation in 1786 was the ordering of supplies, May 23: "wrote for coarse stockings, mittens, two barrels pork, 60 yds check woolen, dried apples, and axe handles." There is no other such entry in the diary except December 16, 1786, when he went to Saint John to get "my necessaries for the winter."

The sawmill business did not seem to interfere with Nase's agricultural activities, as the diary contains the account of sowing and harvesting. On November 20, 1786, he had moved into a new house. The entry for the spring of

1787 contains the first mention of a garden where he planted radishes and lettuce. He evidently now had many oxen and drove them to Hampstead Valley in May to pasture, bringing them back on December 1. Christmas Day 1787, was spent at Major Coffin's "in merriest and good cheer." On December 30 he again visited the Coffins: "I returned home, still bearing in mind that I was driven from home by a set of rebels on this day."

The next year perhaps saw Nase's complete conversion into a New Brunswicker when on March 13 he was married, from which union a large family resulted. Marriage may account for the first mention of the planting of flax, the spinning of which was women's work. Mrs. Nase may also account for the planting in 1789 of beets, carrots, parsnips, cucumbers, pumpkins, and apple trees.

Other new crop entries were oats (1788), and barley and squash (1791). In 1793 there is the first mention of sheep—"May 22nd. Sheared sheep...." There is only one mention of an animal birth (piglets) and of an animal being butchered, though birthing and slaughter must have been commonplace. The technicalities of farming are absent save for several invocations of the method of sowing turnips. "Thumb and finger, four paces, a cast every step." The only reference to fishing is April 18, 1791: "Set a net and 13 suckers and chubbs caught," though it was common to set nets for salmon and any other fish that might come along.

Another activity almost entirely absent is the maintenance of the house, farm buildings, and fences which took place in fall and winter. Also, there is no mention of sugaring, so widespread in the Saint John Valley—presumably he had no maples. Nor is there any mention of hens, ducks, and geese though it is likely he had some. The November 13, 1792 entry—"A small snow, and began to fodder my cattle"—is the only reference to a major farming consideration, the conservation of precious feed. During the season whenever a thaw or rain bared the land in the least way, a farmer would endeavour to get his stock to forage.

On October 23, 1800, Henry Nase informed Edward Winslow: "I have four fine boys and have no other way of providing for them but learn them to work and make them farmers." He had, to quote a recent historian, "learned the lesson of the country."

In the summer of 1785 Joseph Hadfield, an English visitor, wrote of Upper Canada: "It seems as if we may judge it [the American Revolution] as designed by Providence as the only means of peopling a great extent of country, with the very persons who now occupy a part thought too desert and barren to be inhabited." About a dozen years later the Reverend John Stuart, chaplain of the Kingston garrison wrote: "How mysterious are the ways of Providence. How short-sighted are we. Some years ago I thought it a great hardship to be banished into the wilderness.... Now the best wish we can form for our friends is to have them removed to us."

# 5 | FOUND- ATIONS LAID

## LOYALIST CULTURE

*"I have seen the foundations laid of
institutions ... which ... will grow with our growth,
and strengthen with our strength."*

*Richard Cartwright, 1810*

EVERYWHERE THE Loyalists went they had a cultural impact on writing, poetry, theatre, crafts, architecture, education, and religion. The more primitive Upper Canada usually lagged behind Nova Scotia and New Brunswick.

Loyalist printers, as the editor-publishers were called, had an ideal opportunity to provide the new or expanded societies with newspapers, an opportunity that was seized in the Maritimes but not in Upper Canada. Newspapers were much more central than now in their social, economic, political, and cultural functions. They were usually the only indigenous sources of information other than private letters and conversations, and the only outlet for essays (often appearing as anonymous letters to the editor) and poems—the *Saint John Gazette*, for example, printed forty-six locally written pieces of verse between 1783 and 1815.

Loyalists founded three newspapers during Shelburne's boom period, and established the first newspaper in Prince Edward Island. New Brunswick's first newspaper, the *Saint John Gazette*, was established in December, 1783, by two Loyalists, William Lewis and John Ryan. It was at first an opposition organ ranged against the *Royal Gazette*, which had been started in Saint John in October, 1785, by Christopher Sower, a Pennsylvania Loyalist who was also King's printer, publishing such official documents as the *Journal of the House of Assembly*. In 1806 John Ryan, a Rhode Islander, settled in St. John's, Newfoundland, where he introduced the colony's first printing office and founded its first newspaper, the *Royal Gazette*. The same year his son, Michael, founded Fredericton's first journal, the *Fredericton Telegraph*. John Ryan had been apprenticed during the war in New York to John Howe of Boston, who became the most significant Loyalist printer in British North America. In December, 1780, Howe launched the *Halifax Journal*, Nova Scotia's second newspaper; in 1801 he became King's printer and took over the first, the *Halifax Gazette*, which he combined with the *Journal* to form the *Nova Scotia Royal Gazette*. Howe also published the short-lived but lively *Nova Scotia Magazine and Comprehensive Review of Literature, Politics and News* (1789–91) which promoted agricultural improvements and served as an outlet for local writers. Technically, throughout his work Howe "set a new standard of ... printing."

John Howe's son, the famous reformer Joseph Howe, learned his trade from his father and, in 1828, took control of the *Nova Scotian or Colonial Herald* and began his campaign for responsible government. Other sons of Loyalists prominent in Canadian newspaper history were James Douglas Bagnall, who published the *Royal Herald* in Prince Edward Island, and William Buell, Jr., who in 1823 took over the *Brockville Record* and used it to attack the Family Compact.

In Upper Canada newspaper publishing lagged behind the Maritimes. The first newspaper appeared in Niagara in 1793. In 1798 York (Toronto) had one, and in 1810 so did Kingston, but none were published by Loyalists. In 1814, however, the Loyalist Richard Cartwright and others of the elite bought the faltering *Kingston Gazette* from its founder, Stephen Miles, originally of Vermont, whereupon Cartwright, as "Faulkland," became a frequent contributor. John Beverley Robinson's comments on public affairs also frequently appeared in the press.

The second-generation Loyalist and leading Methodist in the province, Egerton Ryerson, founded the *Christian Guardian* in 1829, entering politics as an ally of William Lyon Mackenzie and provoking conservative opponents to refer to "Ryerson's Revolutionary Radicals." Ryerson's loyalism came to the surface by 1833 and he henceforth made his way as a moderate reformer. Like most pioneer societies, Upper Canada had to import much of its literary talent. Its leading journalists—William Lyon Mackenzie, Francis Collins, and even the conservative writers like George Gurnett and Thomas Dalton—were not Loyalists.

Though clergymen might be considered professional wordsmiths and though the occasional sermon was published, apart from the printers no Loyalist was in any sense a professional writer. Yet many wrote. Formal Loyalist literature was largely confined to Nova Scotia and New Brunswick, especially the latter. As with newspapers a combination of primitive frontier demands and a comparative dearth of educated people inhibited literary creativity in Upper Canada with such occasional exceptions as Joseph Brant's translation into Mohawk of the *Book of Common Prayer* and the "Gospel According to St. Mark," published in England in 1787.

About New Brunswick, literary historian Fred Cogswell has written that the decades after the Loyalists arrived was the only period of "significant ... literary activity" before 1880. But he adds, "It is no coincidence that the finest poem composed by a Loyalist poet, 'To Cordelia' by Joseph Stansbury, was a heartfelt rejection of the Maritime Provinces." Stansbury, from Pennsylvania, was not only the best Loyalist poet, he was probably the best American poet of the revolutionary period. He lingered only briefly in Nova Scotia—"Believe me, love, this vagrant life Delights not me"—and returned to the United States.

Perhaps the era's leading American satirical poet, though he also wrote charming, often melancholy odes, and certainly the greatest Loyalist writer to settle permanently in British North America was Jonathan Odell, an Anglican clergyman from New Jersey, who became the long-time secretary of New Brunswick. Most of his verse was composed before 1783, but his aging muse sputtered effectively afterward as well and glowed briefly during the War of 1812. Good satirical and other verses were written by the Reverend Jacob Bailey, who exchanged Massachusetts for Annapolis. Roger Viets, another Anglican cleric, left Connecticut for Digby, Nova Scotia, and in 1788 produced *Annapolis-Royal*, the first "booklet" of poetry published in Canada. Printed in Halifax, it was an "inspirational" poem praising the balanced, calm, Christian growth of Annapolis and the coming of the next generation. "A new born Race is rear'd by careful Hands."

In the late 1790s, Lieut. Adam Allan, one of the first settlers in Fredericton, was in command of a post at Grand Falls on the Saint John River in Northern New Brunswick during a crisis with the United States. His stay inspired a poem about the Falls which was published in London in 1798, appended to his skilful translation from the Lallan (Scottish) dialect into standard English of *The New Gentle Shepherd* by Allan Ramsay.

> From this dread gulf of never-ending noise,
> Resembling that where devils but rejoice,
> The waters rush, like lava from the pits
> Of fam'd Vesuvius, and Mount Etna's lips;
> Foaming with rage, it forward presses on
> From fall to fall, o'er variegated stone;

Allan added an extra scene and a couple of songs of his own. The description of the Falls has been praised by Fred Cogswell: "The poem, unpolished and rough in versification, has a vigour and a fidelity to observation which is refreshing." It seems to have been the first poem written in New Brunswick to have been published outside of the newspapers.

Most Loyalist poetry circulated in good gentlemanly fashion in manuscript and much has doubtless been lost. For example, Roger Viets must have written many more verses than the couple that were published. Some could not be published for private or public reasons. An example of the former was the versatile Benjamin Marston's poem to his Nova Scotian sweetheart, "Elizabeth C." An example of the latter was Bailey's risqué lampoon, "The Adventures of Jack Ramble, the Methodist Preacher." Ramble's many sins included an encounter with a maid in a brothel.

> "Come, lovely youth, to my embrace."
> Jack blush'd and understood the case,
> And when she drew him towards the bed,
> All his expiring virtues fled.

The Loyalist elite typically favoured the "higher" esoteric form of classical poetry over prose, but generally the latter appeals more to a modern reader. In 1817 Walter Bates, a New Haven Loyalist who settled successfully in Kingston, New Brunswick, published *Companion for Caraboo*, later entitled *The Mysterious Stranger*, a best-selling, entertaining prose account of Henry More Smith, "Confidence man, jail-breaker, and horse thief." This slim volume was republished in Saint John around 1837, went through many editions, and is still available in facsimile.

Even better are Loyalist letters and reminiscences, not published until long after the Loyalists were dead. Letters, in those days a decided art form, can best be savoured in *The Winslow Papers* (the most magnificent collection of its kind in Canadian history), letters to and from Edward Winslow, which were edited by W.O. Raymond in Saint John in 1904 and are still available in reprint. In this excerpt from a letter to his wife, Winslow writes from Halifax about his young son, Murray:

> Master Murray made one of a party of pleasure yesterday a fishing, & he's taken cold and it's laughable enough to see the fuss that's made with him—one says, "The dear little creature's oppressed at his stomach"—another says "He's feverish," &c. If they don't hurt him by their nonsense I shall be glad. He is exactly as you have seen him a hundred times, stuffed at his stomach & wheezes, but I am sure that a drink of whey or something warm when he goes to bed will answer all the purpose. The rascal's laughing at them now.
>
> You always thought My Mary that I did not love this precious boy so much as I ought to. How grossly are you mistaken.... Indeed Mama I will not allow that your affection for him is

greater than my own. Since his arrival here he has quite captivated all his relations.... For whenever a company retires and the family & two or three friends form a circle of themselves, he is sure to afford a monstrous deal of real entertainment. He has this evening amused his aunts with a history of the whole family, and has given a character of all the children and servants & of almost everybody in the neighborhood, and he certainly does say some of the most extraordinary things that ever enter'd into the head of a child of his age. But I will not indulge you any farther on this subject, you are already too partial to this little Micmac.

The best reminiscences are Jacob Bailey's, edited by William S. Bartlett in 1853. As the nineteenth century wore on and the Loyalists began to die off, some of the old ones and their children were persuaded to tell or write about their experiences. An excellent collection from Upper Canada is *Loyalist Narratives*, edited by J.J. Talman for the Champlain Society in 1946.

A few children of Loyalists continued the literary tradition. In Lower Canada Chief Justice William Smith's son of the same name wrote a *History of Canada from Its First Discovery to the Year 1791*. It was printed in two volumes in 1815, but did not reach the public until 1826. In 1825 in Saint John, Peter Fisher published *Sketches of New Brunswick*, the first history of the province. He may also have been the writer of "The Lay of the Wilderness," a long, interesting poem, with explanatory footnotes, published in Saint John in 1834, that described conditions experienced by the early settlers.

> Our hearts are loyal, as our minds are free,
> Nor own we such a class as *tenantry*:
> In thee, New-Brunswick, on thy thousand hills,
> Or on thy level, broad, rich intervales,
> A *landlord's due*, ne'er stints the humble board,
> Each farmer here, "Free, happy, his own lord!"

In 1825 in London Oliver Goldsmith (grand-nephew of his famous namesake) born in St. Andrews, New Brunswick, of a Loyalist mother, published the successful and aptly entitled poem, "The Rising Village," which described the "suffering" of "the early settlers," the "difficulties ... they surmounted," and "the rise and progress of a young country." In Nova Scotia in 1829 Thomas Chandler Haliburton, also of a Loyalist mother, published the pioneering *An Historical and Statistical Account of Nova Scotia*, printed appropriately by Joseph Howe. Haliburton, of course, went on to become a best-selling writer and wit of international reputation.

Writing of New Brunswick, Fred Cogswell argues that, after 1808 and the growth of the timber trade, "Inexorably the outlook of the Loyalist gentlemen dwindled to the parochialism of shopkeepers." Nevertheless it is argued that, stimulated by the University of New Brunswick and the genteel atmosphere of Fredericton, the Loyalist literary tradition led much later, beginning in 1880, to the flowering of Bliss Carman, Sir Charles G.D. Roberts (both of Loyalist descent), and others, and to the continuing literary distinction of Fredericton in our own time. In more developed, unified Nova Scotia the intellectual flowering which came earlier (usually dated from the publication of Haliburton's *The Clockmaker* in 1836) can be partly attributed to the stimulus of the growth of Anglicanism and the founding of King's College, both Loyalist phenomena.

Amateur and occasionally professional theatre was cherished by the colonial elite of "the old thirteen." During the war British and Loyalist officers turned thespian to relieve the tedium of garrison duty. There were no Loyalist dramatists but everywhere the Loyalist elite congregated in exile, drawing-room drama was likely, and in Halifax and Saint John they helped to create public, amateur, and eventually professional theatricals.

In Halifax public shows began in 1785, and in 1789 the garrison built the New Grand Theatre on Argyle Street, which was in use for the next quarter century. An announcement for the *Merchant of Venice*, February 26, 1789, added: "The characters by the gentlemen of the navy, army and town." In Saint John the theatre was more purely Loyalist. *The Comedy of the Busy Body* was staged in March, 1789, at Mallard House, a private building where the first assembly had met in 1786. The "gentlemen" of the cast may have included Jonathan and Stephen Sewell, sons of the distinguished Massachusetts Loyalist, Jonathan Sewell, Sr. Years earlier Jonathan, Jr., who ended up as chief justice of Quebec, had been praised by the legendary British actress Mrs. Siddons for a boyhood performance at Bristol Grammar School.

On January 20, 1789, the Saint John *Royal Gazette*, announcing the opening of "a little Theatre," published an anonymous poetic "prologue" which made a still timely plea for the arts. What, it asked, was commercial success (and failure) "without the muse's aid!"

> Make then the muses your peculiar care,
>
> ...
>
> Favour our art: So may your ships increase,

And each adventure prove a golden fleece.

...

What rais'd this City on a dreary coast,
Alternately presenting rocks and frost,
Where torpid shell-fish hardly found a bed,
Where scarce a pine durst shew a stunted head.

The answer was "Commerce—commerce smoothed the rugged strand."

In 1800 some "young gentlemen," including Massachusetts Loyalist George Leonard, Jr., gained permission to use city hall as a theatre. The next year an amateur club called "The Saint John Theatre" was formed, and by 1808 the Drury Lane Theatre, the first building specifically for the purpose, was completed and professional players began to arrive.

In both Halifax and Saint John a lack of sophistication is suggested by newspaper requests that seats must be taken as marked on one's ticket, and ladies asked "to dress their heads as low as possible" so as not to obstruct the view. However, such gaucherie does not detract from the comment by a Scottish visitor to the Maritimes that the Loyalists were "fond ... of ... the Amusements of plays and farces."

Although Loyalist surveyors like Benjamin Marston might do the odd sketch or embellish their surveys, no fine art was produced in Loyalist Canada. Crafts fared better but there were too many practitioners and not enough patrons. Thus, Jeremiah Brundage, a skilled New York silversmith, had to turn to blacksmithing in Saint John; Alexander Ross and James Hunter, cabinetmakers in Fredericton, went bankrupt (partly through importing costly mahogany from the West Indies) in 1788; even during the good times in Shelburne, Charles Oliver Bruff, an outstanding goldsmith and jeweller from New York City, languished while three members of the famous Newport, Rhode Island, cabinetmaking Goddard family were reduced to working as carpenters. They probably moved to Halifax in 1788 but no surviving piece of furniture can be attributed to them. Identifying makers of furniture of the Loyalist period is difficult because of the lack of cabinetmaker's records and the artists' failure to mark their products. Only two works can be very tentatively attributed to Robert Chillas, a New York cabinetmaker, in Saint John between 1785 and 1825. Generally, as with all household furnishings and artifacts, man and time have been the great destroyers. Even less remains of the belongings of the less affluent.

As would be expected, Loyalists' furniture was predominantly American. Thus, despite the presence of English and Scottish craftsmen, Canadian Windsor chairs are of the "rod back" American design, not the "split back" British style. Also there was a strong tendency toward simplicity and conservatism. Few Loyalists could afford the "opulent" Rhode Island fashion of the Goddards. On the land, part-time winter craftsmen made even simpler "country" furniture, often from ash. Silversmiths found the market favoured simple tableware—knives, spoons. A visit to any appropriate Canadian museum shows the elegance Loyalist society was capable of.

The elite brought furniture and household artifacts with them, they commissioned them locally, and they imported them from Great Britain and the United States. A few houses were brought in in sections, but most architecture had to be local.

Again there has been a shameful attrition, but enough houses, churches, and public buildings remain standing or preserved in photographs and pictures to indicate their quality. Rich Loyalists, working from memory, possibly an English copy-book, and in consultation with the abundant local artisans (painters, masons, joiners, blacksmiths, and perhaps a cabinetmaker forced to engage in panelling or moulding) built many beautiful houses, usually of wood, occasionally of stone (as in the limestone area below the Bay of Quinte). Representative of what was possible are: the John Porteous House (occupied for a time by Benedict Arnold) in Saint John (1785); the Spring Hill Farm built by George Duncan Ludlow near Fredericton (c. 1787); the Jonathan Odell House in Fredericton (pre-1795); the "Loyalist House" built by David Daniel Merritt in Saint John (1810); the "White House" built ten miles west of Kingston, Ontario (1793) by William Fairfield; and the Samuel Heck House in Maitland, Ontario (c. 1804).

Typically, domestic architecture was American with a difference, "borrowing ... New England technology and style" in the Maritimes, and New York fashions, such as rubble stone walls, in Ontario, but always "selective and conservative," according to a modern historian. The Loyalist Georgian house, with its clear British and American roots, was "built with little alteration" until 1850, resistant to United States Federalist or neo-classical innovations not only because of comparative poverty (in the Maritimes) but also because of a desire to avoid association with Republican ideology. The Ingraham House, built in 1840 at Bear Island and now located at King's Landing, New Brunswick, "can be taken as evidence of how deeply and how well the Loyalist ideas of architecture established themselves in eastern Canada." (For a general sampling of Loyalist houses, visits to Shelburne, Nova Scotia, or St. Andrews, New Brunswick, are warmly recommended.)

In New Brunswick and Nova Scotia, Loyalist churches appropriately combined American and British styles: the plain meeting house with Wren's classicism. Even more than in New England, the stone forms of old England were scaled and simplified. A splendid example, still extant and little altered, is St. Mary's Anglican Church, Auburn, Nova Scotia (consecrated in 1790), which is a rectangular meeting-house structure with several added classic features, including a Wrenian steeple. The interior is described by the leading art historian Stuart Smith as:

> a blend of pioneer styles and sophisticated classical details. High wainscotting made of very wide boards laid horizontally contrasts with the fluted pillars beneath the west gallery, and the detailed romanesque arch of the chancel opening. The latch and bolt on the main door add a primitive note while the decorative mouldings around the windows and on the pews add a civilized touch.

He concludes: the church's "classical detail and Palladian east window constitute the summation of almost a century of modest North American craftsmanship."

The patron of St. Mary's, Col. James Morden, was not a Loyalist—he was an Englishman living in Halifax with a large Annapolis Valley estate; nor, it seems was the church's designer-constructor, William Mathews, a Master Builder also of Halifax, though his local assistants, Jabex and Michael Benedict, respectively brickmaker and stonemason, and Benjamin Foster, a maker of pine roof-shingles, may well have been, because Auburn was a largely Loyalist settlement. Bishop Inglis, who usually lived in Auburn rather than Halifax, probably personally painted the coats of arms which still indicate the governor's and bishop's personal pews.

More than usual is known about what the bishop dubbed "the neatest, best finished church in the province" partly because in 1890, a century after its erection, the weather vane was blown down, in the process cracking open a copper ball atop the steeple which contained documents concerning its construction. Local pine was used for most material: frame-timber, boards, shingles, panels, moulding. A nearby sawpit was handy for two-man saws (one man in the hole, the other above) such as whipsaws to produce rough boards and clapboards. Various axes were used to finish frame-timber which were put together on the ground and raised "with iron-pointed 'pike poles'." Using a variety of planes, Mathews probably personally made the classical mouldings, but door and window frames and rails were all brought from Halifax. The nails, put in ten- to fifteen-pound lots, were carried by soldiers who marched the hundred-mile-long military road from Halifax to Auburn. Lime for plaster came from Saint John, supplemented in a pinch with burnt local quahog shells. The total cost of St. Mary's was £475, of which Morden paid £165 and Governor Parr £222.

As with houses, Loyalist churches usually had no specific architect. Trinity, Saint John's first church, begun in 1788, was built by the Loyalist firm of Messrs. Bean and Dowling: Thomas Bean was a carpenter; Samuel Dowling was a bricklayer. The Hay Bay Chapel (1792) near Adolphustown, the oldest Methodist house of worship in Upper Canada, is little more than a barn, albeit an elegant one.

Paul Bedell, who laid out the plan of Saint John, was a merchant by profession. The closest thing to a Canadian Loyalist architect, in the gentleman-amateur tradition of Thomas Jefferson and Peter Harrison (to name a rebel and a Loyalist), was Isaac Hildrith, originally from that nest of Tories, Norfolk, Virginia, where he was merchant, surveyor, and carpenter. He fled from there to Shelburne and, in partnership with Aaron White, set up a construction firm that designed and built Christ Church (Anglican) in 1790. A few years later he moved to Halifax and, at the request of the legislature, surveyed a proposed canal between Dartmouth and the Shubenacadie River. In 1800 he became the architect of Government House, probably the first stone building in Nova Scotia, which in 1805 became the official residence—as it still is—of the governor (then Sir John Wentworth). The second stone building in Halifax was Province House, begun in 1811 and completed eight years later, which remains the seat of the legislature. A modern scholar, Brian Cuthbertson, comments: "In Halifax British classicism reigned supreme in the two public buildings most associated with the Loyalists, Government House and Province House, which were monuments to Loyalist taste and pride."

Elsewhere Loyalist public buildings were less grand. In Fredericton, in 1787, Gov. Thomas Carleton moved into an elegant two-and-a-half-storey structure known as the Mansion House, which he paid for himself. It was built by two former members of the New Jersey Volunteers, Sgt. Cornelius Ackerman and Abraham Vanderbeck, who had been a farmer. Ackerman and Vanderbeck constructed several other Fredericton buildings, including the Golden Ball Inn.

Proper quarters for the legislature and supreme court, Province Hall, begun in 1799 and completed in 1802, was a modest wooden building with some plank carved to simulate stone. The first Parliament of Upper Canada met in 1792 at Niagara in Navy Hall, which was little more than a few renovated huts. In 1797 the legislature shifted to York and to two specially built but very modest single-storey, brick structures. Meanwhile in 1794 the Simcoes, who at first occupied a tent at Niagara and at York a canvas house once owned by Captain Cook, personally built Castle Frank overlooking the Don River. Castle Frank was in the form of a Greek temple with large wooden pillars of simulated stone.

Apart from churches and government buildings the largest structures built by the Loyalists were often three-storey saw and grist mills. There were many skilled millwrights among the refugees, including David Brass from New Jersey who built the first water-powered mill in Upper Canada at Niagara in 1783, and Robert Clark of New York who built mills at Kingston in 1784 and Napanee in 1787 and the early 1790s. Although not always considered "architecture," like many functional buildings (such as barns) mills could assume considerable beauty as several contemporary sketches suggest. What is left of the only one still surviving confirms this theory: Capt. John Walden Myers' on the Moira River at Belleville.

Finally, mention must be made of the handsome Cape Roseway Lighthouse, on the southern tip of McNutt's Island, which guarded the entrance to Shelburne harbour. Along with an adjacent house, the remarkable octagonal structure of granite slabs, built by a group of craftsmen and commissioners (mainly Loyalists), used fifty hogsheads of lime and cost the Nova Scotia assembly the considerable sum of well over £2,000. Ten feet square at the base, it towered ninety-two feet in the air from the foundation. Completed in 1790, the lights, which were visible as far as ten leagues (perhaps thirty miles) out at sea, were lit in September, 1792. That December a model of it decorated the table at the Wentworth's Christmas ball in Halifax. A contemporary visitor claimed the lighthouse "was not exceeded or even equalled on the continent of america." The original lighthouse functioned until modern times.

In stark contrast to the civilization and even elegance of the Loyalist towns and large country houses were urban and rural slums. A touching account of the latter was given by Lieutenant Clarkson who, in October, 1791, stopped at Point L'Hébert en route by ship to recruit blacks at Shelburne. He found "a few wretched inhabitants" in the "uncommonly wild" wooded area eking out "a scanty subsistence" from a few rocky acres planted with potatoes and corn. The wealthiest had "a few Sheep or a Cow." At one of the huts Clarkson and his party "met with a most agreeable reception" from Jenny Lavender, a young girl of fifteen, left in charge of two younger brothers while her parents gathered potatoes across the river. With manners that "would have done Credit to a Person of the first rank and Education" Jenny "made a hearty supper" from "potatoes and buttermilk, with a few dried salt fish. Forced by the weather to stay over, the party was made comfortable as Jenny kept the fire going throughout the night.

Clarkson departed next day, "pained to think that so valuable a Mind should be entomb'd in this Wilderness and for ever secluded from the social comforts of Mankind in a state of Society."

The final example of the Loyalist cultural thrust is education. The Loyalist elite, much aware of the need for education, were unwilling or unable to do much beyond their own class. They were not even conspicuously successful in that endeavour. By 1820, one historian asserts, "the justices of the peace of Nova Scotia and New Brunswick were often men completely unlettered in the law or almost anything else." During the first thirty years, elementary and secondary education was primitive. The majority of Loyalists' children received little or none, other than what might be provided in the home. Schools in Upper Canada, recalled one Loyalist's son, were "like Angels' visits, they were few and far between." The affluent relied on private and semi-private academies, often run by Anglican clergy and itinerant school teachers who, in Upper Canada, were often Americans and a source of nervousness. A few grammar schools were established: Fredericton by 1785, Halifax by 1789, Saint John by 1805. In 1799 the Scottish immigrant John Strachan began what became the moulding of almost the entire future ruling class of Upper Canada, when he started tutoring the rich in Kingston and four years later opened a school at Cornwall.

The very rich often sent their children abroad to Britain and the United States for both secondary and higher education. A stimulus to Loyalist educational ambitions was the fear, voiced by Bishop Inglis and echoed by Governor Simcoe and others, that if sent south of the border their children would imbibe Republican principles. However, many Loyalists, particularly in the Maritimes, had no such qualms.

Soon after his arrival, Simcoe petitioned London to finance a university. Secretary of State Henry Dundas' memorable reply was "the Country must make the University, and not the University the Country." Almost a decade earlier, in 1785, Dr. William Paine and six other refugees had made such an attempt when they asked Governor Carleton to set up an academy of liberal arts and sciences in Fredericton. Six thousand acres of land were granted but the result was simply a collegiate school. Ambition outran economic reality. The only Loyalist "country" that could support a university was the most advanced, Nova Scotia, whose assembly, in 1788, granted Bishop Inglis' request for funds for an academy at Windsor. With added British support, King's College (today aligned with Dalhousie University in Halifax) commenced operations in 1789. Inglis' dream was to resurrect King's College, New York, with which he had been intimately connected before the Revolution turned it into Columbia. He also wished to make King's the only university in all British North America, a dream inherited by his son John, an alumnus, who also inherited the bishopric.

The Reverend William Cochran, an Irish Loyalist and co-founder with John Howe of the *Nova Scotia Magazine*, has been called "the intellectual force" behind King's. Cochran wanted widespread, state-sponsored education throughout Canada carried out by well-paid, pro-British teachers. He was a stern, dedicated instructor of the many elite young men, including Joseph Howe, who passed through his hands at Windsor. But his scheme for general schooling remained only an idea, and King's College was something of a failure well before his death in 1833, with flagging discipline, pluralist professors, and, until 1806, Anglican religious tests which excluded most of the population.

Meanwhile, the perennial New Brunswick desire to be free of any dependency on Nova Scotia led to higher education finally beginning in a modest way in 1823. On January 1, 1829, over the objections of Bishop John Inglis, King's College opened in Fredericton in the spanking new building on the hill which is now the centre of the University of New Brunswick, and the oldest university building in use in Canada. The booming timber trade off Crown lands supplied the funds. The faculty, but not the students, had to be Anglican.

Before leaving higher education, mention must be made of Titus Smith, Jr. (1768–1850), a distinguished Loyalist who should be better known. He traversed the interior of Nova Scotia in 1801 and 1802 producing a map which went unchallenged for three decades. A largely self-taught botanist, Smith also listed trees, shrubs, and plants, and by his death had achieved international fame as what a modern scholar calls "a pioneer of plant ecology in North America."

As noted previously, the Church of England, though formally established in the Maritimes, remained a minority denomination deriving its importance from the social prestige and political power of its members. One of the weaknesses of the Anglican Church was that it was far less effective than dissenting groups in what was perhaps the first need of a society close to the pioneer stage: the need for moral police. It is also doubtful that the average representative of the Anglican clergy possessed the intellectual depth of the Congregationalists and Presbyterians who established the first and best colleges in America. What Anglicans brought with them was the essence of Shakespearian England tempered here and there by an anticipation of Gilbert and Sullivan. This was part of the joint heritage of the English-speaking world which dissenting clergy were inclined to neglect or deny.

The ordinary Loyalists were much more inclined to the dissenters, particularly the Methodists and Baptists, who appealed to frontier egalitarianism (one

Methodist clergyman said he was a graduate of the College of "Buck and Bright"—common names for oxen in Upper Canada) and whose ministers were often American. The Loyalists contributed to the religious diversity of Canada by founding or giving solidity to the Methodists, Baptists, Presbyterians, Lutherans, Mennonites, Quakers, and English-speaking Catholics. The German Mennonites came to Upper Canada following the Loyalists from Pennsylvania. Loyalist Adolphustown was "the cradle of Canadian Methodism."

Loyalist Canada was not particularly spiritual but it was a church-going society characterized by self-help and community effort, even among Anglicans and Catholics who possessed a pre-existing organization. Early settlers often relied on family prayers or a simple gathering in a barn or neighbour's house for bible-reading. Communities soon organized to build churches and hire ministers. Many groups arrived accompanied by their ministers, for example the Reverend John Stuart who accompanied the Anglican settlers to Cataraqui, the Reverend John Bethune of Glengarry, the first Presbyterian minister in Upper Canada, and the Reverend George Gilmore who came with some Methodists to Hants County, Nova Scotia.

The Loyalists' role in building the Canadian "cultural mosaic" is illustrated by the way they tended to settle in religious and ethnic groups. Thus, in Upper Canada Roman Catholic and Presbyterian Scots kept apart. When the evacuees from Charleston, South Carolina, arrived in Halifax in 1782, ethnic lines soon transcended geographical lines. The Germans went off to Ship Harbour or Shelburne, the Ulstermen to Rawdon or the Petitcodiac River, New Brunswick.

Although we have characterized the Loyalists as quarrelsome, an equal emphasis must be placed on cooperation. As always in rural societies of that time, lack of inns and amenities made private hospitality a way of life: "the man that would have closed his door against a traveller would have been looked upon as worse than a savage." Loyalists banded together for transportation, educational, and religious purposes. Working bees did not only involve tree-clearing. There were also barn-raising, mill-raising, corn-husking, apple, quilting, butter, stone-clearing, harvesting, and threshing bees. Apart from church, the legal quarter sessions, and the occasional public execution and election campaign, these bees were one of the few chances the common folk had for recreation. A bee would often end with feasting, drinking, and dancing to the fiddle or jew's-harp.

More formal dancing was also a passion with the wealthy. During the winter of 1785–6, a fortnightly dance attended by about sixteen couples was virtually the only diversion in the infant settlement of Cataraqui. In 1789 Sarah Winslow

advised Ward Chipman to come to Fredericton "and dance away your gout.
Everybody's dancing this winter, even Mrs. Carleton...." The hapless elite of
declining Shelburne were known as "the dancing beggars."

The elite were also much given to card parties and to what some visitors
regarded as too frequent repasts that ranged from light afternoon "souchong" teas
to "formal, perhaps extravagant dinners." "Tea, coffee, cakes, and then in an hour
or two cold turkey, ham and a profusion of tarts, pies and sweetmeats; punch,
wine, porter, liquers, and all sorts of drink," was Lady Hunter's half-hearted
complaint in Fredericton in 1804. Ten years earlier in Upper Canada Lady Simcoe
recorded a similar giddy round of teas, cards, eating, drinking, and dancing that
characterized Fredericton and Halifax. According to Patrick Campbell, in New
Brunswick even "Every day-labourer must have his beef, or what he likes better,
pork, twice a day, tea or chocolate, half a mutchkin of rum for grog, and half a
dollar of money *per* day."

The use of alcoholic beverages was widespread. While the poor made do with
rum or spruce-beer, the wealthy imported luxuries such as Madeira. In 1785, a
visitor commented regarding an Upper Canadian Loyalist officer: "The Major
has his guns, fishing tackle, and a large case stocked with all good liquors. I'm sure
he leads a very happy life." Loyalist brewing and distilling began at least as early as
1788 in Cornwall. Joel Stone wrote to his father, January 25, 1788: "I have began
making Malt Brewing beer and Distilling Spirituous Liquors from Wheat barly
Rye ... which are Raised in Abundance in this New Country."

Loyalist society was, of course, provincial. In 1804 Lady Hunter said the ladies
of Saint John "don't look very like ladies of the present day in England, with very
fine-dressed heads of a morning, pink and lilac high-heeled, small toed shoes,
walking over rugged, rocky paths. This strikes me as very odd...."

Visitors found British North Americans isolated and ignorant. News arrived
late and spread slowly. In 1813 British colonel Joseph Gubbins met an old man on
the Miramichi in New Brunswick "who had rather a literary turn." Having found
mention of the *Philosophical Transactions*, he told Gubbins he had commissioned a
merchant to buy him a set. "But he had no idea of their volume and was almost
ruined by his purchase." Another facet of provincialism were genteelisms. Gubbins observed that "the ridiculous delicacy of their expressions are very diverting.
A N.B. lady conceives it indecorous to call a Male Bird a Cock, for which they
substitute Rooster, even to Weather Rooster; Knees they denominate Benders and
so on."

Loyalist society was not only provincial but also in many ways primitive and isolated—improved transportation in the form of roads was very slow. Many and frequent were the complaints of the distance from school, grist mill, sawmill, doctor, and clergyman—hence the do-it-yourself marriages and other home remedies. Upper Canadian families eagerly awaited the arrival of the Yankee peddlers; above Fredericton during the summer it was the monthly Durham boat from which "the women received their supply of Tea, Sugar, Snuff, and sundry other indispensables and the men in their turn were supplied ... with Tobacco, powder shot and clothing, and what was of still greater consequence..., the produce of the West Indies [rum], to cheer their loneliness."

Currency remained in chronic short supply and barter was endemic. In 1790 lawyer Ward Chipman was paid in furniture made in jail at Fredericton by two bankrupt cabinetmakers. In 1811 Gubbins noticed that the New Brunswick Loyalist doctor, Charles Gunter, received his fees in hay, salt fish, pork, and "I have seen him returning with boots." A Cornwallis farmer wrote, in charming doggerel, to the Irish editor of the *Nova Scotia Magazine* that he could not afford the subscription price of twenty-two shillings and sixpence.

> As cash in the country is quite out of use,
> The only way left is to pay in produce.
> Indeed my friend Jacob tells me, he supposes,
> An honest Hibernian will deal in bluenoses. [potatoes]
> If this pay will answer, to be sure sir I shall
> Become a subscriber, and pay every fall.

In the early years before the merchants began in earnest, many items could not be had for barter or cash, especially in isolated Upper Canada. In 1786 Richard Cartwright complained that at Cataraqui neither a "sheet of paper," nor "hair powder," nor a "plate," nor a "tumbler larger than a gill" could "be had at any price." In 1793, at Niagara, Hannah Jarvis asked her father, the Reverend Samuel Peters in London, to send patent medicines, gloves, spoons, clogs, pins, needles, a silver watch, a pewter sun dial, and a pocket compass—"we know neither Time or Points here."

The prevailing tone of Loyalist society that is revealed by travellers' accounts and by the annoyed Loyalist elite is one of frontier egalitarianism, which was primarily the result of the availability of land. Complaints of the difficulties in finding servants or hiring any kind of worker were perennial: "not to be had for love nor money." Publicans, waiters, and servants were "saucy." There was a blurred sense of social distinction. A Loyalist's daughter recalled that in Upper

Canada her father "for many years, used occasionally to take the head of the table with his labourers, to show them he was not too proud to eat with them." Captain Booth, an English officer on duty at Shelburne in 1789, complained that "most ... if not all" the inhabitants were "styled Gentlemen." When his servant would announce the arrival of a "gentleman," Booth would discover "the Poor fellow was either a carpenter, smith or mason begging for employment." He added: "The Spirit of equallity reign'd."

In 1811 Colonel Gubbins arrived at the St. Andrews dock in New Brunswick. "The manners of my boatmen savoured of the American equality. They were perfectly familiar, joined in the conversation and, not seeming disposed to carry our port-manteaus to the inn, we took them under our own arms." In the 1780s in New Brunswick, Sgt. Maj. William Cobbett was amazed to find "thousands of captains ... without soldiers, and squires without stockings," some of whom were happy to sell him a glass of grog. His commanding officer, Lord Edward Fitzgerald, added: "There are no gentlemen; every man is on a footing (provided he works) and wants nothing, everyman is exactly what he can make himself...."

The Loyalist's daughter quoted above, after noting how her mother's help always ate at their mistress' table, went on to assert that "many of these helps of early days have since become the wives of squires, captains, majors and colonels of militia, and are owners of large properties, and they and their descendants drive in their own carriages."

Yet despite the common experience of gentlemen being forced to work with their hands and the dashing of the aristocratic hopes of the New Brunswick elite, life was not entirely equalized by the frontier. Compensation, half-pay, wealth brought from the United States, government patronage, education—any or all of these conferred benefits and advantages on some from the start and in the long run, as the rise of the Family Compacts illustrates.

In 1802, Edward Winslow looked back at the history of New Brunswick. It had been settled by "an order of men who call themselves Loyalists" who "made an election to plunge into a wilderness with their wives and children rather than submit to the humiliating ... necessity of soliciting mercy" from the rebels. "They combated difficulties, fatigues and toils," built their huts "and little holes were cut in the forest." "Immense labour" produced "a few potatoes and a scanty crop of rye." After sixteen years under "a constitution ... similar ... to the British" the situation "was materially changed." "The habitations of the Farmers" were "tight, warm and comfortable," with "robust" families "clad in homespun, feeding upon their own mutton, with bread, butter and cheese in abundance." Agricultural surpluses and the timber trade often won luxuries. At a time when "a calamatous war" was ruining "half the countries in the world," Winslow said of New Brunswickers:

> Enquire among 'em for a Grievance and they'll not be able to
> point out one:
>> Are you oppressed with taxes? No.
>> Do the laws afford you sufficient protection? Why yes.

In 1810 Richard Cartwright looked back at Upper Canada in a similar vein. The Loyalists' efforts "had been crowned with complete success." He continued:

> I have been a resident in this country before there was a
> human habitation within the limits of what is now the Province
> of Upper Canada,... I have seen this wilderness in the course of a
> few years, converted into fruitful fields, and covered with
> comfortable habitations. I see around me thousands, who
> without any other funds than their personal labour, began to
> denude the soil of its primaeval forests, in possession of extensive
> and well cultivated farms,... I see this property unencumbered
> with feudal burdens, undiminished by quit-rents or taxes,
> guarded by the wisest laws, equally and impartially administered.
>
> I see the proprietor himself protected from vexatious arrest or
> arbitrary imprisonment. I have seen the benevolent intentions of
> the British Government towards the Colony, exemplified in every
> measure that could tend to promote its prosperity; and crowned,
> by imparting to it, its own unrivalled constitution, as far as it was
> practicable to impart it to a dependent Province. I have seen the
> foundations laid of institutions and establishments for the
> promoting of knowledge, and diffusing religious instruction,
> which however weak and humble in their present state, will grow
> with our growth, and strengthen with our strength.

# 6

# UNFINISHED BUSINESS

## EXTERNAL RELATIONS

*"It is commonly asserted that without complete independence the United States could not have developed its own peculiar virtue. Yet it was not apparent to him that America was any more individual than Canada or Australia, that Pittsburgh and Kansas City were to be preferred before Montreal and Melbourne or Sydney and Vancouver."*

*—Doremus' reflections on the American Revolution in*
*Sinclair Lewis'* It Can't Happen Here, *1935*

THE LOYALIST migrations affected the balance of power in North America and, through North America, the Atlantic world. Without the Loyalist occupation of their maritime and western flanks, the St. Lawrence Valley French Canadian population of approximately one hundred and thirty thousand—the majority of British subjects in America—would not have been large enough to justify the British presence on the continent.

The foundation of a second state in North America required an informal alliance of French Canadian and British Loyalists, each with their respective cultural and political dimensions. This provided a sufficient population base to warrant the presence of a British garrison in America. From 1783 until the withdrawal of British troops in 1870, the garrison in Canada was roughly equal to the strength of the United States army in peacetime. As Britain renounced "Taxation without Representation" by 1778, the garrison was maintained at the expense of the British taxpayer, substantially subsidizing the Canadian economy.

The Treaty of 1783 registered the independence of the old colonies and the continued British presence on the continent, but there was much unfinished business. A dispute erupted about the boundary between Maine and New Brunswick. Vermont became an independent republic outside the American Union in 1780. There was the serious question of the midwestern American Indians who had supported the British, remained undefeated, and were not included in the peace treaty. In the territory where these Indians were an independent power, Britain retained control of the Ohio posts in defiance of the Treaty of 1783.

Less tangible than these issues of frontiers and power was the unfinished business in the minds of men. Most Americans considered Canada a natural extension of the Republic. Some Loyalists dreamed of drawing the Republic back to the empire by the example of good government. Others hoped to bring the American Midwest under British control and to develop its economy from a

Canadian base. Among the pioneers, for whom land was the first consideration, many wavered between moving west and moving north into Canada.

The dispute about the Maine-New Brunswick border was settled, temporarily at least, by a commission composed of Loyalists and their former enemies. A New York Supreme Court judge cast the deciding vote in favour of Canada after he examined archeological evidence presented to the commission by Loyalist Ward Chipman.

The question of Vermont's status was potentially dangerous. The state had dropped out of the war in 1780, because the Continental Congress would not recognize its independence from New York. The once and future American hero, Ethan Allen, discussed the prospects of Vermont rejoining the empire with the former Vermont Tory, Justus Sherwood, who acted as a British agent. Allen invited Loyalists to resettle in Vermont. Then, when Vermont was accepted into the American Union in 1792, he insisted that the resettled Loyalists take an oath of allegiance to the Republic. Most Loyalists objected and preferred to suffer a second exile. Among these was Capt. John Savage, who claimed compensation a second time for lands lost for the sake of his loyalty. Happily, the Eastern Townships in Quebec were opened for settlement in 1792, permitting Savage and his companions to join the land rush.

The New Brunswick-Maine boundary dispute and the status of Vermont were not the stuff that wars are made of, but the question of the midwestern Indians lingered on until it reached a climax in the War of 1812. Loyalists were involved, in the persons of the British Indian agent, Alexander McKee, and the Loyalist Mohawk chief, Joseph Brant. At the request of George Washington, Brant sought to secure a treaty by which the Indians would concede most of the present state of Ohio in return for recognition of a tribal confederation which would include his own people, the Iroquois. Brant failed because of the overconfidence of the Indians, who had defeated the American forces sent west against them in 1790 and again in 1791. His failure was also partly the fault of his fellow Loyalist Alexander McKee, who encouraged the Indians to believe that they would receive British assistance.

All hope of Indian resistance ended when the American general Anthony Wayne defeated them at the battle of Fallen Timbers in August 1794. Even after this, Lord Dorchester, the governor of Canada, made eleventh-hour efforts to rally the Indians. But the British were seeking a settlement in the West which was secured by the Jay Treaty of November 1794. By this treaty the British agreed to withdraw from the Ohio forts. As a scapegoat had to be found for the false hopes that the Indians had been given, Dorchester was blamed and resigned.

These events decided the fate of the Ohio country, but the Indian question moved west, where Tecumseh and his brother, the Prophet, revived the idea of an Indian confederation. Tecumseh, who might be classed as a late Loyalist, suffered disaster when his brother made an ill-advised attack on the American forces at Tippecanoe in 1811. Yet Tecumseh's activities, for which the Americans held the British responsible, were a major cause of the War of 1812. This war secured for the Indians, at last, the much desired British alliance. Tecumseh joined the British forces in Canada and fought with them until his death at the battle of the Thames on 4 October, 1813.

From the point of view of the Loyalists, the War of 1812 was the last act of the American Revolution, as an American victory in this war would have forced them to accept republicanism or emigrate once more. All the forces involved in the Revolution were again thrown into conflict: the western Indians, the blacks who swam to British warships, the Loyalist militia, French Canadians, and the regular forces of the Crown.

The war did not trigger a resurgence of British loyalism in the Republic but it dragged to the surface the latent power of neutralism, which turned out to be one of the decisive factors of the war. Neutralism was not an important influence in the British-American provinces, but was certainly present in Upper Canada at the outset of the war. Republicanism in Upper Canada at this time was as scarce as British loyalism was in the United States, and those few Canadians who joined the invaders in 1812 seemed to believe that they were joining the winning side. Post-Loyalist American immigrants, who made up over two-thirds of the population of Upper Canada, appear to have shared the neutralism of the northeastern American states. On taking an oath of allegiance, post-Loyalist Americans coming into the province before 1812 had been accepted as British subjects. Some Upper Canadians had doubts about the loyalty of these new immigrants, but their status did not become a political issue until the 1820s.

Just after the 1812–14 war, Lt.-Gov. Francis Gore, at the Town of York, tried to prevent American immigrants from taking the oath of allegiance. Challenged by the assembly, Gore referred the matter to London. The province was then informed that Americans who had accepted American citizenship in 1783 were no longer British subjects and would have to be naturalized under the Act of 1740. This required seven years' residence in the province. A test case arose in 1821 when Barnabas Bidwell, who had come to Canada early in 1812 and had taken the oath of allegiance during the war, was elected to the assembly. His right to sit in the provincial House was challenged on the grounds of his citizenship. As he had fled from the Republic to avoid a charge of misuse of public funds, Bidwell was not permitted to take his seat, but his son, Marshall Spring Bidwell, was then elected in his place.

The question of the status of American immigrants was not settled until 1828 when all those who had taken the oath of allegiance were accepted as British subjects, while those who had entered the province before 1820 could become British subjects by taking the oath. Others had to apply under the Act of 1740.

In the course of the 1812–14 war many American immigrants and some Loyalists fled to the United States, and an act was passed in 1814 enabling the Crown to confiscate the property of those who had left without special permission. By the end of the war there were indictments against seventy who had left the province, and Loyalists who had done so had their names and those of their descendants stricken from the United Empire Loyalist list. As noted previously, Irish-born Joseph Willcocks, who had attempted to form an opposition, was killed in action serving in the American forces—one of the few Upper Canadians who supported the invasion for ideological reasons. In May, 1814, nineteen American-born residents of Upper Canada were tried at the Ancaster Assizes for cooperating with the enemy. Fifteen were convicted and eight hanged. The prosecution was carried out by the son of a Loyalist, the young solicitor general, John Beverley Robinson.

In spite of this, the prevailing mood in the British provinces at the outbreak of the 1812 war was defeatist rather than treasonable. Lt. Gen. Sir Isaac Brock noted that all classes were affected, including the predominantly Loyalist magistrates and militia officers who were convinced that "the Province must inevitably succumb." This mood changed first when General Brock, with the aid of Tecumseh, seized Detroit and then when the American attempt to invade the province was checked at Queenston Heights, where Brock was killed in action.

In the course of the war and after it, the legend grew that the Loyalist militia had saved the province. It had, like the Indians, played a useful and indispensable role. Some of the elite flank companies and volunteers were trained to a professional level, but it was the regulars, including the Fencible regiments raised in the British-American provinces for service in North America, which carried the main burden of the struggle. The Fencibles were raised on the same principles as the Loyalist Provincial Corps that were mobilized during the Revolution. They were often commanded by second-generation Loyalists, and many of those who served were conscious of the Loyalist tradition. They also included French Canadian units like the Voltigeurs, and Fencibles serving in Upper Canada included units recruited from as far away as Newfoundland.

Most conspicuous among these Fencible regiments was the 104th Regiment of

An engraving by Howard Pyle of the last boatload of British leaving the Loyalist haven of New York City. (C-17509 Public Archives of Canada)

Sir John Johnson (above) and Mohawk
leader Joseph Brant (opposite) led one of
the largest overland Loyalist migrations.
They helped liberate Montreal, kept the
frontier in turmoil during the War, and
founded major settlements in the territory of Quebec. (Giles Rivest: Chateau
Ramezay, Montreal)

After fire has cleared much of the town plot for the post-Loyalist (1833) settlement of Stanley, N.B., men pile unburned tree limbs and surveyors (right) move on. The saw-mill (left) and tavern (right-centre) near completion. (C-17:PAC)

A survey party works through the dense forest. (C-117970:PAC)

The sawmill in operation.
(C-3552:PAC)

Stanley from the road.
Men pine-shingle a roof as
houses are completed on
six town lots.
(C-7163:PAC)

The completed tavern, with workmen's
houses (right). Iron-covered wheels, as on
the oxen pulled conveyance, were needed to
haul supplies over rough ground.
(C-4089:PAC)

The city and harbour of Saint John, N.B. (C-14143:PAC)

A black woodcutter in Shelburne in 1788. (C-40162:PAC)

Shelburne, N.S., in 1789, then one of the largest settlements in British North America. (C-10548:PAC)

Cataraqui (Kingston) on Lake Ontario in August, 1783. (C-1511:PAC)

An expanded Cataraqui viewed from Capt. Brant's house in July 1784. (C-1512:PAC)

The settlement at Niagara viewed from the heights above Navy Hall. The American Fort Niagara guards the river mouth on the opposite shore. (C-2035:PAC)

A tiny Loyalist settlement, one of the first in Upper Canada (Ontario). (C-23633:PAC)

C.W. Jeffrey's view of a square-timbered general store in pioneer Upper Canada (C-6849:PAC)

New Brunswick Fencibles, recruited in 1811 in the Loyalist province. They marched overland to Quebec and fought with distinction in Upper Canada. As there was little fighting in the Maritimes, the War of 1812 was as remote as an overseas war to New Brunswick Loyalists such as Penelope Winslow. She wrote that she dreaded the news that finally came in the mail: "Poor James was killed at Lake Erie." In 1814 she married Capt. John Jenkins, a second-generation Loyalist who lost an arm at Ogdensburg on 22 February, 1813.

Among second-generation Loyalists who saw action were William Hamilton Merritt, future promoter of the Welland Canal; John Beverley Robinson, Strachan's most eminent pupil; Christopher Hagerman, leading member of the Family Compact in Kingston; and William Buell of Brockville, later a reformer and ally of William Lyon Mackenzie.

More remarkable, perhaps, were the aging first-generation Loyalists who returned to the field. Sir John Johnson, at seventy, was superintendant general at Montreal. Matthew Elliot, aged seventy-three, left Amherstburg in 1812 to lead the Indians once again. John Coffin, a distinguished Loyalist soldier at the Revolution who later became a general, raised a regiment of New Brunswick Fencibles. At the age of sixty-nine, Capt. John Savage, the founder of Shefford, commanded the second battalion of the Frontier Light Infantry, consisting of two companies drawn from the six battalions of the Eastern Townships Militia. John Francis Wentworth Winslow, son of Edward Winslow, was present at Detroit, Queenston Heights, and Sacket's Harbor with the 41$^{st}$ Regiment of the line. Another son, Murray, was killed while serving on a Great Lakes ship. Some Loyalists, serving with the regulars, fought outside of Canada. James Johnson, son of Sir John Johnson, was killed in Spain, and Alexander McNab, a Virginian Loyalist, once clerk of the executive council in Upper Canada, was killed at Waterloo.

The War of 1812 was a war that British Americans fought together, and, if most of the fighting was done in the Canadas, the Maritime Provinces still managed to interfere with American coastal trade while Halifax was the principal base for the Royal Navy in the North Atlantic. Common membership in the empire provided the basis for shared military effort and shared pride in achievement.

To the Loyalists, the war seemed to be a continuation of the Revolution and, to French Canadians, a continuation of the Seven Years' War. In a sense it was both, for a victory by the Americans would have left the Loyalist settlements in Upper Canada under Republican rule and led ultimately to the assimilation of French Canada. For all the widespread despair and minor cases of disloyalty, the will to resist was bold enough to preserve the existence of the Canadas. Many grumbled, some deserted, and a handful joined the enemy, yet the loyalty crisis was not in Upper Canada, but in the northeastern United States.

Neutralism had been a state of mind during the Revolution and it set limits to what the belligerents could do. In 1812, American neutralism was institutional-ized in the governments of the northeastern states and in the Federalist party. State governors delayed and evaded demands for militia quotas; state militiamen refused to invade Canada; farmers and merchants sold supplies to the British garrisons in Canada with the tacit approval of state governments. The Federalists and regionalists of the northeastern states turned out to be Canada's best defenders. Federalists talked of "Mr. Madison's War" as though the war was a private venture of the president rather than a national effort. Finally, the representatives of the northeastern states met at Hartford, Connecticut, and threatened to secede from the Union.

Tory Loyalists might well feel that their prophecy was at last fulfilled—that the Republic contained the seeds of its own destruction and was disintegrating. What occurred, in fact, was a conservative and regional revolt against a war undertaken by a democratic administration on behalf of western frontiersmen. A short and victorious war would have been acceptable, and that is what the Madison administration had expected. Jefferson himself thought that the occupation of Canada would be a mere matter of marching.

Like many idealists, Jefferson had confidence in the use of moral force in international affairs. In 1807, he had sought to resist the restrictions of the British blockade of Europe by "the Jefferson Embargo," an attempt at economic sanc-tions against Britain which alienated the maritime population of the Republic. While imposing this policy, which could easily have resulted in war, he neglected the armed forces of the Republic. In 1812, Canada was expected to succumb to an armed demonstration—and that was about all the forces of the Republic could muster. Apart from this, the trading Northeast needed the British market and had access to it through Canada, often, but not always, by means of smuggling. It was therefore in the economic interest of the Northeast to keep Canada British.

Federalism, which owed its origin to a belief in the necessity for conventional government, had, by 1812, become involved with regional interests. It remained, nevertheless, a republican alternative to loyalism which many Loyalists came to respect and even admire. In the course of the early colonial resistance to British government, American social conservatives found themselves in alliance with a movement of agitators whom they distrusted. When agitation failed and Congress turned to armed struggle, the military replaced the agitators as the principal arm of resistance. During the long revolutionary war, American amateur soldiers acquired the outlook of professional soldiers and, by the end of the war, the heroes of the Revolution were officers with a conservative outlook on government and society, with socially-conservative George Washington pre-eminent among them.

Whatever the faults of the Republic, Loyalists had to recognize that with Washington now president, it was governed by a gentleman. Moreover, with the outbreak of the French Revolution one year after Washington assumed office, his administration adopted a gentleman's attitude toward the French Revolution and drifted toward an Anglophile foreign policy. When the French Revolution turned toward war and terror, the United States had to decide whether it would join in a republican crusade. Its decision not to, resulted in the suppression of French agents and the passage of the Alien and Sedition Acts. In fact, the American reaction to the French Revolution was much like the British—welcoming what at first seemed a triumph of liberalism, but turning against the Revolution during the ensuing terror. The Continental Congress had itself tolerated and even encouraged the informal use of terror against the Loyalists, but, like the British radicals, Americans had a horror of state-sponsored terror. The American reaction to the French Revolution demonstrated the reluctance of the American public to support European republican crusades, and the War of 1812 indicated its unwillingness to make sacrifices on behalf of Manifest Destiny.

The republican civil religion had its "high churchmen," men like Jefferson who saw the Republic as a model for the world to follow; and it had its "low churchmen" like John Adams who saw the Republic was an acceptable but not necessarily the best framework for conventional government. The Tory Loyalists, who predicted the collapse of the Republic, vastly underestimated the latent conservatism of American society and did not see the Constitution of 1788 as a sheet anchor which would hold the Republic together. Yet their doubts about American stability were not unreasonable. The sheet achor dragged badly in 1812 and cut loose from its moorings altogether between 1861 and 1865. The Federalists did not create a permanent political party, but were representative of the conservative moods and attitudes which have never been wholly absent from American politics.

These moods and attitudes were certainly shared by New Brunswick Loyalists between the years 1788 and 1812. During these years, when New Brunswick was an economically depressed area, six members of the first assembly elected in 1785 returned to the United States. It is unlikely that they had any more difficulty in adjusting to New England Federalism than those late Loyalists had in accepting the British system they found in Upper Canada and the Eastern Townships where they settled. In reporting the election of Jefferson as president in 1801 as "Bad News," the Loyalist press in Canada was reflecting views held in common with New Englanders. Maritime Loyalists had no hesitation in sending their children to be educated in New England, nor did they see in inter-marriage a threat of political contamination. It would seem that a common cultural unity of New England and the Maritimes was strengthened by a conservative mood, shared by Loyalists and Federalists in the years leading up to the 1812 war and during the war itself.

As a party of strong government, the Federalists should have been a nationalist party and should have supported Manifest Destiny. Yet western expansion served neither the regional interests of New England nor the cause of social conservatism. The Federalists consequently prevented effective mobilization of the republican resources for the war in 1812. In so doing, they temporarily became partners of the French Canadians and Loyalists who were laying the foundation for a second state in North America.

American historians have been reluctant to view the War of 1812 as a failure to impose Manifest Destiny and hence a defeat. They legitimately argue that the conquest of Canada was merely a means to an end, the end being the withdrawal of moral support which the midwestern Indians were receiving from Canada. This end was achieved without conquest and, henceforth, the Republic was able to deal with the Indians without external interference.

The American Revolution had partitioned North America just as the Protestant revolt ended in the partition of the Netherlands, and the Irish war of independence brought about the partition of Ireland. In all cases, the "old regime" survived and evolved independently of the revolutionary state. Where such divisions exist, the idea of reunion remains an issue which crops up from time to time. The reunion of the Netherlands, in 1815, brought on a revolt in 1830 that resulted in the Kingdom of Belgium. There are no signs of reconciliation of Ulster with the Irish Republic. Continentalism has never been a powerful force in Canadian politics. Canadian liberalism has suffered in elections when it seemed to be associated with annexation. The issues of the American Revolution have been sleeping a long time, but Canadians in general have been critical of American society and, whatever their origins, are still inclined to look on the United States with Loyalist eyes.

It was no accident that the Imperial Federation League was founded in Canada and in England in the Loyalist anniversary year of 1884. Many of the League's most active Canadian sponsors, such as George Parkin and Col. George Taylor Denison, were of Loyalist descent and zealous promoters of the Loyalist revival which emerged during the last quarter of that century. These descendants of Loyalists, who sought to link the Loyalist tradition to the idea of creating a centralized empire, were favoured by circumstances. North American society had matured to a point where it was possible to have reasonably remote ancestors who had played a part in the history of the continent. Moreover, those possessed of such ancestors often felt themselves neglected in a society where wealth and power seemed to be drifting into the hands of newcomers. Genealogy became a fashionable pastime in the United States and Canada as North Americans introduced their own form of hereditary distinctions.

The "Daughters of the American Revolution," founded in 1890, accepted only those whose ancestors had served in the Continental forces. The United Empire Loyalists Association, founded six years later, was open only to those who could discover Loyalist ancestors. At the same time the ascendancy of the "Free Traders," which began with the repeal of the Corn Laws in 1846, was drawing to a close. The idea of universal peace, based on free trade, was losing its credibility as the Germans, Americans, and even Canadians built up their economies behind tariff walls, and the armament race, which led up to 1914, was already underway. The project of a federation of self-governing dominions and colonies was designed to adjust the institutions of the empire to new conditions.

There was no chance that such a federation could have been created, but the efforts of the Imperial Federation League helped bring about the Conference of Prime Ministers that led ultimately to the Commonwealth. Like most movements seeking support, the League needed enemies to stimulate controversy and found them among those Free Traders, who favoured continentalism. Pre-eminent among these was Goldwin Smith, a former Regius Professor at Oxford, who had married into the Boulton family and presided over a political salon at their Toronto residence, "The Grange." In the ensuing debates, Imperialists treated the annexationist ideas of Smith and others as though they were an imminent danger, and Smith warned against the equally remote danger of a centralized empire.

In the wake of Darwin, racial theories had become fashionable and the Imperial Federalists presented the Loyalists as early champions of "Anglo-Saxon" unity. As "Anglo-Saxon" unity was thought to be a good cause, Smith, in turn, argued that continental unity would be a necessary step toward that desired end.

During the earlier struggle for responsible government, Canadian Liberals had refused to concede the Loyalist tradition to the Tories. During debates about imperial confederation, Smith, the Continentalist, seemed to think the Loyalists more useful as enemies than as friends.

Like most doctrinaires, Smith was inclined to blame reactionaries for the public's unwillingness to accept his ideas. Among these reactionaries he included Tories, Imperialists, French Canadians, clerical Conservatives, and those encouraging the Loyalist tradition. As the Imperialists created a Loyalist myth which presented the Loyalists as self-sacrificing and far-sighted imperial patriots who suffered in the cause of Anglo-Saxon unity, the opponents of Imperial Federation created a "counter-myth" based on the American view of the Loyalists. The counter-myth described the Loyalists as subservient agents of colonial subordination who had rejected the gift of freedom. Neither myth nor counter-myth was firmly rooted in fact, but it was the counter-myth that suited the needs of the national Liberal school of historians who wrote most of Canadian history.

Loyalist supporters of Anglo-Saxon unity would have been surprised to learn that James Otis, a leading figure in the agitation against the Stamp Act, had once denounced their ancestors as un-English and alien. When Loyalist Martin Howard of Newport, Rhode Island, defended the Stamp Act in 1765, Otis declared that the town of Newport was made up of "Turks, Jews, and other infidels with a few renegade Christians and Catholics". He contrasted Newport with the more English and Protestant character of the rest of New England. Race prejudice was common in the eighteenth century, but neither Loyalists nor revolutionaries were concerned with neo-Darwinian views of racial unity.

In one respect the Imperial Federationists were legitimate heirs of the Loyalists. Both were critical of British policy and neither was the least inclined to defer either socially or politically to British officials or politicians. Colonel Denison saw Imperial Federation as an association of equals and expected that, in time, Canadians might emerge as senior partners in the association. William Smith, certainly, and those Loyalists who dreamed of a Canadian-based empire in the Midwest, would have been at home in the Imperial Federation League. But the Loyalists as a group were not empire builders, interested in large schemes, and prepared to support their view by aggressive propaganda. They were suspicious of enthusiasm and inclined to distrust aggressive leadership. A few of Loyalist descent, like Sir Richard Cartwright of Kingston who favoured reciprocity, opposed Imperial Federation and insisted that the role of Canada was to provide a link between Britain and the United States.

Loyalist supporters of Imperial Federation were themselves divided on the question of attitude toward the United States. Maritime Loyalists like George Parkin saw Imperial union as a preliminary to Anglo-American union. Colonel Denison saw anti-Americanism as a necessary means to securing support for the League. In Ontario, which had been invaded in 1812, and where fears of American immigrants had once been a source of political controversy, Denison may well have been right. In the Maritimes, where the War of 1812 had been a source of profit and where there had been no substantial post-Loyalist emigration, anti-Americanism had a limited appeal.

Until Carl Berger's publication of *A Sense of Power*, the national Liberals' view of Colonel Denison, George Parkin, and their supporters as Anglophiles determined to keep Canada in colonial subordination has prevailed. It is now accepted that the Imperialists were Canadian nationalists who sought to assert Canada's position in the world through the means of Imperial Federation. With the wealth of material now being written about the Loyalists, it should be evident that the historic Loyalists were not the political ancestors of the founders of the Imperial Federation League. Those in the United Empire Loyalists Association today stress the social, ethnic, and political diversity of their ancestors.

If the Loyalists laid the foundation of a second state in North America, it is less evident that they founded a separate society. The nature of English Canadian society, how it fits into the North American context, and what part Loyalists played in it are issues raised by the Hartz thesis. Professor Louis Hartz, rising above the more parochial approaches of his predecessors, has sought to put American history into the context of European overseas settlements. This approach proved damaging to earlier views, such as the one that held that democracy emerged naturally out of the pioneer conditions of society, the theory presented by Professor Frederick Jackson Turner's "frontier thesis." Hartz points out, for instance, that efforts to re-enact the American Revolution in another society of pioneer origin—Latin America—did not bring about an American style of democracy. It is difficult to deny his conclusion that former colonial societies are shaped by the political traditions of the country of their origin. It is more difficult to establish, as he contends, that they are bound by the political tradition of the time of their origins. By this reasoning French Canada became a fragment of absolutist seventeenth-century France, that is, France without the Revolution. The United States became a fragment of liberal eighteenth-century England.

In the company of many other American historians, Hartz observes that the political traditions already established in the American colonies were sufficient to provide the ideology of the Revolution and the ideas of Alexander Hamilton and others who produced the Constitution. There might be some dissent, but the weight of contemporary evidence seems to support Hartz. He further insists that the monarchy was already obsolete in America and that Thomas Paine, by utilitarian arguments, brought out the latent republicanism in the American people. This seems a retreat to the "frontier thesis." If this is so, why then the Loyalists? How can we account for the survival of monarchy in Canada, Australia, and New Zealand, born of the same political tradition, and "younger," or at least more recently settled societies? What about the ready acceptance of the monarchy by post-Loyalist American settlers in Canada?

Thomas Paine, who converted America, or at least the Continental Congress, to republicanism, did not derive his antipathy to monarchy from his American experience, but from his position as an alienated intellectual in English society. Monarchy was one of the many things he opposed. He blended his Republican arguments with a case against "big government" which would have an attraction in a society trying to come to terms with the increasing complexities of its own existence. By the end of his career, Paine found "aristocratic" George Washington no more acceptable than George III. Paine was an iconoclast rather than a revolutionary, and disliked authority in any form. It is significant and to his credit that when he was elected a member of the Convention during the French Revolution, he risked his life by opposing the execution of Louis XVI.

Hartz insists that Americans were able to achieve a stability without the monarchy which they could never have achieved with it. But was the United States so different from the Commonwealth countries? Were not some of the tensions in American society stimulated by the presidential system? In one of Jonathan Swift's satires, the "Big-Endians" manage to construct their dwellings without the use of a right-angle, a remarkable achievement, but doing things the hard way. Europeans were impressed not by the fact that Republican institutions worked well in America, but that they worked at all.

Americans proved that Republican institutions could work, but they paid a price. The Civil War was the greatest disaster any society suffered in the last century. In terms of duration, troops engaged, cost, and casualties, it was (in proportion to the American population) equal to the price paid by Europe for World War I. Would this have happened if Abraham Lincoln had been a minority prime minister instead of a minority president? Could Canada have avoided civil war and achieved responsible government and confederation without the dual systems of Baldwin-LaFontaine and Cartier-Macdonald? Could this have been possible under the American constitution?

Professor Kenneth McRae applies the Hartz thesis to Canada and finds Canada composed of two fragments: one of absolutist France and the other a chip off the North American liberal fragment. Professor Hartz might add that this fragment is bourgeois as well as liberal. Much of this is true but it is possible to question the use of the words "liberal," "bourgeois," and "absolutist." First of all, the absolutism of the old regime in France was not totalitarian. There was a good deal of litigation in New France and this enabled the lawyers and notaries to adapt, without much difficulty, to the parliamentary system. Certainly parliamentarians such as LaFontaine, Cartier, Laurier, and today, Trudeau, are part of the liberal fragment and they were and are the leading French Canadians.

.The Loyalist, Professor McRae insists, was essentially a North American liberal, and could be nothing else because he was formed by a bourgeois liberal society. The character of this society would not be altered simply because certain sections of the bourgeois elite, like the Robinsons and the Strachans, had aristocratic pretensions. The word "liberal" could be extended to include anyone in the common law tradition who favoured parliamentary governments. The word "bourgeois" could be stretched to include any elite which was not a military aristocracy. The heart of the matter is the common law tradition preserved by the legal profession, undoubtedly the most important political influence in North American society at the time of the Revolution.

William Blackstone's *Commentaries*, a handbook on the application of common law, was more widely read in America than Locke, Rousseau, Jefferson, or Hamilton, not only in the eighteenth century but in the nineteenth as well. Blackstone was a Tory, opposed to the American Revolution, whose works were much criticized by the rising school of English Utilitarians led by Jeremy Bentham. Common law emerged from a feudal society. The idea of due process, trial by jury, and impeachment, for example, were of medieval origin. The early exponents of common law, Glanvill, Bracton, and Fortescue, and even its later defenders like Bacon and Coke would be surprised to hear that they were part of a rising bourgeoisie. Most of them were either clerics, members of noble families, or the founders of noble families. Tories quoted their words in defence of church establishment and Jacobites in defence of "divine right," a legal concept which had more to do with the origins of royal power than with its extent. Jacobites did not believe in the abolition of Parliament but merely that sovereignty rested in the Crown.

The best-known Loyalist writer to use Jacobite arguments was Jonathan Boucher. He drew on the common law tradition which influenced Jefferson and dedicated his published sermons to George Washington. The Whig caricatures of Tories and Jacobites have induced historians to see Liberal tendencies whenever Tories or Jacobites became champions of civil liberties and popular causes. This is evident in Professor McRae's very useful comparison of American and Loyalist Liberals. The American Liberal, he finds, is dogmatic and self-confident, the Loyalist Liberal troubled by doubt and guilt. Doubt and guilt are qualities of mind found in those who do not believe in the perfectibility of men. They are the essence of the conservative outlook, shared by moderate Conservatives, clerical Conservatives, "Compact" Tories, and American Federalists.

There were, however, dogmatic and self-confident Liberals in Canada, including some Loyalists. McRae seems to think that the Loyalist tradition was the root of Anglo-French tension. Certainly Loyalists like William Smith and second-generation Loyalists like Egerton Ryerson hoped to impose North American cultural uniformity on Canadian society. Yet most of Canada's dogmatic and self-confident Liberals were non-Loyalists like George Brown, the "Free Trader," Goldwin Smith, and the Clear Grits. It was these American-style Liberals who fanned the flame of Anglo-French tension in the last century. Those "Loyalist Liberals" who called themselves Conservatives formed an alliance with clerical Conservatives, personified by the Cartier-Macdonald combination, and it was this combination which carried Canada through the second half of the century. By Laurier's time English Canadian Liberals found common ground with French Canadians in pursuing an isolationist policy which opposed efforts at "Imperial Federalism" and resisted participation in "imperialist wars."

Professor Gad Horowitz, in commenting on McRae's application of the Hartz thesis to Canada, stresses the importance of diversity in Canadian history. He insists, as we do, on the presence of real Tories among the Loyalists. He further suggests that the Canadian Liberals' need to get along with Tories and French Canadians led to their acceptance of diversity in Canadian politics. Consequently, socialism was not a problem for Canadian Liberals. But American Liberals, who were strangers to diversity, had difficulty accepting socialism as part of their political life. These views of Horowitz seem self-evident and raise questions about the long-term effects of the Revolution on liberalism in North America.

There is little doubt that the Revolution was a movement led by Liberals in a liberal society against what appeared to be a threat to liberalism. Yet the liberalism of this society was tempered by the vigilante spirit evident in the lynching of Indians awaiting trial in Western Pennsylvania, and early vigilante movements like the "Regulators" in the Carolinas. The diffused reign of terror unleashed against the Loyalists during the Revolution gave vigilantism a patriotic flavour and enormously increased its role in American society. Whatever the purpose of revolution, its methods are anti-Liberal: conspiracy, war, arbitrary arrest, and summary executions. They are habit-forming and more difficult to live down once they become part of a revolutionary mythology.

In what sense did the American Revolution advance the cause of liberty and equality? The adoption of the Republican form of government was not necessarily a step toward either. There was nothing egalitarian about aristocratic republics like contemporary Poland and not much apparent in the Roman republic from which the Americans borrowed some of their symbols. There was not a spark of liberty in the Venetian republic and twentieth-century republics require no comment. Were the Americans, in adopting a Republican form, setting an example for the world, as Jefferson believed? Or were they, as Adams thought, merely creating difficulties for themselves which would lead in the end to the rediscovery of the monarchical wheel? The Revolution certainly abolished external distinctions but, as previously noted, the externals of egalitarianism can provide a useful disguise for power and privilege. Titles at least make elites easier to identify.

British Liberals, attracted by the egalitarianism of the Declaration of Independence, reacted strongly against "Americanism" in practice. William Lyon Mackenzie tried and failed to enter American politics as a "Jacksonian" Democrat. Two Liberal Fathers of Confederation, the Scots Presbyterian George Brown and the Irish Catholic D'Arcy McGee, tried and failed to come to terms with American politics, in a sense reliving the experience of the Loyalists. Both eloquently and repeatedly denounced the failure of American republicanism. Brown concentrated on the danger of the presidency and the absence of responsible government. McGee denounced the demoralizing influence of American society on family life and the discrimination against Catholics. The Canadian critics of American society and those Americans advocating Manifest Destiny form two sides of an argument which has never resulted in a formal debate. The Loyalists and those following the Loyalist tradition, like most losers, are anxious to open a debate on the justice and wisdom of the Revolution. The Americans, like most winners, consider the matter closed forever. Yet Canada is there, a visible rebuttal to the case presented to the world by the Continental Congress in 1776.

In a world growing smaller, the question of a reunion of the continent will probably be raised again. Americans will likely insist that this should come about by incorporating Canada into the United States. Those Canadians in the Loyalist tradition would probably answer that continental reunion should be an aspect of Anglo-American union, bringing together all peoples separated by revolution.

# CURSED REPUBLICAN SPIRIT

## POLITICS

*"This cursed republican town-meeting spirit has been the ruin of us already"*.

*Benjamin Marston, Shelburne, N.S.*

THE LOYALISTS were victims of the first successful revolution in the New World, the casualties of a conflict which was not of their own making. They had, nevertheless, either actively or passively, and, in some cases, unwittingly, resisted the winners. In so doing they had challenged the moral authority of the Continental Congress to speak for the American people. They denied "the truth" which the Declaration of Independence declared to be self-evident. This was not easily forgiven.

Whether this resistance had been the result of conviction, miscalculation, or circumstances beyond their control, it was the cause of their defeat and exile. Hand in hand with their defeat went the knowledge that agitators and activists who spoke in the name of liberty could turn into persecutors. In addition they were acutely aware of being in various degrees dependent on a bureaucracy which was generally effective, but rarely efficient or equitable. Whatever political ideas, social differences, and assumptions about society divided the Loyalists, they held in common a fear of revolution and a suspicion of those placed in authority over them.

Loyalists had put aside other grievances once they were convinced that revolution was a real danger, but they had not been easily convinced. And in their new home, as the hardships of the Revolution faded into folklore and memory, the experience of living under authority became permanent. The political issues which arose in exile would have more to do with differences among Loyalists and with non-Loyalist Canadians than with fears of revolution. In exile, their most immediate difficulties were with their own government, and their early political efforts were designed to secure an equitable and efficient distribution of the various benefits they had been promised. In spite of this, they were keenly aware of the American Republic's growing power and its course of western expansion which could so easily turn north.

The better educated and wealthier Loyalists, like the Johnsons, De Lanceys, and Butlers, were interested in resuming their roles as great landlords and office-holders, without much concern for abstract definitions or long-term policies. Yet there were still others. Loyalist intellectuals, who had written extensively on the causes of the Revolution, hoped to shape the future course of colonial policy and avoid the spectre of future revolution. Among this relatively small group there were a few who had the ear of the decision-makers in London, where the future of the remaining North American colonies was being decided. There was for the moment at least a disposition to listen to grand designs for the future of the colonies, because decisions of some kind were needed. At this level, distinctions between Whig and Tory had meaning, and it is significant that of the two Loyalists who exercised the greatest influence in the surviving colonies, William Smith, who became chief justice of Quebec, was an unrepentant Whig, and Bishop Charles Inglis was a true Tory.

William Smith and Charles Inglis personify the Whig and Tory aspects of Loyalism. Both represented different sides of the "American story." Smith, son of a Supreme Court judge, was from an established American family, and, like his father, attended Yale. Inglis, orphan son of an Irish Anglican clergyman, born in County Donegal, came to America to seek a professional status not open to him in Ireland. Both had talents, both had a sense of mission, but Smith began with an audience of admiring friends before whom he could exercise his talents, while Inglis had no such opportunity until middle life.

Smith belonged to the mainstream of American liberalism, of Presbyterian background, opposed to the Anglican establishment. As the son of a Huguenot mother, he was convinced that the assimilation of all cultural groups to the English-speaking majority was inevitable and benign. His starting point in politics was opposition to the founding of King's College, which later became Columbia University. Smith argued that as King's was to be an Anglican college, it represented the first step toward the appointment of a bishop and the establishment of an Anglican hierarchy which Smith declared would be the end of colonial liberties. Inglis, who came to America without a university degree and taught school in Pennsylvania before being ordained, saw Anglicanism as a civilizing force in American society and a necessary aspect of political stability. For him an episcopal establishment and an Anglican-oriented system of education were the heart of the matter.

It is not surprising that at the outset of the dispute over colonial taxation Smith, as champion of the popular cause, became a patriot pamphleteer. Because the cause was popular, Smith could campaign openly and soon became known as

"Patriotic Billy." Inglis thought it best to write anonymously and the wisdom of this was confirmed when a mob burned an entire edition of a response he had had printed in answer to Thomas Paine's *Common Sense*.

Smith and Inglis were in rival camps, but Smith remained a firm believer in the force of argument and, by degrees, became convinced that the British government was not the real threat to personal liberty in America. Yet Smith remained an optimist, with confidence in his ability to shape events and to direct the turmoil, stimulated by colonial resistance, toward the creation of a colonial federation. His ideas on federalism were undoubtedly inspired by Benjamin Franklin's Albany Plan of 1754, which was designed to unite the colonies in the war against France. But Smith was an independent thinker whose ideology anticipated and in most respects ran parallel to the federalism of Alexander Hamilton. Smith was certainly the first Canadian Federalist; his scheme for an American colonial federation was adapted to suit the needs of post-revolutionary society and was transformed into a project for the federation of the remaining British provinces.

The American version took contemporary Ireland as a model. There would be a lord lieutenant and an appointed upper and elected lower house. (In the Canadian adaptation there would be a viceroy of British North America who would control the British consular service in the United States and be responsible for Anglo-American relations.) The difficulty with Smith's scheme and a similar scheme actually presented by Joseph Galloway to the Continental Congress was that it was unacceptable to the Congress, whose leaders were determined to establish a republic and sever the British connection. It is less clear that it was unacceptable to the people who had no Republican traditions and might have accepted a Liberal alternative to total independence.

Like the Loyalists, the revolutionary party had its left and right wings, and there was a great deal of affinity between Loyalist left and the revolutionary right. Jefferson saw the Revolution as the beginning of a Republican experiment which would be an inspiration to the world. John Adams merely wanted conventional government and considered monarchy as an aspect of conventional government which the Americans would ultimately adopt. Adams wrote that he did not "consider hereditary monarchy or aristocracy as rebellious against nature...." He added that "our country is not ripe for it in many respects, and it is not yet necessary, but our ship must ultimately land on that shore or be cast away."

In purely administrative terms a federal monarchy would probably have worked as well as a republic in the American context. But for Canada it was clearly premature. Smith's project was read with interest by the authors of the Durham report who, like him, recommended federalism before the provinces were ready for it.

While Smith was maturing his plans for federation, Inglis was preparing a project for an Anglican Episcopate in British America. In this he was acting, unlike Smith, not as an individual but as a leading figure among Loyalist Tories who shared his views of the causes of the Revolution and believed in Anglicanism as insurance against revolution in the loyal colonies.

During the earlier years of the war Smith remained in territory controlled by Continental forces, but his projects for ending the rebellion by mediation soon made him an object of suspicion. In 1778 he was given the choice of taking an oath of allegiance to the State of New York, or moving into New York City, then under the control of Crown forces. By choosing the latter, he unknowingly renounced his place in history as one of the founding fathers of the Republic, as there is little doubt that a man of his prominence, ability, and connections would have played a leading part in American politics. It is a measure of his importance that he was made chief justice of New York in 1780, a civilian post in a city which was under military law.

As chief justice of New York, Smith advocated the introduction of civilian government to replace the military regime. He believed this would make it possible to make New York a model of good government and equitable justice, which would contrast favourably with the irregular procedures evident behind the Continental lines. He would later adapt this policy to suit Canadian conditions, just as he had modified his plan of federation after the Revolution.

Meanwhile, Inglis had become rector of Trinity Church, New York City, in 1777. Therefore, by the time Sir Guy Carleton took over the city in 1782, both men were leading figures among the Loyalists in New York. Both had become accustomed to defeat, and would not be unduly disappointed if their plans were not accepted by those in authority. Carleton, who had been responsible for the shaping of policy which led to the Quebec Act, had a taste for grand designs. It was not difficult for Smith to win his confidence. Nor was it surprising that, when Carleton was raised to the peerage as Lord Dorchester and sent a second time to govern Quebec, he chose Smith to accompany him as chief justice of Quebec.

While Smith plotted out the regeneration of secular government, Inglis, in the company of the Anglican clergy, was planning the creation of an effective Anglican establishment in America, to take effect after the Crown forces had suppressed the rebellion. These plans would later be modified so that they could be applied in the remaining British provinces.

Inglis and many of his fellow Anglicans were under the impression that the Revolution was strengthening the church. It was certainly true that many Loyalists of other denominations and even Congregationalist clergy were coming into the church. The Revolution had assigned the church a new role by making it the rallying point for Loyalists, Anglophiles, and neutralists. Whether it did much to improve the position of the church in society as a whole is unclear. But the British government, which had been lukewarm in its support of the Anglican establishment in America before the Revolution, was now prepared to offer support.

Both Smith and Inglis spent several years in England immediately after the war, Smith returning to British North America with Lord Dorchester and Inglis coming to Nova Scotia as bishop in 1787. The Revolution that had made them allies was over. They were far removed from one another, though their realms intersected. Dorchester, who exercised direct jurisdiction in Quebec, was titular governor general holding a vague jurisdiction over Nova Scotia; Inglis, as Bishop of Nova Scotia, exercised jurisdiction over the Anglican clergy in Quebec. The distance between Smith and Inglis was sufficient for them to work out most of their respective Whig and Tory programs in their own provinces but not sufficient to prevent an occasional collision on matters of importance.

Smith had been a politician all his life. Inglis had acquired skill in the art of politics in the course of the Revolution. He had no experience of working at the higher levels of colonial politics in normal times. For Smith the course was clear: he must retain the confidence of Dorchester and secure control of the appointed legislative council in Quebec City which was under control of the "French Party" led by the Scots physician Adam Mabane. Once that was done the way would be clear for his grand design.

Inglis would be less political in his approach. His own grand design was clear: a strong church and an Anglican-oriented system of education dominated by an Anglican university. Inglis' first task was to convince the decision-makers in London of the political value of religion. As he put it, "Whoever is sincerely religious towards God, from principle and conscience, will also, from principle and conscience, be loyal to his earthly Sovereign." To justify an Anglican system of education, Inglis warned against teachers who were "ignorant, low and fanatical to a degree that is scarcely credible." His second task was to secure influence among his own clergy, who had mixed feelings about his appointment as bishop and doubts about his educational policy.

As a Whig, Smith did not see the causes of the Revolution as stemming from the character of colonial society. He was an instinctive reformer and would never approve fully of any society in which he dwelt, but he shared the ideas and ideals of the average American. He wanted economic progress, and secular education for its own sake and as a means of assimilating minorities into a Protestant culture. These ideas were shared by most of the English population in Quebec, including the recently arrived Loyalist settlers in the Upper St. Lawrence. They had been articulated by the "English Party" (made up of civil servants and fur traders) in the legislative council, whose efforts had been defeated by successive governors. Smith's difficulty was that Dorchester, as the sponsor of the Quebec Act, had been one of these governors.

Smith was not the first educated American to take up the cause of the English Party. Peter Livius, a judge in New Hampshire who became chief justice of Quebec, was dismissed by Carleton in 1776, and James Monk, another New Englander who had taken up the cause of the English Party, was fighting his last battle when Smith arrived.

According to the views of the English Party, French civil law as practised in Quebec was a monstrosity, neither French nor English. They also believed that the seigneurial system was a feudal anachronism which had retarded economic progress under the French regime and continued to do so under British rule. Smith, who had the tidy mind of a trained lawyer, was delighted to find what appeared to be convenient targets for his crusading zeal. In August, 1787, a year after he arrived in Quebec, he wrote to a friend: "I am astonished to find that France neglected all the Foundations for a solid Dominion here, still more so, that the British Instruements since the conquest have, instead of discovering her Errors, recommended an Imitation of her Example." The English Party had been saying this for over a generation, but Smith was able to bring to their cause a wealth of learning and a breadth of vision which they could not provide for themselves.

Smith was not content with mere legal reforms. Quebec, he planned, would be only part of a North American viceroyalty which would provide a more perfect constitutional system than the American Republic could. It would consequently attract non-Loyalist American immigrants and serve as a model to persuade the wayward colonies to consider returning to the empire. The French Canadians would, in time, see the advantages of joining the North American majority, as Dutch and Huguenot minorities had done and as the German Americans were doing. To facilitate this process, Smith devised a scheme of universal education with elementary schools at the parish level and secondary schools for the counties. The system was to be crowned by a collegiate institution "for cultivating the liberal arts and Sciences usually taught in the European Universities; the theology of Christians excepted," Smith explained, "on account of the mixture of the two Communions, whose joint aid is desirable as far as they agree, and who ought to be left to find a separate provision for the Candidates in the ministry of their respective Churches." To finance this, Smith hoped to draw on the revenues of the Jesuit estates which were under control of the Crown.

Like many of Smith's schemes, it might have worked had it been politically acceptable. But like many Americans, Loyalists, and Republicans, Smith misjudged the course of American history.

In spite of the inconvenience which they imposed, French civil law and the seigneurial system of landholding were part of the fabric of French Canadian society, and to more politically-minded French Canadians, they were symbols of cultural survival. Moreover, a system of secular education is understandably an object of suspicion in a Catholic community. Though Smith hoped to make it acceptable by placing Catholics, including the bishop, on the board of governors, this was not enough to recommend the scheme to the Catholic church. The plan was finally defeated by the hostility of Bishop Inglis who, as a firm believer in religious education, was not prepared to support the establishment of a secular university.

Smith was disappointed by his failure to win support for the university, but this was only one aspect of his larger plan for making Quebec a model British American community. His next task was to wrest control of the majority of the executive council away from Adam Mabane's "French Party." He succeeded, but there remained the question of Lord Dorchester's support for Smith's project to reorganize the province. Not caring to repudiate either his former policy or his chief justice, Dorchester remained neutral.

Such neutrality might not have been fatal to Smith's plan had he been able to secure the support of the Loyalists settled on the Upper St. Lawrence. These Loyalists shared Smith's view of French civil law and the seigneurial system, but they did not share his ambitions to assimilate the French Canadians. Sir John Johnson, whom the Loyalists accepted as their spokesman, had been among the great landholders in the old colonies who wanted to resume, in Canada, the role they had formerly played. Johnson had little interest in grand designs and, like the plebeian Loyalists in the new settlements, he saw the creation of a separate province as the most direct means of escaping from French civil law and the seigneurial system.

In order to understand the unwillingness of the Loyalists to share Smith's vision of a province extending from the Gulf of the St. Lawrence to beyond the Great Lakes, it is necessary to consider the manner in which the Loyalists in the western half of the province were defending their own interests. Seigneurialism was nominal in this area because seigneurial rights were held by the Crown, but French civil law was real. The Loyalists had to assert themselves without the aid of an elected assembly, but they were dealing with a government possessing little real force and consequently acutely sensitive to public opinion. Foremost in the minds of the Loyalist settlers was the fear that the nominal seigneurial system would become real by means of grants of seigneurial rights to former officers. These fears emerged in the form of the "McNiff controversy" about the time of Smith's arrival in Canada.

Many Loyalist units had been formed by retired officers and landlords who had been militia officers. Most of these men retained their status in peacetime. But some had acquired commissions as a result of the fortunes of war, and there were among the Loyalists a very large number who had been substantial farmers, and quite a few who might qualify as gentleman rankers. These men were not prepared to see the social hierarchy established in wartime carried into the peacetime Loyalist settlements as was advocated by some conservative Loyalists and favoured by some Loyalist officers. Such a move would leave them in a lesser position than they had held before the war.

The tension between former officers and former rankers came to the surface in 1786 under Patrick McNiff's inspiration. McNiff was a Loyalist from Staten Island who had lost £6,000 in property as a result of his Loyalist convictions. At the opening of the controversy in 1786, he was employed as a surveyor by Maj. Samuel Holland near the site of the present-day city of Cornwall. McNiff was an Irish Roman Catholic, with some gifts for political leadership, but does not appear to have been motivated by ambition.

At the heart of the matter was the fact that nearly all the magistrates and local civil servants in the western settlements of Quebec were former officers, and they constituted the sole link between the average settler and the government. Apart from that, they often received half-pay or pensions: £188 for a major, £88 for a captain, £41 for a lieutenant, and £32 for an ensign. The officers and sergeants had tried to secure choice lands for themselves and within limits succeeded, although Gov. Frederick Haldimand had attempted to enforce the drawing of land by lots.

The first sign of political unrest in the ranks occurred in 1785. Petitions were presented to a local magistrate accusing sergeants of selling rations intended for general distribution. The sergeants cleared themselves by assuring the magistrate that those rations sold were either their own or purchased from others, but the power of political protest had made a strong impression, and suspicion of the officers kept it alive. The officers themselves were active politically and concentrated on petitions against the nominal seigneurial system.

In spite of these petitions, the legislative assembly, with the economy in mind, decided to grant a fifteen-year monopoly to those willing to construct sawmills and grist mills at their own expense. As seigneurs had the exclusive right to run grist mills on their estates, this looked like a step toward establishing a working seigneurial system in the western Loyalist settlements. The first protest came from a group of officers, but it was soon followed by an independent popular petition, spearheaded by Patrick McNiff. Having a suspicious mind, McNiff concluded that not only did the government intend to establish a full seigneurial system, but that the officers were planning to establish themselves as seigneurs. McNiff prepared a draft petition against the mills, hinting that the Loyalists had offers to return to the United States and might do so if the seigneurial system was imposed on them. The officers had, in fact, made similar threats, but their statements were cautiously worded and they acted in a semi-official capacity. McNiff's efforts at independent action brought instant dismissal from his post as a government surveyor and withdrawal of the rations which he drew, along with those of the other Loyalists. This would have proved serious for the McNiff family had not the rations been restored.

McNiff was head of a party which raised questions about favouritism to officers in the original distribution of land. Yet their strongest protest, curiously enough, was against a petition signed by officers which welcomed Lord Dorchester, returning to Quebec for a second term as governor. McNiff and his friends were offended by not being invited to join in the general expression of good will. They were even more offended when the officers sent off a second petition to Lord Dorchester voicing the usual demand of the settlers: requests for roads, schools, and the abolition of the seigneurial system.

Knowing that there was discontent, Dorchester tried to end the conflict by requesting that town meetings be held and representatives be elected to negotiate with government officials. McNiff grasped this opportunity to spread rumours of an officers' conspiracy to transform themselves into seigneurs. The tone of politics in Loyalist Cornwall is indicated by a report to government of a town meeting held in January, 1787, to comply with Dorchester's request. When the half-pay officer Samuel Anderson, a former senior captain in the King's Royal Regiment of New York, ordered McNiff to be silent, McNiff mounted a sled, exclaiming that he was for the liberty of the people and that "this Township was composed of two denominations of men, vizt. Gentlemen officers enjoying half-pay from the Crown, and the Comonality. That they should inform him which of those classes they would choose to Elect from."

Some of the people called out, "No officers, No officers. They have rode long enough and now it's our turn." Others shouted to "turn out all those half-pay Gentry," at which McNiff said it "was by their means that this settlement would be held under Seigniors." At this, Peter Fitzpatrick shouted, "By the eternal God, they should all be murdered." At this point the officers prudently left the meeting. Later those opposed to McNiff made depositions before the officers, denouncing McNiff's actions as subversive. His efforts to influence the Gaelic-speaking Highlanders, in what became Glengarry County, were also rebuffed, but he was able to dominate three of the townships which elected delegates.

Under pressure of petitions, the governor appointed a committee of inquiry, consisting of surveyor John Collins and lawyer William Dummer Powell. McNiff's various charges against the officers were not sustained. He collapsed in the course of the inquiry, being too ill to continue his testimony. In spite of this, Collins and Powell continued the inquiry and condemned the officers for not keeping the rank and file better informed. McNiff expressed his satisfaction with the results of the inquiry and gave up agitation. Yet, after the passage of the Constitutional Act of 1791, it was officers who were elected to the first assembly in Upper Canada.

If the seigneurial system was a source of fear and annoyance in the townships on the Upper St. Lawrence, it proved, for a while at least, a temporary solution to the landholding problems of the Loyalist squatters at Missisquoi Bay. As noted previously, they had been ordered to move by Haldimand and he had cut off their rations. On his departure, rations were restored. Orders to expel them from their farms were put aside, but they remained without legal title to the land they occupied. It was in the interest of the seigneurs, on whose land they were settled, to keep them there, as their presence increased land values and could become a source of income.

The first move toward collaboration between Loyalists and seigneurs took place in 1786. At that time Col. Henry Caldwell, who had purchased the Foucault seigneury which ran along the Richelieu near the frontier, undertook to present petitions to Lord Dorchester from 380 Missisquoi Bay Loyalists. It was probably this petition that induced Thomas Dunn, a member of the executive council, to acquire the nearby seigneury of St. Armand in 1788, which also had attracted Loyalist squatters. Dunn appointed the Dutch Loyalist captain, Henry Ruiter, one of a large family which had been driven out of Albany County, as his land agent. The seigneury was surveyed and land sold at £10 per 100 acres. Similar arrangements were made in the neighbouring seigneuries of Christie's Manor, present-day Noyon, and Caldwell's Manor, present-day Clarenceville. Seigneurial dues of four pence an acre were still collected on Christie and Caldwell Manors. The Loyalists were, in theory, obliged to use the seigneur's saw and grist mills, but no mills existed in the 1780s. It was not until 1792 that the Missisquoi Bay Loyalists were in legal possession of their land. Still the Missisquoi Loyalists had defied Haldimand's authority and, after some eight years of petitioning, won their point.

Meanwhile, 375 Loyalists who settled in the Gaspé had to come to terms with their Micmac, Acadian, and Channel Island neighbours. Like the neighbouring Loyalists in Nova Scotia, they believed that they had both a moral right and sufficient political influence to prevail over the rights of the early settlers. They were soon to be disappointed, as Haldimand would not play favourites. As the Acadians had arrived first they already possessed some of the best land. Loyalists petitioned, demanding a share of this land already cultivated by the Acadians, but Haldimand put aside their demands. He nevertheless protected them against the pretensions of the redoubtable Charles Robin, a Channel Islander who sought control of the local fisheries. Robin's assertions that the land acquired by the Loyalists at New Carlisle had originally been granted to him received short shrift from the governor.

The Loyalist settlement in the Gaspé, like many in the Maritimes, did not attract new settlers, and many of its young people emigrated to Upper Canada and the Eastern Townships. Yet the settlement survived and the presence of the Loyalists was one of the factors which enabled the Gaspé to return an English candidate to the Lower Canadian Assembly after 1792. The candidate was a non-Loyalist, Robert Christie, who was expelled from the assembly on several occasions because of his vigorous defence of the English Party's interests.

The town of Sorel, intended as a military colony, soon became a centre of Loyalist discontent and protest. Haldimand had planned to make Sorel a centre of industrious and subsidized artisans, capable of military service, with a hospital for military pensioners. A hospital was established and survived into the nineteenth century, but the colony did not flourish. The refugee camps maintained during the war at Sorel and Machiche across the river had been centres of discontent, as most camps must be. Yet some Loyalists had hoped to settle permanently in the campsites. Those at Sorel were permitted to do so.

The Loyalists at Sorel, numbering eighty-seven in 1779, had their population suddenly swell at the end of the war when Michael Grass's contingent arrived by sea from New York (carrying with it an epidemic of smallpox). These refugees discovered that they were receiving less rations than they had in New York and, after protesting, were restored to full rations.

All this left a legacy of discontent which festered among the several hundred under-employed Loyalists settled permanently in the town. A report in 1787 described the Sorel Loyalists as "slothfully awaiting the government to feed them," saying that they were tempted to "falsely accuse the officers of the government." It does not appear that the Reverend John Doty, the Loyalist Anglican priest who arrived 4 July, 1784, did much to quiet this discontent. He himself was among the discontented and an outspoken champion of his personal grievances.

Sorel was the first English-speaking town in the province and consequently returned English-speaking members when an assembly was granted in 1792. One of these, the second-generation Loyalist Jonathan Sewell, became a controversial leader of the English party in the assembly.

If the first difficulties of the Loyalists understandably concerned their conditions of resettlement, rations, land grants, and the seigneurial system, the second major issue was their relation to French Canadian society. There were then two points of view. The first was presented by Sir John Johnson, who wanted a simple creation of a new Loyalist province in the West; the second was the view of the chief justice, William Smith, who wanted to use the Loyalist presence in the province as political ballast to secure the repeal of the Quebec Act, and as a support for a program designed to assimilate the French Canadians.

The coming of the Loyalists had, in fact, increased the number of English in the province from 4 to 14 per cent, out of a total population of about one hundred and forty-four thousand. Yet the Loyalists were a majority west of the Ottawa, and if post-Loyalist Americans could be induced to enter the province in sufficient numbers, they might effect a decisive shift in the population balance. This is what William Smith hoped to bring about: that English numbers in combination with English institutions might secure, in effect, the Americanization of the French Canadians.

Smith had no fear of Americanization as he did not, like Inglis, see the character of American society as the cause of the Revolution; nor was there anyone of influence within the province with Anglican Tory schemes to elevate the political and cultural level of North American society. Opposition to Americanization and fear of American immigration could only come from one group and that was the French Canadians. In the course of the generation after 1760,

French Canadians had become acquainted with the British system of government and sought to use their rights as British subjects in defence of their language and culture. They eventually developed their own form of loyalism with which they opposed the policy of cultural Americanization, pursued by the English Party. But this did not happen immediately and the decision to divide the province into Upper and Lower Canada in 1791, which deprived the English Party of its Western support, owed less to pressure coming from the New World than to the inertia of Lord Dorchester, and its appeal as the apparent line of least resistance.

Under the new system, the new provinces of Upper and Lower Canada would each have an assembly. In Upper Canada, the future province of Ontario, there would be no serious clash between the elected assembly and the appointed executive for nearly thirty years. In Lower Canada it became apparent after the first election that the English Party would be dependent on the appointed legislative and executive councils for defence of its interests. Moreover, influence within the appointed councils would count for little without the support of the governor.

This condition was not difficult to foresee. William Smith, who anticipated difficulty with an elected assembly, was in no hurry to see one introduced into the province. Like many authors of grand political visions, his liberal principles were tempered by benevolent despotism. With the passage of the Constitutional Act, it was clear that the seigneurial system and French civil law were secured indefinitely. There was one consolation for the English Party—the Eastern Townships, hitherto closed to settlement, would be opened to Americans and would not be ruled by the seigneurial system.

Smith, who died in 1793, did not live to lead the English Party in the new phase of the struggle, but his son-in-law, the younger Jonathan Sewell, became the leading figure in this party during the next generation.


CONDITIONS WERE very different in the Maritime provinces where Charles Inglis arrived as bishop in 1787. Here there were two large and related questions which were not present in Quebec. One was the plan of Bishop Inglis to set the moral and intellectual tone of the province through higher education. The other was the presence of a greater number of educated and genteel Loyalist families than could be comfortably absorbed into Maritime society. More immediate were the problems of securing land grants and compensation for losses and, above all, finding a place in the politics of the province.

The population of Nova Scotia numbered about twenty thousand before the

Revolution, including some three thousand in what is now New Brunswick. Most of the inhabitants were New Englanders of ten to fifteen years' residence. Outside Halifax the Anglican Church had few adherents. As New Englanders, the Nova Scotians sympathized with the patriots, but they were isolated. There was a small British garrison in Halifax and pockets of loyal men here and there. Under these conditions, the issues had to be openly debated and there was no opportunity for supporters of the resistance to organize committees of safety or to prevent open discussion.

At the same time, the most powerful moral force in the province was the Rhode Island evangelist Henry Alline, who condemned both the Crown and its enemies for the use of force. Neutralism was under the circumstances the obvious recourse of these New England Nova Scotians, a position which was made more acceptable by the fact that the military market created by the war proved profitable. It is impossible to go beyond speculation, but if the issues had been as freely and continuously debated throughout the colonies as they were in Nova Scotia, neutralism, which was a strong force in the Southern Colonies, might have been the option chosen by the majority. Toward the end of hostilities, raids by New England privateers forced Nova Scotia into the conflict by way of self-defence. Consequently, mindful of its own war effort, the indigenous population did not see Loyalists as having a special status in Nova Scotia. Moreover, the governor's council and the Halifax merchants who shared this general outlook were running the province and were not disposed to share power with the newly arrived Loyalists.

On the eve of the Revolution the governor, Francis Legge, through an ill-advised effort to break the power of the Halifax oligarchy of merchants and officeholders, had succeeded in making himself unpopular. His successor, John Parr, was from the moment of his taking office in 1783 an object of suspicion to the Loyalists. Parr, a stout man of over sixty, saw his appointment as a reward for services rendered. Wanting nothing more than peace and quiet, Parr accepted the system as he found it—an oligarchy of Halifax merchants running the province. The Loyalists as newcomers were not represented in the elected assembly. They had arrived expecting to enjoy a privileged position and found themselves outsiders.

Their hopes rose when Sir Guy Carleton appointed Brigadier Henry Fox, the younger brother of Charles James Fox, as commander of the garrison in Nova Scotia. This appointment appeared to neutralize the supposedly hostile authority of Parr. Moreover, it appeared to have immediate consequences. Instructions were given to bring all Loyalist refugees to Halifax and Parr consented to land a substantial contingent in the Saint John River Valley. It was assumed that Parr would soon be recalled and that Henry Fox would be appointed governor. But with the fall of the Fox-North ministry, and the advent of a new ministry by a friend of Shelburne's, the younger Pitt, Parr would remain for a while.

Meanwhile, the presence of a large and growing settlement in the Saint John River Valley lent substance to a plan conceived by William Knox, the under-secretary of the American department, as early as 1779. Knox, a permanent civil servant and a high church Tory, devised a scheme for resettlement of the Loyalists in the present area of New Brunswick. In so doing he hoped to create a society in which the influence of a landed gentry and an Anglican establishment would prevent a re-emergence of the kind of political agitation that had led to revolution. The province would be called New Ireland, after the land of his fathers. But this scheme was premature as much of the territory on which Knox hoped to settle the Loyalists had been granted by charter to the Massachusetts Bay Colony. American independence had not yet been recognized and Massachusetts was still legally part of the empire and could not be deprived of lands under its jurisdiction without a complicated legal process.

The end of the war and the presence of Loyalists in the Saint John River Valley set the stage for a revival of Knox's plan, further stimulated by a petition addressed to Carleton in New York. This document, signed by Fifty-five Loyalists with pretensions to gentility, asked that they be granted 5,000 acres each as a means of supporting their status and enabling them to play their proper role as agents of social stability. Carleton forwarded this petition to Parr without recommending it. Parr thought it best to authorize the survey of lots of 5,000 acres but quickly changed his plans on receiving notice that grants for field officers would be limited to 1,000 acres.

As it turned out, Carleton thought schemes of this kind unworkable, and as the McNiff controversy in the upper province suggests, the rank and file of Loyalists were hyper-sensitive to any project that hinted at seigneurial tenure. In the absence of tenants, large grants to prospective gentry only turned them into land speculators, or absentee owners of undeveloped acres. The effect of the petition of the "Fifty-five" was to arouse further distrust among ordinary Loyalists of the agents appointed to handle their claims, a distrust which equalled their suspicion of Governor Parr and his deputy at the Saint John settlements, Major Gilfred Studholme. This discontent was voiced in a manifesto by the 22nd Company of Militia, denouncing the manner in which lots and rations were being distributed.

By 1784 there were about fourteen thousand Loyalists in the present-day area of New Brunswick sufficiently prosperous to form a viable government and too unwieldly to be managed easily from Halifax. At the same time there was a group of articulate and influential Loyalists in London, men like Jonathan Odell, an Anglican clergyman, Edward Winslow, and Gabriel Ludlow, who had been putting pressure on London to create a separate Loyalist province.

In this case, as in the later division of Quebec into Upper and Lower Canada, the British cabinet followed the line of least resistance. Parr could remain in office with reduced responsibilities. New jobs could be created for needy Loyalist exiles, and the discontented settlers might see in the new arrangements a means of redressing their grievances. The idea of a Loyalist province first conceived by William Knox would be realized, not "New Ireland" but "New Brunswick" in deference to the ruling house.

The Tory ideas of Inglis and the Whig ideas of Smith had thus to be applied to societies already in existence. From the beginning New Brunswick was a Loyalist province, for the handful of pre-Loyalists had no perceptible political influence. Provincial politics, then, was a matter of Loyalists cooperating with one another, and would remain that way until after 1815.

The first governor of New Brunswick, Thomas Carleton, brother of Sir Guy Carleton, was a military man who thought of himself as governor of a frontier province and, until 1792, he was in command of the forces stationed in Nova Scotia. He brought with him, as his advisors on the appointed council, an impressive array of Loyalist talent, including Jonathan Odell, Ward Chipman, and Gabriel Ludlow. These men formed a Loyalist oligarchy which would dominate the government of the province for over a generation and would be faced with much the same charges as those levelled against the Halifax oligarchy and the Family Compact in Upper Canada.

Those New Brunswick Loyalists appointed to the ruling council were more intellectual than the Butlers and Johnsons who settled in Quebec. Yet, like them, they were primarily concerned with resuming the roles of officeholders and landlords which they had held in the old colonies. Their ideal seemed to be a secure and genteel society in which they would play a leading part. They shared most of the assumptions held by Tory Loyalists about the causes of the Revolution, but they had no grand designs like Inglis and Smith. The constitution of New Brunswick was substantially the same as those of Virginia and New York, and this to them seemed sufficient since they controlled all the appointed offices. As most of the Loyalists surrounding Carleton were New Englanders, they were particularly anxious to avoid town meetings, a form of local assemblies in the old colonies which had become centres of disaffection. Loyalists found some comfort in the fact that the majority of the settlers were from New Jersey and New York.

The province was divided into counties and parishes and the town of Saint John was given a charter based on that of New York. In spite of these precautions against popular politics, all white males of three months' residence in the province could vote. Representation in the projected twenty-six-member assembly was by population, which was heaviest on the seaboard.

Carleton decided to locate the capital at Fredericton, seventy miles up the river from the metropolis. Carleton's decision was probably influenced by military considerations, rather than by a Jeffersonian-like fear of cities and commerce, common among many of the Loyalist elite. As the Supreme Court met in Fredericton and most of the legal business was conducted in Saint John, this decision had serious consequences for the province. In spite of this, Carleton and his Council opposed all demands that the Supreme Court meet in Saint John or that the jurisdiction of the lower courts be increased. This attitude would later make the location of the capital a political issue, but it did not receive much attention in the first election, probably because the government business was still being conducted from Saint John when the first election took place in 1785.

To make the system work, Carleton had to secure a majority in the assembly. As there were no provincial parties, the first election resolved itself into a series of local contests where government candidates were usually returned. There were notable exceptions, as in Charlotte and Northumberland counties, and a very vigorous contest in Saint John, where six seats were at stake. Although this election involved a small city and lasted only a few days, it is of special interest because it brought to the surface the latent social tensions within the Loyalist community. There apparently were similar tensions in most urban centres where Loyalists were present. In Saint John the government party was known as "the Upper Cove," which was based on the more prosperous residential areas located on the the higher ground. It was opposed by a popular party labelled the "Lower Cove."

The "Upper Covers" were characterized by their gentility and connections, and included among their candidates the attorney general, Ward Chipman, and the solicitor general, Jonathan Bliss. Defeat of these candidates would have been serious for the government even if it secured a majority in the assembly. The opposition "Lower Covers" were identified with the opponents of the "Fifty-five." They were led by tradesmen of some substance but who had no claim to gentility and were without connections.

Neither Upper nor Lower Covers were at home in their new environment, and were prepared to believe in the presence of conspiracies and the imminence of disaster. The Lower Covers undoubtedly included former tenants on the estates of the Dutch Patroons (landholders like the seigneurs) such as the Van Rensselaers whose loyalism was founded on resistance to revolutionary landlords. It was not difficult to arouse their latent fear of being reduced to tenant farmers. On their part, the officerholders who led the Upper Cove Party were inclined to see revolutionary intent in mere opposition.

Neither side played their cards well. When the election seemed to be going against the Upper Cove, they placed the polls on their own territory where they were less accessible to the opposition. The Lower Covers' response was a riot, during which troops were called out and the polls closed for several days. When the polls reopened the Lower Cove still won by a comfortable majority of 100, out of 1,100 votes cast. It is possible that some of the marginal votes included former residents who had moved out of town and were not eligible to vote. On the pretext that a majority had been won by fraud, the government scrutinized the voting list and arbitrarily eliminated two hundred electors, thus ensuring a victory of the government candidates.

This dramatic event left understandable bitterness behind, but the Lower Covers did not have the kind of unanimous support enjoyed by John Wilkes in the famous Middlesex election in England or by William Lyon Mackenzie in the Upper Canadian elections of 1831. Moreover, the mutual suspicions which led to confrontation would not burn with the same intensity once the governed and the government had settled down to a routine existence. It is significant that no permanent political movement grew out of this early political turmoil.

Yet this election marks the first time that the "Loyalty Cry" was raised by a government party in Canadian elections. In this case it failed to secure a majority, as it failed again later when first employed by the Family Compact in Upper Canada. The "Loyalty Cry" was effective only in the hands of popular leaders, as was shown in Upper Canada during the election of 1836, when it was raised by the Roman Catholic Bishop Alexander Macdonell, Orange Grand Master Ogle Gowan, and Methodist Egerton Ryerson, or in New Brunswick on the eve of Confederation when it was raised by the formidable Leonard Tilley.

After electing his candidates by abuse of administrative power, Carleton had a secure majority but would still face a vocal opposition. As the salaries of the leading officials were paid by the imperial government and revenues of the province rarely exceeded £2,000, however, the opposition in the assembly could do little more than embarrass and inconvenience the government. Furthermore, as about a third of the revenue paid the members of the assembly for their attendance, they could not reject the budget without penalizing themselves. The opposition crystallized around Elias Hardy, an active opponent of the "Fifty-five," whose dislike of Loyalist agents had induced him to support Parr's efforts to prevent the creation of a separate province. Hardy and his friends concentrated their attack on placemen—those senior civil servants including judges who held seats in the assembly. They also made much of the fact that most of the council members were New Englanders, while the majority of Loyalists were from New York and other provinces.

Serious opposition began when the non-Loyalist James Glenie was elected from the Sunbury constituency in 1789, a district where the pre-Loyalists were in the majority. Glenie, a gifted Scot born in Fife, was a Latinist, an author of a dissertation on mathematics, and a member of the Royal Society for the Advancement of Science. He had a gift for making influential friends, but difficulty in getting along with his immediate superiors. He was cashiered by Sir Guy Carleton in a court-martial, attended by Thomas Carleton, reinstated in the army through influence, and became deputy surveyor general under John Wentworth, who later became governor of Nova Scotia. Being a non-Loyalist was not a serious disadvantage for a man of unusual ability because the Loyalists enjoyed a majority in the province. William Hazen, the non-Loyalist merchant, for instance, was acceptable as a member of the council just as Glenie was to the opposition.

Glenie had the art of championing real grievances but did so too often, with assertions of his own intellectual and social superiority to those in the governing councils. By the time he was elected there was a serious schism between merchants and agricultural interests with the governor opposing the merchants. Trade had collapsed in the 1790s when American ships were admitted to the West Indies market, thus eliminating the New Brunswick middlemen who had been carrying American goods. At the same time an act of the secretary of state, not enforced in other colonies, prevented further free gifts of land. This discouraged immigration and was considered by larger landowners and would-be land speculators as a major cause of the economic stagnation of the province.

In the election of 1793, only twelve of the twenty-six original members were re-elected. Nothing could be done about the depression, but it was possible to quarrel about the division of the meagre revenue and the degree to which the practices of both the government and opposition conformed to British parliamentary tradition. In a province well stacked with political talent, this could become an absorbing occupation.

Even if the assembly made no contribution to the development of the province, it provided a means of political education, establishing a level of debate which could not be equalled in other provinces. By 1795 the opposition was holding up budget money, insisting that initiative in financial matters must come from the assembly, not from a budget prepared by the council. In the course of this dispute, the familiar opposition moves, practised in the old colonies and in England, were attempted. Pre-eminent among these was tacking, by which the opposition added its own legislation to government money bills, a device which goes back to the reign of Queen Anne.

In a petition to the Crown, the opposition charged that the council, by denying initiative in money matters to the assembly, departed from true British practice. The council, in turn, accused the opposition of taking that dangerous road which in the old colonies had led to revolution. Neither could claim to be strictly following British practices because the British cabinet, which corresponded to the New Brunswick executive, was based on a majority in the House of Commons.

This dispute and similar disputes between elected assemblies and appointed councils in other colonies had little in common with the agitation that had preceded the Revolution. In the old colonies, the protest had been against imperial policy. In the British American provinces, the dispute involved a quarrel between two groups within the colony in which the imperial government was appealed to by both sides as a mediator. Authorities in London were careful to maintain this role and were not much inclined to support their appointed civil servants. British mediation was possible because the members of the council were rarely mere civil servants, but were possessed of considerable personal influence in the colonies. The attorney general and the solicitor general, for instance, normally held seats in the assembly. In the case of New Brunswick, even judges held seats and there were many seats held by members friendly to the council. There were always some members who would support government measures in the interest of tranquillity; still others who merely disliked the opposition. It seems likely that the officeholding oligarchy could have organized a popular party at this time, but did not do so because its members were opposed to popular politics on principle and thought of themselves as administrators rather than politicians.

The initiative was therefore with Glenie and his supporters in the assembly. Glenie himself seems to have sympathized with that vanishing group of British radicals who in turn sympathized with the principles of the French Revolution. His opposition to Anglican privilege, for example, reflected his own views rather than those of his supporters. He nevertheless could rally a majority on particular issues, as illustrated by his successful move to prevent the creation of a government-sponsored secondary school, Fredericton Academy. Ultimately, Glenie's tactics were self-defeating as the opposition penalized both themselves and the province by holding up supplies for four years (1795–9). Moreover, the limits of his influence were clear when a vote of censure, introduced by Glenie against Carleton in 1797, was rejected by a substantial majority.

As might be expected against a background of economic stagnation, there was talk of annexation to the United States, and some Loyalists returned to the old colonies. Yet many of those who left went to Upper Canada. The younger Jonathan Sewell found a place in the civil hierarchy of Quebec and later became a leading figure in the English Party of Lower Canada. The argument for annexation rested largely on economic grounds. It was assumed that joining the Americans would bring New England prosperity to New Brunswick, and that the prevailing economic tendencies were permanent.

When Carleton left New Brunswick in 1803, he had little cause for satisfaction. After nineteen years of government the province had a population of 25,000, much of it engaged in subsistence farming. His departure coincided with the brief period of the Peace of Amiens and signalled a turning point in the economic fortunes of the province. Gabriel Ludlow replaced Carleton as president of the council, holding office until 1808 when he was succeeded by Edward Winslow. Both men were Loyalists, and the appointed council remained in Loyalist hands. There was thus no change at the top, but the opposition withered as the economy recovered. This was not altogether cause and effect. The tension between the assembly and the appointed councils brought no tangible results and opposition had lost its novelty.

The decade of conflict was undoubtedly a useful political experience, and it is perhaps significant that there was more tension between the New Brunswick Loyalist council and the Loyalist opposition in the assembly than there was in any other province. The common experience of revolution and exile had not obscured conflict of interest. A glance at the history of the Loyalist province of New Brunswick during this period should dispel any lingering assumptions about the conservative and tory predispositions of the Loyalists. It is also significant that many of them accepted Glenie as their leader, who was, in ideological terms, a radical, with no previous connection with political opposition.

The Loyalists in the opposition ignored the charges of their fellow Loyalists, like the Ludlows and the Chipmans, who accused them of re-enacting the early phase of the Revolution. Yet among these opposition Loyalists and those who voted for them, the fear of republicanism survived. When the "Chesapeake-Leopard" affair of 1807 raised the spectre of war with the United States, the militia turned out to a man. It was necessary to ballot to determine who would remain at home instead of who would serve. As the danger subsided, the militia lost interest. Desertion and discipline became a problem, but the point had been made: the Loyalist spirit was alive beneath the surface of opposition politics.

MOST OF THE Maritime Loyalists who remained in peninsular Nova Scotia had to find a place in an established society. As the Loyalists made up about half the population of Nova Scotia, the creation of the province of New Brunswick weakened their position, just as the division of the old province of Quebec weakened the position of the English Party in French Canada. In time they might hope to exert political influence, but as they were virtually excluded from the councils and soon quarrelled with Governor Parr, they had no influence on the provincial executive. Moreover, as the existing assembly had been elected before their arrival, they were at first without representation. This disadvantage was modified in 1785 when ten Loyalists were elected to the assembly. Clearly there would be a Loyalist-led struggle for power between the assembly and the council.

As a group, the Loyalist half of the population felt themselves not only morally superior because of their loyalty, but culturally superior. They had come from a more advanced society and many among them had the benefit of the higher education offered in the old colonies. Their ability to write, and to speak publicly, and their knowledge of law and parliamentary procedures were undoubtedly superior to that of the officeholders who surrounded the governor. However, they fell short of a majority in the province and under the existing system were under-represented in the assembly. The Loyalist bloc of ten seats could not exert much influence as mere champions of Loyalist grievances. To establish a place in politics, they would have to gain the support of the outports against the "Halifax oligarchy" and the circle of officeholders around the governor.

While in New Brunswick the Loyalists were divided between Tory officeholders and an opposition invoking Whig principles, in Nova Scotia the logic of the Loyalist position made the entire Loyalist community behave like Whigs. There was a precedent for this in English history as the Tories were forced into the role of opposition after the Revolution of 1688, forming a Tory country party in opposition to the court policy of the Whigs. Tories had, in fact, formed the opposition in England until the accession of George III to the throne in 1760. In England, the Tory country party combined the usual role of opposition with high church principles. But in Nova Scotia this was not appropriate because Parr and the council were strong supporters of the church. The Nova Scotia Loyalists who had been called "tories" during the Revolution adopted the classic role of a country party, that is, they became champions of popular grievances, borrowing freely from the arsenal of the Whig opposition in contemporary England.

As in New Brunswick, the Nova Scotian Loyalists insisted on the right of the assembly to introduce money bills and denied the council's right to amend them. The familiar process of impeachment was employed against judges accused of misconduct. Yet most remarkable was the motion by the Pennsylvania Loyalist, Isaac Wilkins, calling for the dismissal of the governor's Privy Council. Speaking in support of this motion of non-confidence, Loyalist major Thomas Barclay assured the assembly that it was "most usual for His Majesty's Commons to pray [for the] dismission of his Ministers." The motion was defeated 21 to 8, but it is significant that it was introduced in 1789, just seven years after Lord North's ministry had resigned on a vote of non-confidence, the first to do so in British history.

Supporters of Parr labelled the opposition leaders as "New York office grabbers" but parliamentary opposition has always been associated with the quest for patronage. Without the Loyalist presence in the assembly, an opposition of this degree of vigour and sophistication is inconceivable. By doubling the population of the province the Loyalists advanced the timetable of settlement. In a similar manner they advanced the calendar of political maturity by bringing with them the experience acquired in the old colonies.

Yet the justice of the charge that the Loyalists were office seekers became manifest soon after the death of Parr in 1791, when Loyalist Sir John Wentworth became lieutenant-governor of the province. Barclay, who had introduced the motion of non-confidence, secured a well-paid post. Seven of the eleven new appointments to the council went to Loyalists, as did about 40 per cent of all appointments made by Wentworth, the better-paid jobs as a rule being awarded to Loyalists. There was a noticeable softening of the opposition as the Halifax oligarchy made room for the more able Loyalists. Henceforth, Loyalists in Nova Scotia would be divided in politics and no longer represented as a distinct group, but their work of political education was done. They had instilled the habit of opposition in the assembly.

With the turn of the century the opposition was taken over by William Tonge, who entered the assembly during the election of 1799. He became champion of the outports against the reconstituted Halifax oligarchy, which had been enlarged to include Loyalists. Tonge, a former naval officer and personal enemy of Wentworth, kept up his connections with the Halifax garrison, and belonged to the same social group as many Loyalist leaders. But in 1803 he even sought to take loyalism from the Loyalist-dominated civil administration by seizing the initiative in securing an assembly vote of £10,000 in support of the war effort.

THE ADVENT OF the Wentworth administration coincided roughly with the beginning of the war against revolutionary France. The wartime prosperity which followed Wentworth's years (1792–1808) also synchronized with the efforts of Inglis to create an effective Anglican establishment in Nova Scotia and New Brunswick. Anglican establishment was perhaps the only aspect of toryism which could be applied in the New World. Loyalty to the Crown and British connections was shared by the Whigs. Tory schemes for the creation of a landed gentry, as contemplated by William Knox and recommended by the "Fifty-five," could not be implemented when capital and labour was in short supply, even if such projects had been acceptable to the majority of the Loyalists. Moreover, in the old colonies, it was the large estate owners like the Livingstons and Van Renssalaers of New York, and the Washingtons in Virginia, who had provided the leadership of the Revolution. Loyalist memory was still vivid.

Anglicanism itself was an imperfect guarantee of loyalty as Washington and most of the Southerners supporting the Revolution were nominal Anglicans. Yet nearly all the Anglican clergy of the old colonies opposed the Revolution. From the perspective of the British government, this was a point in favour of the Anglican church. Still, the majority of Loyalists, like the majority of Americans, were of dissenter background. Given the general willingness of pioneer communities to accept resident clergy of any denomination, Inglis' idea of a strong Tory-oriented Anglican Church would have been possible if most of the exiled Anglican clergy had come to the Maritimes. But as it turned out, Inglis could not fill the religious vacuum in the new communities and most remained without clergy until they found dissenting ministers to supply their needs.

In England the Anglican clergy were the principal link between the Tory Party and the people. In Upper Canada, John Strachan and the Family Compact created a church party composed largely of Anglican officeholders which formed a Tory minority within the Conservative ranks. By creating a church party, Strachan made church establishment a political issue in Upper Canada and for a while drove the Loyalist Methodist, Egerton Ryerson, into an alliance with William Lyon Mackenzie. Inglis was a Tory and had acquired political experience as a Loyalist pamphleteer during the Revolution, but he made no move to anticipate Strachan by creating a church party. His Irish experience had given him a sense of the limitations of church establishment and the futility of efforts to use political and social influence to secure religious uniformity. In dealing with dissenters, Inglis had learned "to avoid in my conduct what would give them disgust and shock their prejudices."

Apart from this, Inglis did not have full control of his church or full cooperation from his clergy. The Anglican church had been established in Nova Scotia in 1758. Lt.-Gov. John Parr was a strong supporter of the church and insisted upon interfering with church patronage and administration. Under the system of establishment he had the right to do so, and without his support Inglis could not get financial assistance from the two English missionary societies—the Society for the Propagation of the Gospel and the Society for the Propagation of Christian Knowledge. Inglis was not given a seat on the council by virtue of his office as bishop, and he did not acquire one in his own right until 1809. Moreover, his clergy were not accustomed to working under episcopal jurisdiction and many felt that he was not the best possible choice as bishop.

Before the coming of the Loyalists, there were six Anglican missionaries in Nova Scotia, including several Loyalist clergymen who had settled there before the general exodus. Apart from Halifax, there were no large Anglican congregations in the province. Inglis saw the folly of attempting missionary work among the "old Nova Scotians" who made up half the population, and he sought to maintain good relations with the dissenting clergy. His church would have to be based on the twenty thousand or so Loyalists in the province, of whom less than a third had any previous connection with the Church of England. About two-thirds of the clergy who came to Nova Scotia were Loyalists and of these about one-third had been converted to Anglicanism from other denominations. Some had attended Harvard or Yale. Few shared Inglis' ideal of making the church a cultural influence which, by a diffusion of refined manners and deference to superiors, would create a fertile atmosphere for political conservatism.

Anglican clergy were caught between the demands of their congregations for popular preaching and the convictions of the bishop and more influential Anglican laymen that the church should be a school of manners. In spite of the desire of Inglis to keep on good terms with the dissenters, he clung tenaciously to the privileges of his church, insisting, without altogether gaining his point, on the exclusive right of the Anglican clergy to perform marriage services. Although he made arrangements for Presbyterian ministers to receive small sums from government sources, he insisted that they receive the money as individuals, not as clergymen.

By the 1790s it was clear that the dissenting churches were winning over the majority of the Loyalists in the Maritimes and, with the outbreak of the French Revolution, Inglis reiterated his belief in the nefarious connection between political and religious dissent. It was difficult to build up a formal church establishment without provoking political controversy. Yet, if the establishment was nominal, the endowment was real: 20,000 acres in glebe lands were awarded to the Anglican church. The assembly would not vote stipends for clergymen, but was prepared to support educational projects of the church. Thus, if the church could not fill the religious vacuum, there was still a chance that it might, with government support, create an Anglican-oriented system of education. Inglis did not attempt to do much with the charity schools that the church provided, although they seemed to have turned out some polite and obedient servants. His main effort was in the field of higher education which, as discussed in another chapter, achieved very little. The sole legacy of his policy, King's College, functions today as part of Dalhousie University in Halifax.

In 1785 the New Brunswick Assembly established the Anglican church in the province and, because of the Loyalist majority, the prospects for Anglicanism seemed more favourable. Still, there were only six Anglican clergymen in the province, under the distant jurisdiction of Inglis at Halifax. They had no chance of filling the religious needs of the pioneer society. Moreover, as Inglis tried to build up the infant King's College, which had an enrolment of only nine students in 1812, he also opposed the creation of a rival institution of higher learning in New Brunswick, which did not acquire a college until 1829.

Given the resources at his disposal, Inglis did the best he could. By patient and cautious work, he created a formidable minority church and a small college. Yet this church and college, as will be made clear, contained the seeds of an Anglican culture which had political consequences. The religious history of the Loyalists suggests that James I's statement "No Bishop, No King" does not apply to the British North American settlements. The majority of Loyalists were either dissenters or highly susceptible to dissenter influence. Anglicanism was not essential to loyalty, but its established practice of blending art with religion by means of ritual made it easier for Loyalists to accept the practice of introducing an element of poetry in government which is the essence of monarchy. The cultural influence of Anglicanism, which stretched far beyond the church as such, had much to do with the style of government in Canada.

In 1784, the year the Loyalists arrived in Cape Breton, the Island was placed under a separate jurisdiction from Nova Scotia, with its own lieutenant-governor, and was not reunited with the mainland until 1821. As the population was small and much of it Acadian, no assembly was granted. As in Quebec before the Constitutional Act of 1791, politics revolved around the executive council and, to some extent, around the vestry of the Anglican parish of St. George's in Sydney.

Gov. J.F.W. Des Barres, with the support of 130 British settlers who arrived in 1784, was soon at odds with the 400 Loyalists who drifted in over a period of several years. The 400 or so Acadians kept out of politics. Leading the Loyalist opposition on the executive council were Abraham Cuyler, a former mayor of Albany, New York, and David Mathews, former mayor of New York City. Cuyler as registrar and Mathews as attorney general, with the support of two other Loyalist councillors, opposed the lieutenant-governor and three other councillors drawn from recently arrived British settlers.

As a result of a quarrel over disbursement of Loyalist supplies, Des Barres was recalled in 1786. Other quarrels followed with the Loyalist Anglican clergymen, Ranna Cossitt, joining the British settlers in their disputes over education and church affairs. In 1793 Cuyler was driven from Cape Breton, but he returned in 1795. Cossitt was purged from the council in 1799, but returned in 1800 when Mathews was dismissed as attorney general. However Cossitt soon found himself transferred by Bishop Inglis to Yarmouth. These shifts in the council reflected little more than personal quarrels but had the effect of retarding the development of Sydney and Cape Breton generally.

After 1802 the influx of Scots Highlanders overwhelmed the Loyalists, but the latter's influence is marked by the work of Richard Gibbons, the younger, who led the move for the creation of an assembly in Cape Breton. Following the reunion of Cape Breton with Nova Scotia in 1821 Loyalist influence on the Island withered away.

The Loyalist settlers on the Island of St. John, as Prince Edward Island was then known, numbered about a fifth of the population. As in Nova Scotia, they brought with them a political sophistication which gave them influence in excess of their numbers. This was further enhanced because large portions of the Catholic population, particularly those who spoke Gaelic and French, took no part in politics. William Schurman of New Rochelle, New York, who founded a prominent Loyalist Island family, was a member of the assembly, as was Joseph Robinson, a former lieutenant-colonel of the South Carolina Royalists, who became Speaker of the House. When Loyalist Edward Fanning became governor in 1787 he appointed Loyalists to the council, including Robert Gray, an ancestor of John Hamilton Gray, a Father of Confederation.

Just as the Loyalists in Quebec faced the seigneurial system, those on the Island confronted the question of absentee proprietors. In 1781 Gov. Walter

Patterson had arranged the escheat and sale at bargain price of huge acreages to himself and his cronies. The move was overruled by London, but an agreement was finally reached which enabled Loyalists and others to settle on the Island. Under these conditions, the Loyalists supported Patterson against the elitist "Country Party" of Stewart Desbrisay. The Patterson faction won the election of 1785 and the assembly refused to reverse the land sales of 1781, as London ordered them. As a result Patterson was recalled, leaving the land question unsettled and the Loyalists without a clear title to their land.

Even the Loyalist governor Fanning failed to improve the situation, so by 1806 Loyalists were prepared to form a fringe opposition party. This was led by an Irish lawyer, James B. Palmer, and the son of a Rhode Island Loyalist, William Haszard. They formed a democratically inclined, if narrowly motivated, society called "the Loyal Electors" whose principal demand was for a clear title to their lands. The ubiquitous, now octogenarian, governor, J.F.W. Des Barres, who had governed Cape Breton in 1784, was now governor of Prince Edward Island. At first he supported the Electors, but their patriotism was put in doubt when, with war fast approaching, the assembly refused to pass a militia grant. The absentees had Des Barres recalled. The governor had tripped over the Loyalists again, just as he had, in different circumstances, a quarter of a century earlier in Cape Breton.

The Electors, charged with subversion, abandoned open opposition during the war, though they re-emerged as the nucleus of the nineteenth-century Liberal Reform party. But the broken promises of 1784 continued to fester. The land question simmered and boiled and was not resolved until 1873 as part of the Island's arrangements for entering Confederation.

In New Brunswick the Loyalists were free to quarrel among themselves, while in Nova Scotia they played a leading part for a while as the driving force behind the opposition. In Lower Canada, however, the Loyalists were a minority within a very small minority but, because of their education and abilities, were able, as individuals, to play a leading part in public life.

When the Constitutional Act became a working document in 1792, the politics of manoeuvre in the appointed councils and the politics of petitions were overshadowed by the creation of two elected assemblies in what had been the old province of Quebec. In Upper Canada this meant a belated emergence of parliamentary politics in a predominantly Loyalist province. In Lower Canada, it meant that the struggle between the French and English Parties, which had characterized the appointed councils, would now be fought out in an elected assembly.

William Smith, who won his last battle against Adam Mabane's French Party, died in 1793, leaving his son-in-law, the younger Jonathan Sewell, to continue the struggle in the new arena, a role Sewell was eminently suited to fill. Coming to the province as solicitor general, the Loyalist Sewell became attorney general and eventually chief justice. He was, like Smith, an intellectual attracted by large ideas. Sewell wrote about French law as it applied to Quebec; he produced papers on the commercial possibilities of the St. Lawrence, and drew up a plan for a federation of the British provinces. Apart from this, he played the violin and had a talent for amateur dramatics. Between 1796 and 1808, he held the seat for Sorel and acted as government leader in the assembly, being the most eminent member of what became known as the "Chateau Clique."

Second only to Sewell as upholder of the English interests in Lower Canada was John Richardson. He represented the merchant interest in Montreal and was the moving force behind the digging of the Lachine Canal. Richardson had been a Loyalist privateer during the Revolution and had come to Montreal some years afterward. Also closely associated with Montreal business interests in later years was Edward Ellice, who acted as their agent in Montreal. The Ellices were a fur-trading family from the Mohawk Valley who acquired the seigneury of Beauharnois, south of the St. Lawrence River. These three Loyalists—Sewell, Richardson, and Ellice—held key positions within the two centres of English influence: the administration at Quebec City and the merchant community in Montreal. Within the elected assembly there were sixteen English members out of a total of fifty. Less than a third were Loyalists, the majority coming from pre-Loyalist fur-trading interests. In 1792, at the sitting of the first assembly, about ten thousand out of a population of one hundred and forty-six thousand were English. Of this ten thousand, not more than two thousand had Loyalist connections.

When it became apparent after the first session that the English Party could not control the assembly, both the Chateau Clique and Montreal merchants directed their efforts toward convincing London that constitutional revision was necessary. Their program was essentially the program that William Smith had taken over from the English Party: the abolition of French civil law, the seigneurial system, and the special position of the Roman Catholic church, and the encouragement of American immigration. To this they added reunion of the provinces of Upper and Lower Canada and, after the outbreak of war with France, they insisted that the natural sympathies of the French Canadians with France made them a security risk. This last point does not appear to have been the result of Loyalist memories of the American Revolution, as its most persistent advocate was Herman W. Ryland, a permanent civil servant without Loyalist connections. French Canadians in the assembly vigorously asserted their support of the war effort against revolutionary France, and charged the English Party with endangering the British connection by encouraging American immigration into the Eastern Townships.

Nothing could be done by Sewell and his friends without the support of the British government, and this meant winning over the governor of the province. Although Dorchester's successors showed some sympathy to the English Party, it was only when Sir James Craig became governor in 1807 that the English Party found a champion. This proved to be a most unfortunate combination. In a series of confrontations with the majority, Craig dissolved the assembly several times and ultimately suppressed the opposition paper, *Le Canadien*, and arrested its staff. Craig then wrote a lengthy despatch appealing to London for support—a` futile gesture that ended in London's repudiation of his policy and that of the English Party. Craig's term of office ended in 1811 and his successor, Sir George Prevost, excluded the English Party, including Sewell, from his circle of friends.

Meanwhile the French Canadian opposition, which had been making a careful study of English law and constitutional tradition, found welcome allies from among second-generation Loyalists, especially James and Andrew Stuart, sons of the Reverend John Stuart, chaplain of the Second Battalion, King's Royal Regiment of New York. James Stuart had been dismissed as solicitor general by Craig in 1809 and undoubtedly his subsequent moves were partly influenced by personal pique. Yet he was formidable because of his command of legal technicalities and parliamentary procedure. Having lived in Nova Scotia, James Stuart was aware of the use of impeachment of judges in that province and he instituted proceedings against Loyalist chief justice Jonathan Sewell. By undertaking this, Stuart became virtual leader of the opposition party in the assembly. Proceedings against Sewell were ultimately defeated because the governor did not support the impeachment. Yet, for a time, the politics of the province revolved around a conflict between two Loyalists: Stuart, representing the French interest, and Sewell, the English.

By a curious twist of circumstances, similar conditions prevailed during the rebellions of 1837–8. Attorney General Charles Richard Ogden, a second-generation Loyalist of Lower Canada, directed the intelligence services of the Crown forces. Opposed to him as leader of the Patriote forces in Montreal and during the Richelieu Valley uprisings in 1837 were the New Brunswick-born Loyalist Thomas Storrow Brown, and the Sorel-bred Loyalist doctor Wolfred Nelson. Nelson's brother, Dr. Robert Nelson, took the lead the next year in the raids of the Hunters Lodges across the Quebec frontier from the United States, raids that were designed to provoke hostilities between the United States and Great Britain and ultimately to secure independence for Lower Canada.

The region west of the Ottawa, which became the province of Upper Canada, had grown from under ten thousand at the time of the first Loyalist settlements in 1784 to twenty or thirty thousand by the time the new province was created in 1792. It was the only province to attract post-Loyalist American settlers in great numbers, and it was the least political and least intellectual of the British provinces in America. The first lieutenant-governor of the province, John Graves Simcoe, was not a Loyalist, but had commanded the Queen's Rangers, a Loyalist unit that was organized more like a task force than a regiment.

Like most Tories, Simcoe took the view that the Revolution was the work of a minority and, like Bishop Inglis, he was a firm believer in church establishment. Thus he wanted a resident bishop appointed to the new province. But in other matters, Simcoe's outlook was more like that of William Smith. He wanted imperial support for economic development and for a provincial university that he hoped would make the province an intellectual centre. Above all, he aimed to make Upper Canada an economic success by attracting American immigrants and expected that this success would induce the errant colonies to return to their true allegiance.

As in the other colonies, the salaries of the civil establishment were paid by the imperial government and provincial revenues were insignificant. As the McNiff controversy proved, a pioneer community, given a grievance, could organize a protest. But in the years before 1812, there were not enough grievances to force the pioneers to organize loud political protest. Nor was there a class of professional or amateur politicians capable of creating an effective opposition to the government.

What opposition there was came from two sources. The first were prominent Loyalists like Richard Cartwright of Kingston, who kept a library, had intellectual interests, and was a member of the appointed legislative council. Cartwright took up a popular grievance by protesting Simcoe's efforts to award the exclusive right to perform marriages to the Anglican clergy, some three in number during the early days of the province. More personal was his objection to senior civil servants holding dual membership in the executive and legislative councils. Cartwright and his supporter, Robert Hamilton, appeared republican in spirit to Simcoe. But at the heart of the matter was the resentment of a man of wealth and influence in the community pitted against the authority of an imaginative and strong-minded lieutenant-governor who would neither consult him on matters which he (Cartwright) thought important nor defer to his advice.

There was some popular feeling in favour of regular New England-style town meetings, much feared by Loyalists, and Simcoe was prepared to permit local meetings under the supervision of an appointed justice of the peace. Nothing came of this concession, though, as there was little enthusiasm for local taxes, however democratically voted. Simcoe had no serious difficulties with his sixteen-man assembly. Neither did his successors.

It is significant that the post-Loyalist Americans, who out-numbered the Loyalist and British immigrants three to one by 1812, were not organized into a political movement and seemed content to let Loyalist and British civil servants run the government. They were, however, a source of anxiety to those in authority, who were also worried about the weakness of the Anglican church and the fact that the religious vacuum was being filled by dissenters, principally itinerant Methodist preachers from the United States. The retreat of Anglicanism was marked by the Marriage Act of 1798 which extended the right of performing marriage ceremonies to Lutherans, Calvinists, and Church of Scotland clergy. Roman Catholic clergy had enjoyed this right by virtue of the Quebec Act of 1774.

Opposition or, more correctly, efforts to create a permanent opposition came not from Americans or dissenters, but from Anglicans from the British Isles. William Weeks, an Irish-born lawyer, was elected to the assembly in 1805 and introduced a motion calling for a "discussion of the disquietude which exists in the province." It was voted down ten to four, and Weeks was killed in a duel the following year. Another Irishman, Joseph Willcocks, who was dismissed from the office of sheriff of the Home District in 1807, founded the first opposition newspaper, *The Upper Canadian Guardian*. Elected to the assembly in 1808, Willcocks continued in opposition to the government until 1812 when he joined the American forces and was killed in action. A third Irishman, Robert Thorpe, an associate judge of the court of King's Bench, used his office to sponsor grand jury petitions and, securing a seat in the assembly in 1807, he sought unsuccessfully to form an opposition. He left the province, having been dismissed from office in 1807.

The efforts of these energetic and capable, if not always stable men, were premature. They enjoyed enough local support to acquire seats in the assembly, but once there they excited curiosity rather than sympathy. On the eve of the War of 1812 there was a good deal of concern on the part of officials about the loyalty of the population, but there was no organized opposition to the government in the Upper Canadian Assembly.

In spite of this the "War Hawks" in Congress and even Thomas Jefferson assumed that the Canadians desired annexation to the Republic and that a mere demonstration of force would be sufficient to occupy Upper Canada. There was, in fact, much pessimism and defeatism in the province, partly dispelled by Maj.-Gen. Sir Isaac Brock's energetic military action that led to the American surrender of Detroit and the repulse of the American invasion at Queenston Heights. The real loyalty crisis was in the United States, where the state militia refused to cross the frontier to invade Canada. Some Canadians, including a few Loyalists, sought safety by crossing the frontier to the American side. A few like Willcocks joined the American forces. While the assembly gave verbal support to the war effort, it would not agree to the introduction of martial law in the province. Fifteen of those who had joined the enemy and had been captured were brought to trial at Ancaster. Of these eight were hanged. In March, 1814, the legislature made it possible to seize the property of those who had taken refuge in the United States, and Loyalists who had gone to the United States had their names stricken from the Loyalist list.

The 1812 war had two results: it created a post-Loyalist sense of patriotism (for a time, the myths arising out of the war overshadowed the Loyalist tradition); second, those American immigrants who had been welcomed by Simcoe would henceforth be objects of suspicion. The war had a further effect—the emergence of John Strachan.

A Presbyterian Scot, John Strachan came to Canada as tutor to the children of the Loyalist Cartwright family in 1799. In 1803 he was ordained an Anglican clergyman and opened a school at Cornwall. Here he gathered around him the sons of many of the leading families of the province. In the course of educating his pupils, Strachan assumed the Loyalist-Tory view of politics and for half a century became the personification of Anglican-toryism in the province. He was the intellectual force behind the Family Compact, a combination of officeholders that included most of the leading Loyalist families. Pre-eminent among them was John Beverley Robinson, son of a New Brunswick Loyalist family which moved to the upper province. Robinson became attorney general of Upper Canada (1818–28) and later chief justice. The Compact included non-Loyalists like the Boulton family of York and Niagara and those not originally associated with Strachan, like the Loyalist Christopher Hagerman of Kingston, who became solicitor general in 1829 and later attorney general, and Allan MacNab who built up a sphere of influence in Hamilton. Each district had its cluster of Loyalist Compact families like the Sherwoods and Joneses of Brockville and the Andersons, McLeans, and Farrands of Cornwall.

Most prominent Loyalist families held militia commissions and commissions (or justices) of the peace and in that manner were associated with the Compact. There were exceptions. The Buells of Brockville, headed by Colonel William Buell—a second-generation Loyalist who had served in the War of 1812— represented the reform interests for Leeds County. Egerton Ryerson, a leading Methodist in the province and for a time a leading reformer, was the son of a Loyalist who had left New Brunswick for Niagara. Somewhere between the Compact and the reformers was William Hamilton Merritt, a second-generation Loyalist who promoted the Welland Canal with Compact aid, but became a reformer in the 1840s when the reformers were in power.

Until the 1840s the Conservatives were really a government party and within this group the Loyalists played a leading role, but there was a popular conservatism developing which, in the 1840s, formed a liberal wing of the party personified by newcomers like John A. Macdonald. Even in the 1830s the Tory claim to a monopoly on loyalism was challenged by the Orange Grand Master, Ogle R. Gowan. In the election of 1830 he had refused to cooperate with the Loyalist Tory Henry Sherwood, and then, finding that they would not share patronage, Gowan denounced the Loyalist Tories. The Orange leader declared on January 29, 1833, "The Loyalists were entitled to the lasting gratitude and ample remuneration, and have not they been amply remunerated? Has not the entire province been placed at their feet—judgeships, colonelcies, shrievalties, magisteries, and officers in them?" Gowan pointed out that there were only fifteen immigrant militia officers out of 115, although two-thirds of the ranks in his county were immigrants. Later, during the 1838 visit of Lord Durham, Gowan declared that the Loyalist descendants were loyal only to their privileges and that the only unselfish Loyalists were the immigrants from the United Kingdom.

Loyalty was clearly an issue in the Upper Canadian elections of 1836 and 1844. In the first instance, Compact Tories, Orangemen, Egerton Ryerson, and the Roman Catholics under Bishop Alexander Macdonell united in support of the government party whose real leader was the lieutenant-governor, Sir Francis Bond Head. The use of nativist propaganda by reformers had convinced both Orange and Catholic Irish that it was in their interest to maintain the old country connection. In 1844 Gowan and Ryerson again supported Compact Tories, but this time the question of loyalty was mixed with fears of French domination, a fear not shared by the Catholic population.

By the 1830s Tory Loyalist families in Upper Canada had to share their loyalism with recent immigrants. In the 1840s these Tory Loyalists formed the leading element in the right wing of the Conservative party. Henry Sherwood headed a short-lived government in 1847–8, and Allan MacNab led the Upper

Canadian wing of the MacNab-Morin government of 1854, the first partnership between Tories and French Canadians, which led to the lasting partnership of George-Étienne Cartier and John A. Macdonald.

There is nothing in the Canadian experience that suggests that the words "Tory" and "Loyalist" were synonymous. In Nova Scotia Loyalists laid the foundation for political opposition; in New Brunswick they were divided. William Smith, the leading Loyalist in Quebec, was a Whig of long standing. The "Chateau Clique" and the Montreal merchants were conservatives politically, but stood for a program of economic development which made them opposed to the social status quo. Jonathan Sewell, the younger, and John Richardson had quite a different view of the world than Charles Inglis, Ward Chipman, or the circle around Strachan. There was virtually no republican sentiment in Canada during the half-century which followed the Revolution, and the efforts of Tories to make a political issue out of loyalism met with no success. When republicanism became an issue in the 1830s, there is no evidence that the Loyalists' reaction to the threat was more acute than any other sector of the population. Individual Loyalists, like the Nelsons and Brown in Lower Canada, were prominent among the Patriotes. The Orange Grand Master, Ogle Gowan, expressed doubts about the loyalty of the Buells in Brockville, and the lieutenant-governor of Upper Canada was alarmed by rumours that members of the prominent Loyalist Nelles family of Niagara planned to throw in their lot with the Hunter raiders in 1838. Some of the most active supporters of the government in Lower Canada were French Canadians such as Louis Guy, who helped mobilize the first Montreal volunteers in 1837, Chief of Police Pierre-Edouard Leclère, and the French-speaking Swiss, Augustus Gugy. Post-Loyalist American merchants who settled in Montreal were foremost in offering their services during the rebellions of 1837-8, as were the Irish Roman Catholics.

In Upper Canada, William Lyon Mackenzie's effort at rebellion was based on the post-Loyalist American population, but the most active opposition to the rebellion came from the non-Loyalist Orangemen. As the Tories hoped to profit politically by the Loyalist tradition, they were most anxious to keep it alive and be identified with it. For this reason, reformers and liberals have regarded the Loyalist tradition with apprehension and have been inclined to discourage its manifestations.

The Loyalist tradition underwent an eclipse in the mid-decades of the century, but it enjoyed a revival in the centennial year of 1883-4. This revival had more to do with family history and local traditions than with politics. Yet it coincided with the increase of imperial sentiment manifested in the Imperial

Federation League. This, in itself, as Professor Carl Berger has pointed out, was a manifestation of Anglo-Canadian nationalism. It made some use of the Loyalist myth, in which the Loyalists appear as true Tories and Conservatives and even Anglo-Saxons. This did much to convince French Canadians and Liberals that the Loyalist tradition was a threat to their interests. The Loyalist tradition also obscured the political diversity among the Loyalists and the distinction they shared with French Canadians as dissenters from the North American majority.

The Loyalists' greatest contribution was one which neither Loyalist Whigs nor Tories could foresee. By joining French Canadians in preserving the Crown and the British connection, they kept the door open for the emergence of a system of cabinet responsibility.

# 8 | THE PROMISED LAND

## BLACK LOYALISTS

*"The Year of Jubilee is come*
*Return ye Ransomed Sinners Home"*

*—hymn sung by black Loyalists*

MOST EDUCATED people have heard of George Washington and his role in the American Revolution. Lund Washington and Henry Washington, on the other hand, are known to only a few. Lund, a cousin who was left in charge of Mount Vernon, gave supplies in 1781 to a British frigate that was roaming Chesapeake Bay. This action, considered "exceedingly ill-judged" by the general, shows how easily even well-placed rebels could risk charges of Toryism in the face of British power. But cousin Lund was no Tory. He was seeking absconded slaves.

British offers of freedom to rebels' slaves who would come over were an embarrassment throughout the war. Ex-slaves were a large proportion of the more than three and a half thousand free blacks evacuated in 1783, mainly to Nova Scotia. Among them were at least three former Mount Vernon slaves, including Henry Washington who was, in a sense, both related to the father of the great Republic (he bore his name) and a Loyalist. After a few unsatisfactory years, Henry, with over a thousand other blacks, moved to Sierra Leone, West Africa, where in 1800 he took part in an unsuccessful uprising for independence, for which he was banished. If he had lived and known, would the old general have applauded his former slave's suspiciously American behaviour? Probably not.

BLACKS, WHO numbered nearly half a million (mainly slaves) in a total population of three million at the start of the Revolution, comprised a higher proportion of Americans than they do today. They could not be ignored when hostilities exploded. But few American rebels had any intention of extending the liberty for which they were fighting to blacks. The result was a distinct nervousness, fuelling the perennial dread of slave revolt. As early as September, 1775, it was reported that "a TORY Negro was hanged, and burnt at Charleston, for endeavouring to excite the Negroes to sedition and burned down the town."

The immediate question was whether to use blacks in the armed forces. The

British, with little to lose, acted first. On November 7, 1775, Lord Dunmore, governor of Virginia, proclaimed freedom for all rebels' slaves who would join him, and soon nearly three hundred blacks, known as "Lord Dunmore's Ethiopian Regiment" with "Liberty to Slaves" inscribed across their chests, were in service. Dunmore's offer was extended throughout the colonies in 1779 by the commander-in-chief, Sir Henry Clinton.

Until the success of Dunmore's scheme was seen to be growing, according to George Washington "as a snowball, by rolling," official American policy forbade the enlistment of blacks, slave or free. In January, 1776, Congress reversed itself and allowed the recruiting of free blacks, a policy most states followed and sometimes extended to include slaves.

Perhaps five thousand of the thirty thousand patriot troops were black, while a few thousand fought for the British and many thousands more fled within the lines. Some blacks were probably present in every major battle of the war, but both sides were reluctant to arm them, preferring them as pilots, seamen, pioneers, and musicians, or as auxiliaries—to spy, dig, build, drive wagons and, in the case of women, to nurse. The blacks' war effort was not decisive for either side. Indeed, as the *Annual Register* suggested, the British offer of freedom may have been counterproductive: "This measure, rather invidious than powerful, tended infinitely to inflame the discontent..., without adding anything to the strength of royal arms."

The majority of blacks were too unsophisticated or oppressed to take much personal part in the Revolution. As in the Civil War, most slaves simply followed their masters. But a minority did join George III, just as later others joined Lincoln.

> Now, farewell, my Massa, my Missy, adieu,
> More blows and more stripes will I ne'er take from you.

Motivation was simple: blacks wanted freedom and advancement, concessions more likely to come from the British.

Slavery was abolished in the North after the Revolution and was even questioned in the South, and numerous talented blacks were able to emerge—a challenge to white racial theories—but blacks must generally have been disillusioned with their white countrymen.

The British and the Loyalists delighted in the hypocrisy of a revolution in the name of a liberty that sanctioned slavery. And ironically, with the impediment of the Southern slave economy removed, the British did abolish slavery throughout the empire in 1833, whereas by the same date the South was totally committed to it. But during the Revolution neither the British (with West Indian interests) nor the Loyalists (most of whom, especially Southerners, upheld slavery) had any more intention than Lincoln at a later date of waging an abolitionist crusade. British offers of freedom did not apply to Loyalists' slaves. As the war drew to an end the Loyalists either sold their chattels or carried them into exile. Slaves were "snatched as last minute booty by British, Hessian, American and French troops alike."

What happened to the blacks who fought for the British? Most who had been slaves received their liberty, as did those who fought for the revolutionaries. Whether slave or free-born, the black Loyalists were promised the same treatment as the white ones. A few thousand black Loyalists were among the approximately twenty thousand blacks (mainly Loyalists' slaves) evacuated by the British, who resisted American demands for the return of runaways. For economic reasons slaves were usually taken to the Bahamas and the Caribbean, sometimes via East Florida (temporarily held by Britain). The freemen were given their choice of destinations. Some went to the Bahamas and the West Indies, and some who remained in the army were posted to Jamaica, St. Lucia, and Granada, but most avoided areas of large scale slavery and went to Nova Scotia; some went to Britain; a few even went to Germany—as military musicians.

An unknown number of black Loyalists, probably a few hundred, reached Great Britain where they generally joined the black poor of London. In the 1780s, as a contemporary put it, "the streets of London were swarming with a number of blacks in the most distressed situation, who had no prospect of subsisting in this country but by depredations on the public, or by common charity." The majority of the poor blacks could not have been Americans but their arrival increased and highlighted the problem. A 1787 pamphleteer noted the metropolis was "lately infested with American Negroes." The solution was a plan to found the colony of Sierra Leone on the coast of West Africa, a scheme backed by various evangelicals—facetiously dubbed 'Saints'—including the notable Granville Sharp, city businessmen, some black leaders, and the British Treasury, ever anxious to get rid of the burdensome poor.

Black interest in Sierra Leone, especially black Loyalist interest, was stimulated by the promise of land grants; unlike all other Loyalist refuges, Great Britain offered no such prospect. The conditions of settlement in Sierra Leone were generally similar to those offered the Loyalist refugees in North America and elsewhere. In addition to land, settlers were promised free transportation and, on arrival, further provisions, seeds, clothes, building materials, knives, various agricultural tools, and other implements.

Although almost seven hundred of London's thousands of black poor contracted to go, death and desertion left a mere 350 to sail from Portsmouth on April 9, 1787. They were joined by about sixty whites, "chiefly women of the lowest sort" most of whom had "intermarried with the black men." At least half, probably more, of the blacks were Americans. Granville Sharp described them as "chiefly Seamen, that had served in the Royal Navy, last War, or as Rangers with the Army in the American Woods."

The reluctance of blacks in Britain (in contrast to those in Nova Scotia a few years later) to immigrate to Africa can be traced to the existence within London's demi-monde of a flourishing, albeit poverty-stricken, black community. It preferred "'a crust of bread and liberty' in Old England, to ease, plenty and slavery in the W. Indies," which was able to assimilate runaway slaves and black refugees. Few blacks were actually from Sierra Leone so it was only the African-born minority, as well as the English- and American-born, who regarded the settlement as foreign and forbidding. The enthusiasm of the Canadian blacks is a telling comment on the desperation of their life in the Maritimes.

The bold Sierra Leone experiment, involving black self-government, turned out a hopeless failure. Poor planning, a hostile climate and environment, and the opposition of the local tribes caused its downfall. In February, 1791, a relief ship could round up only sixty-four "Old Settlers," as they came to be known. But an African toe-hold was established which prepared the way for the arrival of the Nova Scotian blacks, whose success was partly the result of the lessons learned from the initial failure.


THE HISTORY OF the blacks in Nova Scotia and New Brunswick reflects well on the blacks, ill on the whites. A few blacks arrived from Boston in 1776, but most came at the end of the war: a trickle from Savannah and Charleston in 1782, a few from East Florida in 1783, the bulk, about three thousand, with the evacuation of New York the same year. A "conservative" total is 3,550, which is at least 10 per cent of the whole Loyalist influx, a surprising figure not widely known or acknowledged in Canada today.

In addition an unknown number of slaves (perhaps three thousand) accompanied their white Loyalist owners. Some were also brought to Quebec. Although British North America was not well suited to it, slavery on a small scale preceded the Loyalists. Many of the prominent refugees brought their slaves as servants and labourers. The slaves were widely distributed in the Maritimes, including a few in Prince Edward Island, but their population was concentrated in the towns, particularly Saint John, New Brunswick, and Shelburne, Nova Scotia.

The most important location of the free black Loyalists in Nova Scotia was Birchtown, named after the beloved Col. Samuel Birch who had issued certificates allowing them to leave New York. It was located close by the white Loyalist boom town of Shelburne, where a little over 1,500 or 40 per cent, settled. There were two other all-black Loyalist communities: Brindley Town, near Digby, with over 200 settlers, and Little Tracadie, on St. George's Bay, with about 170 settlers. Within white communities important locations were the Halifax area with 700 blacks (400 in Halifax, 300 in Preston, near Dartmouth), Chedabucto with 350, Shelburne with 200, Annapolis with 100, and Liverpool with 50. Saint John, New Brunswick, had 180 black settlers.

Loyalists, black or white, needed supplies, land, and rights of citizenship in their new homes. The disappointments of whites have already been described: it comes as no surprise to find the blacks even more disappointed.

Land, in those pre-industrial days, was the *sine qua non* for a decent life for most people. The fate of the black Loyalists is easily summed up: the majority got no land; the minority, who did, received smaller, poorer, less accessible grants than whites. By November, 1786, when grants to whites had been completed in Shelburne, none of the Birchtown blacks had received farms, although a few town lots had been issued. Two years later when the Birchtown grants were completed only about a third of the settlers had been awarded farms. They averaged thirty-four acres compared to an average seventy-four acres for whites. In the Digby area the situation was worse. After more than six years' travail, though the blacks had a few acres in Brindley Town, they were completely without farms. It was somewhat better at Little Tracadie and Preston, but at Halifax the 400 blacks living there in 1791 had received no land whatsoever.

Conditions were probably worse in New Brunswick. For example, in 1785 Thomas Peters (later the black leader of the exodus to Sierra Leone) and a group of dissatisfied Loyalists from Digby and Annapolis moved to Saint John with Governor Carleton's comforting assurance that they would be granted land on a par with the whites. This assurance proved false. While small, town lots were granted, many farms were so far away (up to eighteen miles) as to render them "worthless." Throughout New Brunswick a permanent, successful black farm was a rarity.

All Loyalists had been promised provisions for three years. Whites did not always receive their full allowances; blacks suffered far more. The leading authority on the subject, historian James Walker, concludes that "generally speaking they fared as badly with provisions as they had with land." At Digby, for instance, blacks were given provisions for only a few months and then only if they worked on the roads, a condition seldom required of whites.

While black Loyalists were required to fulfil the duties of citizenship, such as tax-paying and militia service, they failed to enjoy its privileges. They were not allowed to serve on juries or vote in elections. Governor Carleton bluntly told the New Brunswick sheriffs in October 1785, "the votes of blacks are not to be admitted." The charter (April 30, 1785) of the city of Saint John was democratic for whites, but blacks could not be freemen, which severely limited their work opportunities—"only freemen ... could practice a trade or sell goods," as a local historian points out—and prevented them from fishing in Saint John harbour. In Nova Scotia there is evidence of blacks being treated more harshly than whites in the law courts. Early in its history the town of Shelburne ordered "that fifty handbills be printed immediately, forbidding negro dances and frolics in this town."

Blacks suffered twin disadvantages deriving from the whites and from themselves. Whites, with some exceptions, looked upon them as, at best, second-class citizens, an attitude reinforced by their experiences in the slave-holding American colonies, and by the legality of slavery in the Loyalist provinces. Governor Parr of Nova Scotia, his successor John Wentworth, and much of officialdom did try their best for the blacks, but they acted with an assumption of black inferiority. Governor Carleton and the Fredericton oligarchy were less sympathetic.

The blacks themselves, usually ex-slaves, were ill prepared for the task of clearing the wilderness and starting farms. Their small number of children, compared to whites, was a further disadvantage. To all this was added the prevailing confusion, incompetence, and sometimes corruption—all the difficulties of settling so many Loyalists on so little good land with so few surveyors. The eighteenth century had a well-established pecking order and, in the view of even liberal whites, blacks came last.

It is not surprising that the black Loyalists sank to the bottom as sharecroppers, day labourers, and indentured servants. Thomas Clarkson, who came to recruit immigrants to Sierra Leone in 1791, has left an outraged, but fair description of Nova Scotia which is summed up by the laconic, "Justice [is] scarcely ever done to the Blacks" who were considered "no better ... than beasts." Hundreds of black sharecroppers cultivated whites' land in return for half the produce. Clarkson called it "a state of slavery," whereby the whites got their land "cultivated for nothing."

The wide availability of land for whites caused a labour shortage that drove up wages—but not for blacks, who were exploited as cheap labour. For example, the Black Pioneers working on construction in Halifax, Saint John, and Shelburne did not receive the high white wage rates. Clarkson reported that it was common for a white man to hire a black, then when the work was almost done to quarrel and take him to a justice of the peace "who gives an order to mulch him of his wages."

Tension between blacks and whites erupted in a ten-day race riot at Shelburne and Birchtown in July, 1784. The causes were doubtless complex but, as in our time, economic competition within the working class was central. The diary of Benjamin Marston, the Shelburne surveyor and friend of the blacks, recorded on July 26, 1784: "Great Riot today. The disbanded soldiers have risen against the Free negroes to drive them out of Town, because they labour cheaper than they—the soldiers." Twenty houses in Birchtown were destroyed, Marston fled to Halifax, and Governor Parr had to send the army and navy to restore order. The riot was unique, but the violence, plus the fact that some white Shelburners had tried to engross their land, left the blacks feeling insecure.

Many blacks were driven into indentured servitude to survive. They were often exploited and cheated. Henry McGregor agreed to work for a white man, Alphea Palmer (who became notorious for sharp practice) for £50. McGregor quarrelled with Palmer after eighteen months and was "turned off without pay." Zimrie Armstrong was cheated by his master, Samuel Jarvis, who agreed to buy the freedom of Armstrong's family, still slaves in the United States, but in fact simply re-sold them. Armstrong got no satisfaction from the New Brunswick authorities and, not surprisingly, later welcomed the chance to move to Sierra Leone.

John Clarkson, Thomas Clarkson's younger brother, recorded a sorry story which, he claimed, was but one of many. A young black named Lydia Jackson, deserted by her husband, was induced to become a companion to the wife of Henry Hedley of Manchester, Nova Scotia. The illiterate girl was tricked into signing an indenture she believed to be for one year but was in fact for thirty-nine years! Hedley sold the indenture for £20 to Dr. John D. Bolman, a former Hessian soldier residing in Lunenburg, who treated his servant with inhuman cruelty. When she complained to a lawyer, Bolman threatened to sell her as a slave to the West Indies. Finally, after three years of misery, she escaped and was befriended by Clarkson.

Clarkson sought the release of several indentured children so that they could join their parents going to Sierra Leone, but with little success. He recalled that all his pleas to a Mrs. Hughes to give up the daughter of Caeser Smith fell on deaf ears.

For black children, more common than indentured servitude and its equivalent was apprenticeship, which could also lead to abuse. Clarkson met a black Loyalist who had stolen his apprenticed son from his master, a Shelburne butcher "of a most vile & abandon'd Character," because the butcher was moving to Boston, taking the boy with him. It was bad enough that the boy would be taken away, but it was also suspected that he would be sold as a slave, once in the United States.

Indentured servitude and apprenticeship could be a form of neo-slavery and sometimes led to actual slavery. There was also the danger of being kidnapped to the United States and sold there, or of being claimed in court as a lost slave by a white Loyalist. These fates do not seem to have been common, but were threats that amplified black anxiety.

Conditions deteriorated still more for the blacks in the late 1780s. Shelburne's bubble burst. Everywhere blacks grew more dependent on local and English charity. Indenturing and apprenticeship increased; so did the beggars in Halifax. As in Lower Canada, 1789's severe winter resulted in famine. Boston King, a black preacher, reported that many blacks at Birchtown were forced to sell their clothing and "even their blankets" to get food. Some ate cats and dogs; some starved to death.

Even before the famine, Birchtown was a sad place. Lieut. William Dyott, a British visitor in 1788, found the place "beyond description wretched, situated ... in the middle of barren rocks." The blacks lived precariously in "miserable huts." "I think I never saw wretchedness and poverty so strongly perceptible in the garb and countenance of the human species as in these miserable outcasts."

As a group, the blacks' great weakness was a lack of farming and commercial experience. But their economic record is not one of unrelieved gloom. Many were successful fishermen. Some did well as navigators, pilots, and seamen aboard merchant vessels. Black Pioneers helped clear the land and build Shelburne and Birchtown, while others were engaged on public works at Halifax and Saint John.

Many of the ex-slaves had learned skilled trades on the plantations. They had most commonly been millwrights, blacksmiths, sawyers, caulkers, and coopers, but also boatbuilders, lumbermen, masons, ropemakers, carpenters, and chimney sweeps. Some were able to continue, albeit at unfair wages, in their new homes. At a lowlier level many blacks were domestics, seamstresses, liverymen, cooks, and tavern servants. Some had successful gardens.

The blacks' greatest success was religious organization, by which they developed "as a distinct separate community." Blacks were hungry for the Gospel of the dominant whites and needed institutions in their struggle for survival.

The Church of England remained the official church in Nova Scotia and later New Brunswick, and was strengthened by the arrival of a host of Anglican Loyalists, including many clergymen and the establishment in 1787 of a bishopric. The interest of Bishop Inglis and the church's missionary society, the SPG, resulted in the conversion of many blacks. Anglican blacks were usually segregated.

At St. Paul's in Halifax (where the rector John Breynton wrote in early 1785, the blacks "daily crowd me for Baptism") they were at first confined to a specially built gallery, then when whites elbowed them out they met privately with their own instructors. At Christ Church in Fredericton, in 1794, a special section of the North gallery was reserved for "servants & people of colour," but by 1815 black worshippers were kept behind a partition. At Brindley Town blacks also met separately and between visits from the Anglican priest at Digby were led by one of their own, Joseph Leonard, who by 1791, as Inglis was shocked to find, was virtually acting as a regular priest. Similar situations developed elsewhere. Church policy alone was sufficient to develop in the black community the same kind of Anglican congregationalism that had marked white Anglicanism in the Southern Colonies.

The Methodists, both Huntingdonian and Wesleyan, and the Baptists made many black converts. The Calvinistic Huntingdonians had the advantage that their Nova Scotia missionary, the Reverend John Marrant, was a black Loyalist of a sort, who had been converted in colonial Charleston by George Whitefield and later pressed into the British navy during the Revolutionary War. Marrant's brother, living in Birchtown, persuaded John to come over in 1785 and, assisted by another black Loyalist, William Furmage, he converted over forty Birchtown families and ordained Cato Perkins. Marrant returned to England but Perkins took over as leader of Nova Scotia's black Huntingdonians, most of whom soon migrated to Sierra Leone.

Wesleyan Methodism began with the arrival in 1780 in the Maritimes of the Reverend William Black—a white man. In 1785, to help him cope with the Loyalist hordes, the Baltimore Conference of Wesleyans dispatched the Reverend Freeborn Garrettson, a white American who had been a pacifist during the Revolution. By 1790 more than one-quarter of Nova Scotia's eight hundred Wesleyans were black Loyalists.

As with the Anglicans, though whites initiated action, the blacks developed their own organization and leadership. Blind Moses Wilkinson became pastor at

Birchtown and converted Boston King, who became an outstanding evangelist in Shelburne, Digby, and Halifax, and in 1791 was appointed pastor at Preston by William Black.

The black Loyalist Baptists followed the famous Congregational revivalist Henry Alline's path, but were entirely self-created, mainly by one of the most able black refugees, David George. George, who had been converted while still a slave in Georgia, was a founder in 1773 of the Silver Bluff Baptist Church in South Carolina, the first black congregation in North America. Arriving in Shelburne in 1784 he had immediate success with both races, but during the riot was attacked in his chapel by the angry whites and fled to Birchtown where he continued his ministry. There he encountered further opposition from white and black Anglicans alike, the latter led by Stephen Blucke, a colonel of militia, the area's leading citizen and largest black landowner.

George expanded his mission beyond Nova Scotia to New Brunswick, where he had great success among the blacks of Fredericton and Saint John. George recalled when he landed at the Port City that "some of the people ... were so full of joy they ran out from waiting at table on their masters, with the knives and forks in their hands, to meet me at the water-side." At Preston he converted Hector Peters, a black Loyalist from Charleston, who became an elder and later a gifted evangelist.

Like his flamboyant white predecessor Henry Alline, to whom he was a worthy successor, George was a classic, rousing revivalist, the most influential black preacher, offering a message that went beyond "salvation from sin" to "salvation from white domination." This and his success with a few whites led to white opposition which left him as a strictly black spokesman. In 1792 George became the first Baptist missionary in West Africa.

The blacks must not be portrayed as a band of completely united brothers. Like white Loyalists they were prone to quarrelling. For example, in Shelburne County all four of the political-religious leaders, Blucke, George, King, and Wilkinson, and their followers distrusted each other. Although some of the revivalists preached to slaves and some slave children were admitted to black schools, the black Loyalists seem to have felt themselves superior and generally kept themselves aloof. This was an attitude to be repeated in Sierra Leone.

Apart from those in military units, notably the Black Pioneers, the black Loyalists, hailing from different parts of Africa and America, were rather split originally. Some groups must have formed in New York City in the years before the evacuation, but it was in Nova Scotia as Baptists, Methodists, and Anglicans, "only loosely tied ... to any white hierarchy," as historian Walker states, that they developed a sense of cohesion. Black churches assumed a central role in black life; black preachers became both secular and spiritual leaders. Black Christians, rejected by whites, adopted an elitism, a "tradition of religious anarchy," and added to their burning desire for land their equally burning desire "to practice their own brand of Christianity."

Closely connected with the church was a secondary pillar of the black community, schools. There were five in Nova Scotia, all Anglican in origin, four sponsored by the "Associates of the late Dr. Bray," one by the Society for the Propagation of the Gospel, of which Bray was a founder. Dr. Thomas Bray, an Englishman, had pioneered the education of American slaves and after his death in 1730 the work was continued by his Associates. Naturally the Associates were interested in the black Loyalists. The result was the establishment of schools at Brindley Town, Halifax, Birchtown, and Preston where the school, started by the blacks themselves under Catherine Abernathy, was soon adopted by the Associates. The SPG School, sponsored by Bishop Inglis, was at Little Tracadie. All the school teachers were black Loyalists and all the schools, like the churches, were semi-independent. Occasionally white children attended but generally the schools reinforced black exclusivity.

Black educational efforts in New Brunswick are not as well documented. But in 1790 some black Loyalists, hearing news of Nova Scotia, requested government assistance for a school where their children might be brought "from a state of ignorance and darkness to an enlightened understanding and rectified heart." The government does not seem to have responded but in 1798 Bishop Inglis visited a Bray School for blacks in Fredericton.

The black schools offered only a limited curriculum based on memory drills and practical skills like sewing and "manual industry." Writing and arithmetic were not stressed because, in the official view, they were "unnecessary accomplishments in children who would subsequently be required to perform the meanest tasks." Only a small number of children attended. Black support was so poor that white benefactors complained, accusing the blacks of being "negligent and indifferent." But given the blacks' general illiteracy and slave origin the wonder is that so much educational progress was made. Up to three hundred black children did learn something of the three Rs, and as time passed several black women won the rare chance of a profession as teachers.

A third and final institution important to black society was the family. Unions were frequently common-law; attitudes to sex were casual by white standards. Another difference was that blacks carried from Africa and slave-America the concept of a family that could extend beyond blood relatives and

God's children to "simply people of the same community." Community spirit was vigorous. Groups paid individuals' debts so that all might go to Sierra Leone, where debtors were not accepted. When the inhabitants of Preston petitioned to be settled as a group in Africa, in turn the Birchtowners petitioned to be settled next to the Prestoners "as they and us Are Intimately Acquaint'd."

In judging the history of blacks in Eastern Canada the simplistic transfer of twentieth-century values must be avoided. Their plight must not be viewed in isolation: life was hard for what the eighteenth century called "the lower sort," poor white Loyalists were no strangers to poor land, poor wages, exploitation, official neglect, and even starvation. Indeed, Clarkson noted many disbanded white soldiers shared the blacks' troubles and "with tears in their eyes" begged to go to Sierra Leone. Segregation did not necessarily stem from prejudice. Loyalists of all kinds tended to settle in exclusive groups. In 1791 Bishop Inglis wrote reprovingly that the blacks "seem to want to be entirely independent and separate from whites and to have a church of their own." The blacks' religion set them apart from, and engendered a feeling of superiority to, the whites. Their segregation was often the blacks' choice.

Nevertheless, the whites had reneged on their promises of equal treatment. Blacks were the most disadvantaged group of Loyalists. They lacked land, and their lives veered toward peonage. But they had developed leaders and distinct communities. In 1790 circumstances conspired to give some of them the chance for a fresh start.

This was the year that Thomas Peters, a former North Carolina slave who served throughout the Revolutionary War as a Black Pioneer sergeant, decided that, after six years of frustration in Nova Scotia and New Brunswick, enough was enough. Probably in November, with "much Trouble and Risk," Peters arrived in England bearing a petition from over two hundred black Loyalist families. Some wanted their "due Allotments" in North America, others were "willing to go wherever the Wisdom of Government may think proper."

At this time the Sierra Leone Company (incorporated July 1, 1791) was being formed to take over the moribund colony. The directors included Thomas Clarkson (John's older brother), who a few years earlier had written a prize-winning anti-slavery essay at Cambridge and was destined, before his death in 1842, to become the leading white abolitionist in the world.

It has always been assumed that Peters' connection with the Company was fortuitous. But a recent historian, Ellen Gibson Wilson, marshals strong evidence that the Nova Scotia blacks had heard of the Sierra Leone experiment before 1790. More precisely she quotes an article written by Thomas Clarkson for an

American magazine in 1792. Some white Nova Scotians were overheard discussing Sharp's schemes by a black waiter who "took the opportunity of spreading them among his countrymen. The hope of relief animated them, and they resolved to send over their agent, one Thomas Peters ... and learn if they might go to the new colony...."

The idea of going "back to Africa" dates naturally from the first abducted slaves. For those born in the Western Hemisphere the idea faded but, through folk traditions, never died out entirely and was renewed by fresh captives to the slave market. Among the majority of blacks, it has always been a minority goal. It comes as no surprise that upto half the Nova Scotians who went to Sierra Leone in 1792 were African-born. In fact, "back to Africa" has been mainly a *white* pipe-dream, a hope of losing the "tiger by the tail," espoused by such otherwise intelligent persons as Presidents Jefferson and Lincoln. The first tangible result was the Sierra Leone settlement of 1787 (later the colonization of Liberia in 1822 was a United States' version). The Nova Scotia exodus of 1792 began the most successful of all the back-to-Africa schemes.

In London, Peters' activities induced Secretary of State Henry Dundas to order Governors Parr and Carleton to investigate and right any wrongs: any black not satisfied could go to Sierra Leone or sign up for West Indian army service. Peters recrossed the Atlantic and began recruiting settlers from the Saint John Valley of New Brunswick and from the Digby-Annapolis area of Nova Scotia.

Meanwhile the Company, unwilling to rely on a black man disliked by both Parr and Carleton, needed a white man to take charge. Twenty-seven-year-old John Clarkson, "strengthened in my determination" by Peters' "dismal accounts" of black "sufferings," volunteered, was accepted, and arrived in Halifax on October 7, 1791, a few days after Peters. The meticulous, circumspect yet outspoken John Clarkson had joined the Royal Navy at the age of eleven, risen to lieutenant, but so hated the bloodshed that he resigned his commission, converted to pacifism, and had been working with others to combat the slave trade.

In Halifax Clarkson found that Parr had already published the Sierra Leone proposal and appointed four emigration agents. The agent for Halifax was a New Jersey Loyalist and Halifax merchant named Laurence Hartshorne, who in contrast to the other three enthusiastically helped Clarkson in his mission. To any free black with satisfactory character references as to "Honesty, Sobriety and Industry," Clarkson offered free transportation to Sierra Leone where each adult male would receive twenty acres of land, each wife ten, and each child five. Racial equality and a ban on slavery were also promised. From Halifax Clarkson went to

Preston, then to Birchtown and Shelburne where David George became his "steady friend" and recruiter.

Although Clarkson, appalled by conditions in Nova Scotia, was convinced the blacks would be well advised to leave ("it would be impossible for them to make a change for the worse"), he waged a nominally neutral campaign, partly to avoid alienating white officialdom. He scrupulously outlined the pros and cons of staying in Nova Scotia or enlisting for the West Indies. He warned of the uncertainties of the African venture ("a prospect extremely precarious"), urging careful consideration (especially by those who were tolerably well off) before any decision was made.

The fact that only fourteen blacks were recruited into the army while about 1,190, or one-third of the black Loyalists, departed for Sierra Leone suggested a massive dissatisfaction with life in the Maritimes and at the very least an acceptance of the "precarious" prospect of Africa.

Substantial as the number is, it does not even represent all the blacks who wanted, or might have wanted, to go. A few debtors' obligations were paid by the Company, some were settled by other blacks, but as a group debtors were barred from leaving—a category that included many sharecroppers who had borrowed seeds from their landlords. Indentured servants were stuck unless their indenture-holders agreed to release them. Despite Clarkson's entreaties few did. The fleet that left Halifax in January, 1792, was slated to be the first of several, but the British government, surprised by the number and expense, decreed there would be no more free transportation, thus leaving an unknown number of hopeful emigrants stranded.

No settlers came from such places as Little Tracadie, Manchester, and Chedabucto that were presided over by the uncooperative government agents. Emigrants came from areas personally visited by Clarkson or Peters, where the result was frequently startling. Almost all the free blacks left Preston, probably three-quarters left Brindley Town, 40 per cent left Shelburne-Birchtown, and a majority left New Brunswick. David George led almost the entire congregations of his Birchtown and New Brunswick Baptists to Sierra Leone as did Hector Peters from Preston; Joseph Leonard took the Brindley Town Anglicans en masse; the Wesleyans, the largest black Loyalist sect, were led in great numbers from Shelburne county by Moses Wilkinson, Boston King, and Richard Bell, as were the Huntingdonians, by Cato Perkins and William Ash. Most of the school teachers emigrated: on November 19, 1791, the *Halifax Weekly Chronicle* reported "a very considerable proportion of the Sooty Brotherhood seems determined to emigrate."

The only substantial body of blacks who rejected Sierra Leone by choice were some Birchtowners led by Stephen Blucke, the most successful black Nova Scotian "with the closest ties to the provincial establishment." They were the happiest and most susceptible to white pressures to remain. Although some encouraged the blacks to leave so that "they may purchase their property on the most shameful terms," generally whites opposed emigration. These pressures were strong. Officialdom did not welcome evidence that it had failed to care adequately for the black Loyalists. Apart from Hartshorne, the Nova Scotia agents opposed black emigration. So did the New Brunswick agent, Jonathan Odell, whose conduct Clarkson described as "reprehensible." White society was loathe to lose its source of cheap labour. Opposition was selfish, unscrupulous, and at times vicious. Thomas Peters was physically assaulted in Digby, forcing Clarkson to cancel plans to visit that area for fear of a similar attack. Sierra Leone was denigrated in the press and by word of mouth. For example, the climate was described as deadly, and official advertisements used the word "Guinea" with its slave connotations, instead of Africa. But often to no avail. In Saint John four blacks led by Richard Crankapone, prevented by trumped-up charges of indebtedness from sailing to Halifax to emigrate, intrepidly walked the entire 340 snow-covered miles in fifteen days.

Blacks' motives for emigrating were a combination of complaints about Nova Scotia and hopes for Africa. Their complaints were a summary of their woes in Nova Scotia and New Brunswick. The evils of inequality, neo-slavery (share-cropping and apprenticeship), and fears of actual re-enslavement were mentioned, but the central theme was land. Many had some, but it was poor, insufficient, insecure. "It is ... too late for the greatest part of us to reap any benefit in this country." Clarkson's promise of improvement, the "Governor would see they had their lands," was answered, "Massa Governor no mind King, he no mind You." The emigrants saw in Sierra Leone the promise of not just land, but land in the secure setting of religious and political independence. As with most American immigrants the word was betterment, particularly for the next generation. Clarkson reported that at Birchtown the "greatest part" wanted to go "for the sake of their Children whom they wished to see establish'd (as they express'd it) upon a better and more certain foundation."

Clarkson's diary for November 2, 1791, records an evocative interview with an applicant "originally from the Coast of Africa" who spoke English "indifferently":

> "Well my friend, I suppose you are thoroughly acquainted
> with the nature of the proposals offered to you by His Majesty."

"No, Massa me no hear nor no mind, work like Slave, cannot
do worse Massa in any part of the world, therefore am
determined to go with you Massa if you please."

"You must consider that this is a new settlement & should
you keep your health, must expect to meet with many difficulties
if you engage in it."

"Me well knows that Massa, me can work much, and care not
for climate, if me die me die, had rather die in my own country
than this cold place."

This is a rare black reference to the fearsome Canadian climate, although the
official white explanation for the exodus was that the cold climate completed the
ex-slaves' lack of fitness for pioneer life. The climatic argument is mainly white
myth. Who, apart from modern skiers, relishes a six-month winter? (Conversely,
who enjoys labouring in a humid 85°F? Blacks, no more than whites, do it—if
they have to.)

Halifax was the designated gathering-spot for final departure. Only a couple
of hundred had been expected but almost twelve hundred turned up, mainly in
ships hired by the Company. Clarkson, a most efficient "Saint," coped expertly,
lodging his charges in barracks, supplying food and clothing at a cost of £6,000.
The blacks, organized into companies commanded by their own captains, were
well disciplined, their five-week stay remarkably free of trouble or crime.

This cohesion augured well for their future in Sierra Leone. Unlike the black
poor of 1787, the Nova Scotians of 1792 were mainly families, which were in turn
part of military, religious, and community groups, with effective leadership. One
profile is provided by an analysis of 155 Birchtown emigrants. Nearly all were
married, but children averaged only just over 1.5 per family. Most of the adults
were in their prime—about 72 per cent were aged between 30 and 50; many had
trades—tanners, coopers, sawyers, blacksmiths. Over 43 per cent had military
experience and over 31 per cent owned muskets. Clarkson noted that most
emigrants had "tolerable good musquets" and many were excellent "Sportsmen."
Typically, he added he would purchase ball and powder "unknown to them" and
keep it in reserve for emergencies. Clarkson's high opinions—"the majority ... are
better than any people in the laboring line ... in England"—might be suspect, but
Stephen Skinner, the reluctant Shelburne agent, admitted that at least two-thirds
were "good settlers." Indeed, a white fear was that Sierra Leone would drain off
the best, leaving the idle and crippled.

Clarkson, not surprisingly, loomed large in the hearts of the blacks. As one of them wrote: it was "the handy work of Almighty God that you should be Our leader as Moses and Joshua was bringing the Children of Israel to the promised land." This view was shared by Clarkson himself who did not flinch from the "arduous task" of arranging the evacuation of over a thousand people, some of whose debts, at the last minute, he paid from his own funds.

Ever solicitous, he made sure the emigrants had a decent passage to Africa. For shipping he designated a generous two tons per adult, one and a half tons per child. Slave-traders took five men per ton. There were to be no echoes of the first middle passage (the notorious slave run from Africa to America) in this second one.

That Christmas just before they sailed was special for the emigrants. A petition to Clarkson dated December 23, 1791, requested a day's allowance of "Irish Beef for a Christmas dinner ... as it is the last Christmas day that we ever shall see in the amaraca." On January 15, 1792, the fleet of fifteen vessels sailed, bearing 734 adult blacks and 456 children. By the beginning of March all the ships had reached St. George's Bay. On Sunday March 11, two days after the last transport arrived, David George preached a sermon under a cotton tree. Clarkson wrote: "the delightful manner in which the Nova Scotians sang the appropriate Hymn, The Year of Jubilee is come [Return ye ransomed sinners home], created such sensations as I have not power to describe."

Sixty-five settlers had died during the passage, but some babies had been born, and the eldest emigrant, a woman 104 years old (who may have been Cato Perkins' mother), had survived. Clarkson had acceded to her request to come so "that she might lay her bones in her native country."

The black Loyalists' arrival in 1792 began the Nova Scotian period of Sierra Leone history which lasted until at least 1808. To this day the black Loyalists have been known as the Nova Scotians, though Afro-Americans would be a term of equal or greater accuracy. Unlike any other large group of Loyalists, except the East Floridians, the Nova Scotians were twice moved. Their second chance in Africa proved to be turbulent and relatively successful.

They built Freetown, which became the largest city on the West African coast, and they evolved into the Creoles, a sophisticated elite that remained powerful until independence was attained in 1961.

Most Canadian blacks then and now would probably agree with the black Halifax student who commented of Sierra Leone in 1971: "We all should have gone over there when we had a chance." Today in Freetown there are doctors, lawyers, and teachers who are descendants of the black Loyalists, whereas in New Brunswick and Nova Scotia there are none. Despite all setbacks, the Nova

Scotians in Sierra Leone have retained a strong place among the elite; their brethren in Canada have retained an equally strong place among the lowest classes.

The exodus of 1792 "beheaded" the black community rather like the conquest of Quebec did the French community in 1763. Deprived of so many preachers, teachers, and skilled workers the remaining population, top-heavy with the old, the sick, indentureds, and sharecroppers, did not fare well. Government assurances that adequate land would be allocated were not honoured. The black churches and schools collapsed. Nearly all the black settlements suffered severe losses in population. Preston was completely vacated. Indentured servitude, apprenticeship, and poverty increased.

THE SITUATION in the old Province of Quebec was somewhat different. As there had been no massive evacuation of runaway slaves to Montreal and Quebec, free blacks were the exception. Most blacks in the province were either slaves of Loyalist or non-Loyalist owners, or had been claimed as the spoils of war during forays into the old colonies, and could be bought or sold. On May 13, 1784, an advertisement appeared in the *Quebec Gazette* offering for sale "a likely, healthy negro wench between 15 and 16 years; brought up in the province of New York; understands all sorts of housework and has had small pox."

The King's Royal Regiment acquired some forty or so slaves and Jessup's Rangers about thirty. Loyalist families had slaves attached to their households. John Stuart, the Anglican clergyman at Kingston, had several, as did Joseph Brant, the Indian chief. Some, like Matthew Elliott of the Indian Department, had fifty or more, who constituted part of the workforce on his estate. Altogether there were about three hundred blacks, slaves, and free, on the Niagara Peninsula. Sir John Johnson was not sympathetic to claims of some black slaves for land. He argued that land grants earned by blacks serving as soldiers were valid, but by law such lands belonged to the slaves' owners.

Blacks received more sympathy from John Graves Simcoe, who was determined to put an end to slavery in Upper Canada. On July 9, 1793, he secured the consent of the Upper Canadian Assembly to an act which made buying and selling slaves illegal and declared that children of slaves would be free on reaching their twenty-fifth birthday. Of the sixteen members of this assembly who voted unanimously, six were slave owners, among them Solicitor General Robert Gray, the son of a Loyalist, Maj. James Gray of Cornwall. (Similar measures were defeated, however, in the assemblies of Nova Scotia and Lower Canada.)

Public opinion was hostile to slavery. In England, Chief Justice Mansfield had decided in 1774 that slaves were and always had been free under English law. Slavery remained legal in the colonies, but Mansfield's decision influenced the Canadian judiciary and judges like the Loyalist, Ward Chipman, who deliberately neglected the claims of slave owners. This neglect by degrees phased out slavery, the last vestiges of which had disappeared by 1820. Some land was given to free blacks in Upper Canada, but Simcoe felt that the blacks should be dispersed among the general population and he rejected at least one petition by blacks requesting a land grant designed to set up a black community.

The War of 1812, as far as the black community was concerned, was a continuation of the Revolution. Like other sections of the community, they profited by the need for labour and provided 120 volunteers for the Halifax militia. In Upper Canada, where most of the fighting took place, blacks formed part of the militia and could be found in most volunteer companies. Richard Pierpont, an African-born black who had served with Butler's Rangers, petitioned for the formation of a black company. This company, commanded by a white officer, fought at Queenston Heights and at most of the more important battles in Upper Canada, at times alongside Scots from Glengarry County and the Newfoundland Fencibles.

When the Royal Navy entered Chesapeake Bay, slaves responded to a summons to desert their masters. Some twenty-four hundred or so swam out to British warships and were evacuated to Nova Scotia. In the same war the black Carolina Corps, raised in 1779 as a Loyalist unit, and evacuated to the West Indies with headquarters at Granada, continued on active service and took part in the British attack on New Orleans in 1815.

Many of those evacuated to Halifax were then settled in Preston, once the home of black Loyalists who had since emigrated to Africa. Another 520 were sent to New Brunswick. These refugees were not at first accepted as equals by the old black Loyalists, but by degrees merged with them in the face of poverty and racial prejudice. Interest in their Loyalist past was overshadowed by the influence of religious revival, inspired by the black American Richard Preston. Blacks received the vote in Nova Scotia in 1837 and the right to serve on juries in 1839 but these rights were not extended to blacks in New Brunswick until 1840. Efforts to promote a second black exodus in 1820, this time to Trinidad, met with little response. The Loyalist migrations brought a black population to the Maritimes which, if it has not prospered, has at least endured.

Conditions were slightly better in Upper Canada, which was to become the terminus of an underground railway, guiding runaway slaves to freedom in the decades before the Civil War. Although William Lyon Mackenzie was opposed to the institution of slavery, blacks feared that his rebellion would lead to annexation to the United States. Nearly one thousand blacks turned out to serve in the Loyalist Militia in 1837. The lieutenant-governor, Sir Francis Bond Head, noted that wagons loaded with blacks turned out at their own expense "to beg in the name of their race, that I would allow them the honour" of sharing in the anticipated attack on Navy Island, where Mackenzie's followers had formed a Canadian provisional government. Blacks did, in fact, take part in the burning of the *Caroline* which was bringing supplies to Mackenzie at Navy Island. Line companies of blacks were also raised in the western part of the province to guard the frontier against the raids of the "Hunters' Lodges" which posed a threat until 1839.

Canadian blacks, like blacks throughout the continent, had to face prejudice which could not be abolished by the mere removal of legal disabilities. Yet black Loyalists helped to make Canada possible and, by their opposition to the Revolution, they helped to create a refuge for future generations of runaway slaves. The movement which began with the flight of blacks behind the British lines during the Revolution continued until the American Civil War.

# 9 | THE LOYALIST INDIANS

## SHAGANOSH

*"Use those Indians in easy manner about land matters at this present unhappy times for us..., it gives the dam Rebels larger mouths against us."*

*Capt. Joseph Brant to Sir John Johnson*
*May, 1784*

THE INDIANS, if not refugees in a political sense, were the first displaced persons in America. For them, the American Revolution was another episode in the inter-European struggle, and the enemy was always the power most likely to push the pioneer settlements westward. The French, because they had been less anxious to develop the interior of the continent, had been more attractive to the Indians than the English, and for the same reasons the British and Loyalists were more attractive than the Continental Congress. Yet these considerations were tempered by two others: first, there was a price to pay for supporting the losers, and no point in paying it if the losers were to withdraw from the continent; second, Indian tribes were opposed to one another and, in choosing European allies, the Indians had to consider the effect of their choices on the tribal balance of power. They could not afford to strengthen their hereditary enemies.

In any conflict between the colonist and imperial powers, the latter would be more attractive to the Indians if only because it was the colonists who were most concerned with expanding their territory. This was certainly the case in the era of the Revolution. One of the grievances of the colonists was that the imperial government was using its power to put a brake on western expansion.

Apart from this, there was a less tangible consideration. The institution of monarchy was more comprehensible to the Indian than the egalitarian ideas of the Declaration of Independence. There was among the Indians a sense of dignity which respected the red-coated regulars more than the ragged militia, and preferred ritual and ceremony to the easygoing familiarity which was common among the Continental forces.

At the close of the war, most western Indians had to face the consequences of having opposed the winners—they would have to move. And if the Indians suffered the disadvantage of being associated with the losers, there were certain consolations. In a divided continent, the Indians might still hope to find European allies, as the losers were still present in sufficient force to be formidable.

The Indians thought of themselves as an independent people who made treaties with European powers in accordance with their own interests. They would recognize the claims of the king as an ally, but did not consider themselves his subjects. For the Micmacs in Nova Scotia and the Mississaugas north of the Great Lakes, their interests and obligations were clear: power was in the hands of the Crown forces; they would support the king, their ally. The Malecites, who occupied the upper regions of what became New Brunswick, felt no strong obligations to support the Crown and were impressed by the apparent strength of the New Englanders, who sought to invade Nova Scotia. They indulged in the luxury of supporting the losing side, but suffered no severe consequences, because the Loyalists who settled in post-revolutionary New Brunswick had no immediate designs on Malecite lands and were content to offer conciliation.

The western Indians were less fortunate because their hunting grounds stood in the way of the advancing line of settlements. Those in the Middle West would remain beyond the reach of the American government for a decade after the Revolution. But the Iroquois, a federation of Six Nations whose lands straddled the Mohawk Valley, had no such respite. Had there been no revolution, they would have undoubtedly been pushed anyway by the land-hungry pioneers.

On the eve of the Revolution most of the influence in the Mohawk Valley was in the hands of Sir William Johnson, the enterprising Irish immigrant whose combination of ability and family connections secured for him the important post of Superintendent of Northern Indians. Johnson linked his control of Indian affairs with the management of a great commercial empire based on trade with the interior and an enormous landed estate.

During the later years of his life, Sir William Johnson's household had been managed by Molly Brant, the daughter of an Iroquois warrior of the Mohawk tribe, who bore him eight children. As she had carried cakes of sagamite in her hand on entering Sir William's house as proof of her ability to cook, she was, according to Mohawk tradition, his wife. She presided over an establishment that included black slaves and, during the frequent visits of Indian chiefs and officials to the Johnson estate, she acted as hostess. Her brother Joseph Brant became a protégé of Sir William, who sent him to More's Indian Charity School, an institution run by the dissenting minister Eleazar Wheelock, at Lebanon (now Columbia), Connecticut.

Wheelock, who became president of Dartmouth College (where Brant later sent his two sons) was the principal link between Continental Congress and the

Indians. Brant was impressed by Wheelock, but on returning to the Mohawk Valley, he came under the influence of the Anglican missionary John Stuart, later chaplain of the King's Royal Regiment of New York and rector of Kingston in Upper Canada. As an officer of the Crown, Johnson was committed to loyalism. Brant, as his protégé and an Anglican, shared his commitment.

The sudden death of Johnson in 1774 during a great Indian council understandably left a gap in the leadership of the Loyalists in the Mohawk region. His estates passed to his son, Sir John Johnson. His office as Indian Superintendent went to his son-in-law, Col. Guy Johnson. Col. John Butler, head of a family second only to the Johnsons in influence, became Guy Johnson's deputy. Guy Johnson was also served by Col. Daniel Claus, a master of several Indian languages, who was made deputy Indian agent with jurisdiction over the Canadian Indians.

Shortly after the outbreak of hostilities, both sides appealed for Indian support. The Crown continued to work through its established Indian agents, but Congress needed to create Northern, Middle, and Southern Departments to handle Indian affairs. As there was little hope of winning over the Iroquois, Congress sent messages to them to try to secure at least their neutrality. Several hundred tribesmen from the Oneidas, one of the Six Nations where the influence of Wheelock, Samuel Kirkland, and other dissenting ministers was strong, negotiated with Congress for several weeks, but most of the Iroquois Federation remained under the influence of the Johnsons, partly due to the efforts of Joseph Brant and the Reverend John Stuart.

In their character as an independent people, the Indians exercised their right to decide policy, but to most of them the facts were plain. With the outbreak of the Revolution, there were really two wars in progress: the Revolution itself and the permanent war between Indians and the settlers intruding on their hunting grounds. In the South, tribes like the Creeks and Cherokees, who were resisting the advance of settlers across the mountains, kept in contact with British agents. They sought help from the Spanish as well. None came to Canada in 1783, but a small colony of Creeks founded a settlement on the outskirts of Nassau in the Bahamas. It is only the Iroquois who can be properly considered Loyalists, as they opposed the Revolution from the beginning and were resettled in Canada along with the other Loyalists.

When the Johnsons and Brant commenced their efforts to secure Iroquois support for the Crown, the Johnson estate was turned into an armed camp, patrolled by recently arrived Scots Highlanders. It was evident that supporters of

Congress in Tryon County, which covered most of Western New York, would make some move against the Johnsons. In anticipation of such a move, Guy Johnson gathered a party of 120 Iroquois chiefs and warriors together with Brant, Butler, and Claus, and set out for Oswego. There, at a council of Indian chiefs, Brant was elected war chief of the Iroquois and the party proceeded to Montreal to consult with the Canadian Iroquois.

Carleton had a host of problems. He had appointed Maj. John Campbell as Superintendent of the Indians in Quebec. The presence, then, of Johnson and particularly of Colonel Claus, who also had jurisdiction over the Indians in Quebec, was embarrassing. Moreover, Carleton was preoccupied by the war with Continental Congress. He was not prepared to alienate public opinion in the colonies by turning the Indians loose on the frontier settlements which included both patriots and neutrals, the latter potential Loyalists.

Matters were further complicated by the presence, among the Canadian Indians, of Louis Le Nègre, an agent of Continental Congress. Le Nègre was a part-black Indian who was received cordially by George Washington and returned to Canada with flattering messages to the Indians from American generals. Yet another worrying factor was the influence of Jesuit priest Father Pierre-René Floquet, who recommended caution to the Indians and encouraged them to adopt an attitude of neutrality. His influence was formidable among the Caughnawagas, a branch of the Iroquois who had settled near Montreal when Canada was still New France and had come under Catholic influence.

Upon their arrival in Montreal, the Loyalist Iroquois met with the Canadian Iroquois, the Caughnawagas, at their settlement, Sault Saint Louis. Here the question of neutrality was heatedly debated. The eloquence of Colonel Claus prevailed as he reminded the Indians of past injuries received at the hands of the Southern colonists. Before Claus' harangue was over, the Indians were "determined of attacking and laying waste the New England Frontiers." However, Claus urged them first to attend an Indian congress at Lachine near Montreal to declare their sentiments personally to the governor, Sir Guy Carleton. Here some six hundred Loyalist and Canadian Indians continued the debate on neutrality for four long days from July 26 to 29, 1775, finally confirming their decision to take up the hatchet against the Bostonians.

To their dismay, Carleton forbade them to take any action without his express permission. On scouting patrols, the Indians were to fire only in retaliation. Johnson and Claus were dumbfounded. They did their best to convince Carleton that the Indians must be given some leeway, but the governor refused to unleash the Indians on the frontiers. The congress broke up with irritation on all sides.

Whatever enthusiasm had been aroused by Johnson, Brant, Claus, and Butler was thus dissipated. The American Loyalist Indians moved on to Niagara or drifted back to the Mohawk Valley, while most Caughnawagas returned to Sault Saint Louis. In November Butler departed for Niagara to establish a base there for Loyalists and Indians. After a summer of inactivity, Brant and Guy Johnson left for England.

During August, 1775, a small party of Caughnawagas under the Chevalier de Lorimier patrolled the frontier areas, as rumours circulated that Continental agents, including Montreal merchants, were active among the Indians. A mixed force of Caughnawagas and Mohawks assisted in the defence of Fort St. Jean when it was besieged by Continental forces that September. One hundred Indians actually drove back an early attempt of the invaders to land near the fort. As Indians were able to pass with relative ease between the lines, they were used as reinforcements during the early stages of the siege, but deserted when the fall of the fort seemed inevitable. When the fort fell on 2 November only two Indians remained. Along with the rest of the garrison, they were imprisoned and taken captive to the Southern Colonies.

During the occupation of Montreal, western forts were still held by British forces and the western Indians supported the Crown. When the fortunes of war turned against the invading Continental forces in the spring of 1776, the St. Regis Indians on the Upper St. Lawrence joined with French Canadians in harassing the American invaders on their western flank. In June just before the Continentals' withdrawal from Montreal, Sir John Johnson arrived from the Mohawk Valley with a party of Indians and 170 tenants. This group joined local Indians and French Canadians to form a party of about five hundred who arrived in Montreal on the heels of the retreating invaders, and a few hours before the regulars arrived. It was thus a party of Indian, French Canadian, and American Loyalists who liberated the city.

After the collapse of the invasion of Canada, two events shaped the fortunes of the Iroquois. Col. John Butler was building up a base in Niagara which served as a refuge for Loyalist and Iroquois refugees and a springboard for forays against the frontier settlements. At the same time Joseph Brant and Guy Johnson were in London, where Brant enjoyed a considerable social success. He was interviewed by James Boswell, painted by George Romney, invited to dinners and balls, and even presented to the king. On the political side, he visited Lord George Germain and agreed to secure the support of the Six Nations for Burgoyne's projected thrust into New York from Canada. Brant was given a gold watch by the king and a silver gorget (neck armour) denoting his rank of captain.

Brant returned by way of New York, arriving at the time of the British occupation, making his way secretly to the Mohawk Valley. Here he found the Iroquois in a state of armed neutrality, but prepared to attend a council called by John Butler at Oswego. Of the eight hundred who attended, some four hundred were prepared to follow Brant. These included the Mohawks, Senecas, Cayugas, and many Onondagas. The Oneidas remained neutral and under their influence, so did the Tuscaroras. Thus the Iroquois Confederation, founded three hundred years before by the legendary Hiawatha, was at an end.

In spite of this, Brant secured arms and supplies from the base at Niagara and prepared a war party, which united with a contingent of Butler's Loyalists and those organized by Sir John Johnson at Lachine. This force was placed under the command of Lieut.-Col. Barry St. Leger and was assigned the task of taking Fort Stanwix (Rome, New York) and moving down the Mohawk Valley to support Burgoyne's descent on Albany. Meanwhile, about four hundred Indians accompanied Burgoyne, as did Maj. John Campbell and most members of the Quebec Indian Department.

The double defeat—that of St. Leger's force at Oriskany near Fort Stanwix, and the surrender of Burgoyne at Saratoga—that resulted, left the Mohawk Indians open to reprisals by the Continentals. These were not long in coming and by May, 1778, 2,700 Iroquois had taken refuge at Niagara, where most of them had to be fed at government expense, supplies being sought as far afield as Detroit.

The force of Loyalists and Indians under control of Butler and Brant needed to be used effectively in the war. It was clear that their most powerful and perhaps only role could be harassment of frontier settlements thus threatening the food supplies of the Continental forces and drawing off troops from the main centres of warfare. In the course of 1788 they made raids into the Delaware Valley, a descent on Wyoming in Western Pennsylvania, the raid on the village of Cherry Valley, and even a raid against the neutral Oneidas.

Guy Johnson and Brant had favoured attacks on frontier settlements at the outset of the war, but Carleton understood that the political consequences would be serious. As military operations, the raids had a large measure of success and, had it not been for French and Spanish intervention, they might have helped bring the war to a successful conclusion. As it was, they left behind bitter memories, which folklore has blown into a black legend. Similar atrocities were committed by the Continentals—but the winners wrote most of the history.

Retribution came to the Indians when Congress sent Gen. John Sullivan into the land of the Senecas to burn their villages and destroy their stores of grain, and the state of Virginia sent George Rogers Clark into the Northwest. When the balance of atrocities is measured, it is worth mentioning that Clark induced a British garrison to surrender by having four bound Indians tomahawked in view of the fort.

Under the terms of the Treaty of 1783, the territory south of the Great Lakes was unceremoniously assigned to the Republic, although most of it was still in the possession of Indian tribes friendly to the Crown. Matters were further complicated by the fact that the key points south of the Lakes, including Detroit, remained in British hands until the Jay Treaty of 1794: In order to bargain effectively with the United States government, Joseph Brant sought to create an Indian Federation among those living on lands assigned to the Republic. At the close of the Revolution, Brant, hopelessly as it turned out, still saw the Indians as an independent people who could decide major questions of policy for themselves. He did not realize they had now become merely subjects of the government which claimed jurisdiction over the territory on which they resided.

Brant's immediate task was to secure resettlement of Loyalist Indians, who were granted government supplies similar to those awarded the whites. Those already on Canadian territory were the considerable contingent at Niagara, with whom Brant was in direct contact, and a smaller group who had taken refuge under the leadership of Chiefs John Deseronto, Isaac Hill, and Aaron Hill. A Mohawk village of 125 Indians, of whom 40 were warriors, had grown up near Lachine. In accordance with his policy of moving Loyalists away from French Canada, and possibly to separate them from the Caughnawagas (who had an indifferent record for loyalty), Haldimand ordered this group to move west. Land was not a problem as Brant had secured land for resettlement of Loyalist Indians as early as 1779, in the Bay of Quinte area.

Like other Loyalists, the Indians at Lachine did not have much enthusiasm for the move to the West, but Haldimand was firm. As one chief put it, "You tell us to go with the earliest opening of the river, and not to leave a soul behind. This is our intention as soon as the ice is broken." This group arrived at the Bay of Quinte on 22 May, 1784, and survives today as the Tyendinaga Reserve, covering some twenty-seven square miles between the city of Belleville and the village of Deseronto. They have enjoyed a relatively quiet existence, separate from the mainstream of Indian history.

It was the original intention of Brant to move all of the Iroquois into the Bay of Quinte region, but he had to consider the plight of Indians on both sides of the frontier. The Oneidas and Tuscaroras who had supported the Revolution would be permitted to remain on their lands. The Senecas who, after Sullivan's depradations, had rebuilt some of their villages, decided to remain within the

American frontier. They persuaded Brant that a move to the Bay of Quinte would mean permanent separation and for the sake of keeping the tribes closer together, he received a second grant along the Grand River.

This move west was part of Brant's scheme for an Indian Federation, and required the Crown to purchase land from the indigenous Mississaugas. Brant also asked for a grant of £16,000 to cover the cost of resettlement and £1,500 to deal with immediate needs. The land was purchased from the Mississaugas on 25 October, 1784, but the money was not immediately forthcoming. Under the agreement, 67,000 acres were placed in the hands of the Iroquois "to them and their heirs forever." This land was held free of taxes and other obligations, but it could not be sold by the Indians.

Settlement began in the spring of 1785; over a thousand Indians came in the first influx and over eighteen hundred were in the settlement by the end of the year. Brant journeyed again to England to secure further concessions. He was particularly interested in attaching Indians to the Anglican church, and supervised a translation of the Prayer Book into the Mohawk language, translating the Gospel of St. Mark himself. A church completed in 1786 at Brantford was given the royal coat of arms. Four pieces of plate given to the church in the Mohawk Valley by Queen Anne in 1712 were brought to the Brantford church in 1788. According to folklore the silver plate was buried near Fort Hunter when Deseronto fled in 1775 and was retrieved at the end of the war. When the Indians reached the Bay of Quinte a service was conducted, with the plate, using an upturned canoe as the altar.

The Grand River settlement flourished after a fashion and attracted to it "late Loyalist" Indians who faced the pressure of the advancing pioneer frontier in the United States. There were, nevertheless, serious difficulties for the new settlements. Game was not abundant in the new hunting grounds and Indian agriculture was too primitive to secure more than a marginal existence. Brant's solution was to sell land to white settlers, hoping that saw and grist mills which they could construct would prove a stimulus to the Indian economy, and the money received would then supply capital for further development.

Toward this end, he secured the support of the Grand River chiefs in 1786 for the transfer of land to ten white Loyalist settlers. In this Brant exceeded his power, and Deseronto at the Bay of Quinte protested the transaction to Sir John Johnson who had been made Superintendent of Indians in 1782. Johnson then declared that the terms of the Royal Proclamation of 1763 had forbidden the sale of lands reserved for the use of the Indians. Nothing was done to expel the white settlers, but they could not secure a clear title to their lands until after the War of 1812.

As the prohibition against the sale of Indian lands was designed to protect Indians against land speculators, those sympathetic to Indian interests hesitated to accept Brant's point of view. When the province of Upper Canada was organized he quarrelled with Simcoe over the question, threatened to move his people to the United States, and opened a correspondence with the Superintendent of Indian Affairs in New York State. Simcoe, in turn, threatened to limit Indian settlement to one side of the Grand River but nothing happened as neither party was in earnest. Brant was able to win over Simcoe's successor, Peter Russell, and as a result of this more land was transferred to white settlers. Yet Russell had exceeded his powers and was overruled by the home secretary in London, who was then in charge of colonial affairs. The only result of Russell's efforts to help Brant was to increase the number of whites who were tolerated as squatters on Indian lands. Brant was still attempting to secure the right to sell Indian lands at the time of his death in 1807.

His tribe's loyalty and his own had been disastrous. Many Indians had died during the war. Many more perished in the epidemics that swept the Niagara refugee camps. The Confederation was split, its autonomy fatally compromised. However, the fate of the Loyalist Indians merely anticipated the fate of all tribes west of the Appalachians. If the Loyalist Indians suffered before the rest, their suffering was mitigated by the sanctuary and subsidies provided by the Crown. In the long run, they fared better than most American Indians.

MEANWHILE, THE Indians in the American Midwest had been resisting growing settlement. In 1793 a group of Delawares, under the influence of the Moravian missions, sought to avoid this conflict by resettlement in the Grand River area. The battle of Fallen Timbers in August, 1794, ended resistance in the Ohio territory, but the Indians further west found new leaders in Tecumseh and his brother, the Prophet. They, in turn, suffered defeat at the battle of Tippecanoe in 1811, which might have been final had it not been for the outbreak of war the following year.

For Tecumseh, the War of 1812 presented an opportunity of salvaging the fortunes of the American Indians in the Midwest, but the Canadian Iroquois were primarily concerned with their own security. Like most Loyalists and other immigrants in Upper Canada, they had kinsmen on the American side of the frontier. The Seneca chief, Red Jacket, persuaded the Iroquois on American territory to remain neutral and informed the Grand River Indians of their intention. The desired effect, however, was offset by the seizure of Michilimackinac by the western Indians and the spectacular capture of Detroit by Sir Isaac Brock, with the aid of 600 of Tecumseh's Indians. As Tecumseh was given the rank of brigadier in the British army, it seemed, in the summer of 1812, that the war was being fought in Indian interests and that the Americans were likely to be the losers.

At Queenston Heights, Joseph Brant's son, John Brant, saw action in the service of the Crown. The Grand River Indians were clearly committed and served in most of the significant actions throughout the war. The defeat and death of Tecumseh, on 5 October, 1813, was a serious blow to the Anglo-Canadian war effort, but the West was not a decisive theatre of war. In the last year of the war, American Indians crossed the frontier in support of United States forces and in the battles of Chippewa and Lundy's Lane, Iroquois fought Iroquois.

This did not alter the fact that Indians had been indispensable to the defence of Canada during the war. Tecumseh's warriors had turned the tide in favour of the British at the outbreak of the war and the neutrality of the American Iroquois, while it lasted, had been very useful. Indian support understandably had its price. Both sides paid five dollars for live prisoners. The British government paid $100 to a chief who had lost an eye or a limb, and $70 to a warrior. Widows of chiefs received an annuity of $200, and widows of warriors $110. Tribes engaged in military operations had to be fed at government expense, as they had little time for hunting and agriculture.

After the war, responsibility for Indian Affairs, formerly exercised by the lieutenant-governor of Upper Canada, was given to the commander of the forces. The Indians remained on the military budget until 1832, after which they were supported by an imperial grant until placed on the Canadian budget in 1860. After 1844, the civil secretary of the governor of the United Provinces of Upper and Lower Canada managed Indian affairs.

The principal item on his budget was the annual cost of presents to the Indians, such useful items as hatchets, kettles, fish hooks, and tomahawks. These were given not only to Indians resident in Canada, but to those tribes living in the United States who had supported the British war effort. This latter practice was discontinued in 1841, cutting the cost by a third and encouraging a modest influx of American Indians into Canada in order to qualify for the gifts. Annual presents came to an end when the Canadian government took over in 1860.

John Brant, who had served in 1812, was elected to the Upper Canada Assembly in 1830, but was not allowed to take his seat on the grounds that most of those who voted for him did not have property qualifications, as Indian ownership of land was not freehold. Indians were finally enfranchised in 1857, but by this time it was a question of the status of all Indians, rather than Loyalist Indians.

The Loyalist tradition nevertheless remains part of the life of Indians along the Grand River and in the Bay of Quinte. And although the direct line of the Brants died out, one descendant of Molly Brant enjoys a conspicuous place in Canadian cultural history. The daughter of Chief G.H.G. Johnson, a grandson of Sir William Johnson and Molly Brant, was Pauline Johnson, the poet.

By all the tests that matter, the Iroquois who came to Canada were Loyalist. They fought for the Crown and fought well. After the war they were resettled on British territory and, like the Loyalist blacks, served again in 1812. They differed from other Loyalists in claiming that they were allies, and not subjects, of the Crown.

In 1876 the remarks of Sitting Bull to Inspector J.M. Walsh, when the Sioux chief brought his people to Canada after the defeat of Custer at Little Big Horn, suggest that the Sioux considered that they had always had a Loyalist option. Sitting Bull told Walsh that they were originally Shaganosh (British) and that during the War of 1812 they had been told by a representative of their Shaganosh father (George III) that they could move into British territory if they found things difficult in the United States.

# THE LOYALISTS IN HISTORY

## EPILOGUE

Spem Reduxit: *"Hope Restored"*

*New Brunswick motto*

Ut Incepit Fidelis Sic Permanet: *"As She Began, So She Remains, Loyal"*

*Ontario motto*

THE LEGACY of the Loyalists is rich even today. They cannot be dismissed as mere losers. Their migration to Canada made possible the founding of a second state in North America. French Canadian culture survived because of Great Britain's commitment to the Loyalists, which prevented the capture of British North America in the nineteenth century by the forces of United States expansionism. Within the Republic, the French would have been absorbed in the "melting pot."

Loyalists were the victims of an angry mood in colonial American society, a mood preserved in the patriotic mythology of the United States which presents the British, the institution of monarchy, and George III, in particular, as the enemies of liberty. Like their enemies, the Loyalists had their fits of anger, but since they preserved an existing system of government which was shared by others, their grievances were never knit into an authorized civic religion. The "Loyalist myth," woven by the more conservative Loyalists, was only the property of those Loyalists who cared to claim it. It had some basis in fact, but the impression it left was misleading. Very few Loyalists were genteel Anglican Tories drawn from the privileged elite. Yet the prevalence of this myth has shaped the thinking of Canadians about the Loyalists.

Canadians have never been able to accept the Loyalists as founding fathers in the way Americans have championed the revolutionary leaders. The Whig-democratic tradition in Canada, which takes an American view of the Revolution, deemed the Loyalists somewhat "un-Canadian." One of Canada's best-known syndicated columnists, Charles Lynch, recently called the Loyalists "Canada's first welfare recipients" and dismissed them as rich "failed counter-revolutionaries." Their aristocratic, Anglican proclivities, real and imagined, have rubbed against the Canadian grain and indeed were opposed at the time by many rank and file Loyalists. Later immigrants—the Irish, the British poor, the Ukrainians, the Italians, and the original French—have not found the Loyalist tradition congenial.

The real Loyalists cannot be ignored as mere losers, neither can they be dismissed as reactionaries, subservient to authority and uncomfortable in a free society. (The Revolution freed not only the Americans but also the Canadians who proved that "subjects" could be just as happy as "citizens.") Most Loyalist intellectuals, including the more conservative, suffered because they tried to use their constitutional right to free speech. This reality is illustrated by two quotations. In the 1830s, Sam Slick, the famous character created by Thomas C. Haliburton, grandson of a Loyalist, proclaimed, "There is no tyranny on airth equal to the tyranny of the majority." Decades earlier, in 1771, the Reverend Mather Byles watched the funeral of the victims of the Boston "massacre" and observed: "They call me a brainless Tory; but tell me ... which is better—to be ruled by one tyrant three thousand miles away or by 3,000 tyrants one mile away."

The Loyalists previously engaged in public life took an active part in politics after 1783, but not primarily as Conservatives. They reflected all shades of political opinion. Some second-generation Loyalists, like the Nelson brothers of Lower Canada who were distant relatives of Admiral Nelson, and Samuel Edison of Upper Canada, grandfather of the inventor Thomas Edison, supported the rebels of 1837. The presence of the Ryersons and Buells among the popular reformers of this period, along with New Brunswick's Lemuel Allen Wilmot, grandson of a Poughkeepsie Loyalist, and Nova Scotia's Joseph Howe, son of a Massachusetts Loyalist, indicated that Loyalists made a contribution to all political movements. But their contribution to conservatism has received the most attention because it is so easily visible.

Loyalists like John Beverley Robinson and Allan MacNab were among the founders of those early Tory groups known as the Family Compact. This small body of officeholders holds its place among the founders of the present-day Progressive Conservative Party. The fact that this party is called and, on the whole, accepts the name of "tory" is an aspect of the continuing influence of the conservative Loyalists.

The Loyalists' respect for the conventions and procedures of the British parliamentary tradition permeated all parties. The degree to which Canadians were insulated from the ideas of the American Revolution is shown by Louis-Joseph Papineau's speech at the time of the death of George III in 1820. Papineau described George III as "a Sovereign respected for his moral qualities and his devotion to duty."

Republican sentiments have arisen among Canadians. These affected French Canadians in 1837 and induced English Montreal merchants in 1849 to demand annexation to the United States. But these impulses have been temporary. In Canadian politics, although not essential, it was always an advantage to have Loyalist credentials, much like being of Mayflower stock in the United States. Groups like the followers of William Lyon Mackenzie and the Clear Grits of the 1850s, who repudiated the Loyalist tradition, never secured more than a temporary or local influence.

In reprisal, Canadians could be harsh, but they were not unforgiving. After the rebellions of 1837, both William Lyon Mackenzie and Louis-Joseph Papineau resumed their seats in the provincial Parliament without relinquishing their points of view. The Americans offered no such option to the Loyalists or, for that matter, to the Confederate leaders after the American Civil War. The acceptance of former rebels was a measure of the milder tone of Canadian politics, a bequest from the Loyalists. Extremists and even fanatics had no trouble gaining a hearing in Canada, but few were awarded a following. Isolationism, nativism, the immoderate fear of conspiracy, so common in the United States, can be found in Canadian politics, but they tend to evaporate. Movements like the Anti-Masonic Party in the 1820s and the Know-Nothings, which flourished in the Republic, never gained a footing in Canadian society.

Canada's relatively peaceful western expansion and the absence of lynching must owe something to the Loyalists who were among the early victims of "Lynch Law." It is even argued that because of the Loyalists several Canadian provinces have elected socialist governments (admittedly very mild) during the last few decades. Those who believed men "free and equal" expected them to be self-sufficient; hence the suspicion of state-enterprise and welfarism in the United States. It is argued that the Canadians, free from such suspicions, have accepted medicare and a public broadcasting system, the CBC. This favourable disposition towards the role of the state in society had its critics. A Scottish professor at the University of New Brunswick, John Davidson, writing in 1904, found the Loyalist tradition baleful. He quoted a local: "In this country men think five dollars of government money is worth ten dollars from anybody else."

In such intangible ways the Loyalist tradition has exercised a profound political influence. Canadians thus have a distinct political tradition. It is less evident that they have a distinct culture.

The cultural impact of the Revolution on the continent may well be overestimated. Canadian patriotism grew up around loyalty to the Crown, not around a revolutionary tradition. But in other respects, Canadians and Americans share a common American culture which includes baseball, Thanksgiving Day, and apple pie. The prize-winning entry of Nova Scotia in the 1974 Rose Bowl Parade was a float representing the unity of the Canadian and American peoples.

American families who moved into Canada long after the Revolution, families like the Masseys, the Shaughnessys, and the Van Hornes, had no difficulty adjusting to British-style democracy. Royal visits are popular in the United States where English ancestry is prized and English-style boarding schools flourish. Outside of Newfoundland and Quebec, the public school system in Canada is much the same as that in the United States. But while the North American spirit of conformity is strong in Canada, it is not reinforced by a revolutionary tradition. This has worked in favour of the survival of French culture in Quebec and has made it easier for Catholics outside Quebec to establish separate schools.

As we have seen, the Loyalists in New Brunswick were eventually swamped and assimilated by British immigrants who arrived after 1815. The post-Loyalists who came into Upper Canada had a similar effect in that province. In 1900 it was estimated that one-seventh of the Canadian population was of Loyalist descent. Today the most generous estimate is no higher than a tenth.

Whatever the percentage of Loyalist ancestry among the present Canadian population, the role of descendants of Loyalists in Canadian society is self-evident. A precise tally made in 1900 included such cultural figures as Charles G.D. Roberts, Bliss Carman, and W.F. Ganong, as well as sixteen lieutenant-governors, eighteen chief justices, three provincial premiers since 1867 and fifteen ministers of the Dominion. A more recent list includes Norman Bethune, T.S. Woodsworth, and Pierre Elliott Trudeau.

Apart from biological happenstance, can these and other worthies be linked to anything specifically Loyalist? Only if they chanced to be adherents of a Loyalist outlook which, of course, needs no genetic restrictions. Most Loyalist children shared this outlook, as did some non-Loyalist contemporaries like John Strachan who, within a few years of his arrival in Upper Canada, was converted from the pro-American views he had brought with him from Scotland. But how real is the Loyalist philosophy today in Canada? To distinguished Canadian historian Professor James Talman, it is "intangible and hard to measure."

Loyalist history lends colour to contemporary Canadian life. Genealogy has become a North American pastime and Loyalist ancestors, when they can be found, are usually welcomed to the family tree. The United Empire Loyalists Association is today a growing organization of some two thousand Canadians who boast Loyalist ancestors. Moreover, local history societies and the tourist trade help to keep the Loyalist sentiment alive. On both sides of the American frontier, bicentennial celebrations of the Revolution have led to a proliferation of military societies which have painstakingly reproduced the uniform and drill of Loyalist regiments. And local Loyalist tradition enhanced the visit of Prince Charles and Lady Diana to the Maritimes during the 1983 bicentennial Loyalist celebrations.

American tourists' fascination for these rites of celebration should raise doubts about the necessity of a total separation between Britain and the colonies. Separation kept Americans out of Britain's wars, but created political tensions on the American continent; for instance, the Jefferson Embargo and the War of 1812. It is clear from the rise of the Dominions that any imperial connection which the Americans maintained with Britain would have been an association of equals. Such a partnership in 1914 or 1939 might have preserved world peace. The Loyalists' cry "Unity of Empire" was not ignoble.

It may be true that there is a certain Canadian dourness resulting from three losing traditions: the French, the Gaelic-speaking Scots, and the Loyalists. Yet legend tells us that Rome was founded by Aeneas, the loser in the Trojan war. Loyalists were losers who refused to drop out of history. As Canadian poet William Kirby put it:

> Not drooping like poor fugitives they came
> In exodus to our Canadian wilds,
> But full of heart and hope, with heads erect
> And fearless eyes, victorious in defeat.

# bibliography

WITHOUT CONSULTING original sources, it is still difficult to write about the Canadian aspects of the United Empire Loyalists. Nearly all government and most private papers covering the years from 1776 to 1800 have some bearing on the subject. These can be found in the Public Archives of Canada (PAC) or the Provincial Archives of Ontario and the Maritime provinces; the more useful ones are listed in the bibliography under *Unpublished Manuscript Material.*

Two sources deserve special mention: the Haldimand Papers at PAC and the Winslow Papers at the University of New Brunswick. Gov. Frederick Haldimand was responsible for the reception and resettlement of Loyalist refugees in the old province of Quebec. Edward Winslow was a Loyalist member of the council in New Brunswick during the formative years of the province. There is a wealth of secondary sources dealing with various aspects of Loyalists in Canada.

Although there is much writing that focusses on parts of the Loyalists' experience in Canada (otherwise this book could not have been written), it is astonishing that, with the partial exception of Egerton Ryerson's *The Loyalists of America and Their Times, from 1620 to 1816* (2 vols., 2nd ed., Toronto: W. Briggs, 1880), only two attempts have been made at the totality: William S. Wallace, *The United Empire Loyalists* (Toronto, 1914) and Arthur G. Bradley, *The United Empire Loyalists* (London and New York, 1932). They share the same title, but not the same quality. Wallace's book is good popular history, Bradley's much less so; both are dated. The best modern account is L.F.S. Upton's *The United Empire Loyalists: Men and Myths,* an excellent collection of readings and documents, but not a history.

L.F.S. Upton's *The Loyal Whig, William Smith of New York and Quebec,* and Judith Fingard's *The Anglican Design in Loyalist Nova Scotia 1783-1816* provide the best treatment of William Smith, the leading Whig Loyalist, and Charles Inglis, the leading Tory. Wilbur Siebert's series of lectures, based on the Haldimand Papers and published in the *Transactions of the Royal Society of Canada,* provide a detailed treatment of Loyalist settlement in the old province of Quebec. Esther

Clark Wright's *The Loyalists of New Brunswick*, together with David G. Bell's *Early Loyalist Saint John: The Origin of New Brunswick Politics, 1783-1786*, provide the best guides to the study of the Loyalists in New Brunswick. The recently published *The Loyalist Governor: Biography of Sir John Wentworth* by Brian C. Cuthbertson gives useful support to the unpublished Ph.D. thesis of Neil Mac-Kinnon, "The Loyalist Experience in Nova Scotia 1783-1791," which offers the best general coverage of Nova Scotia loyalism. To this should be added the unpublished Ph.D. thesis of Robert J. Morgan, "Orphan Outpost: Cape Breton Colony 1784-1820."

Mary Beacock Fryer's *King's Men: The Soldier Founders of Ontario* offers a recent and thorough coverage of the military aspects of the Loyalists. Robin Winks' *The Blacks in Canada* gives a fair account of the black Loyalists, while C.M. Johnston's *The Valley of the Six Nations* provides a recent account of the Iroquois settlements. For information on British subsidies to the Loyalist settlements, Howard Temperley's article, "Frontierism, Capital and the American Loyalists in Canada," is very useful. Those interested in the intellectual aspects of loyalism can consult Janice Potter's scholarly treatment of the subject in *The Liberty We Seek: Loyalist Ideology in Colonial New York and Massachusetts*. William H. Nelson's *The American Tory* remains the best and most readable general introduction to the Loyalists in America.

*Unpublished Manuscript Material*

Audit Office papers, vols. 12 and 13. Public Record Office, London.
Dorchester, Guy Carleton, First Baron. Papers. PAC, Ottawa.
Haldimand, Sir Frederick. Papers. PAC, Ottawa.
Inglis, Charles. Transcripts, journals, papers and letters. PAC, Ottawa.
Marston, Benjamin. Diary. University of New Brunswick, Fredericton.
"The Narrative of Hannah Ingraham." PAC, Ottawa.
Nase, Henry. Diary, 1776–1797. New Brunswick Museum, Saint John.
Powell, Anne. Description of a Journey from Montreal to Detroit in 1789. Public Archives of Ontario, Toronto.
Powell, William Dummer. Papers. PAC, Ottawa.
Winslow, Edward. Papers. University of New Brunswick, Fredericton.

*Primary Sources*

Bates, Walter. *Kingston and the Loyalists of the "Spring Fleet"*. Edited by W.O. Raymond. 1889. Reprint. Woodstock, N.B.: Non-Entity Press, 1980.

Campbell, Patrick. *Travels in the Interior Inhabited Parts of North America, 1791–92*. Edited by H.H. Langton. Toronto: Champlain Society, 1937.

Haldimand Papers. Calendar printed in *Public Archives Reports 1884–89*, Ottawa.

Hunter, A., ed. *The Journal of Gen. Sir Martin Hunter and Some Letters of his Wife, Lady Hunter*. Edinburgh, 1894.

Inglis, Charles. *Steadfastness in Religion and Loyalty recommended, in a Sermon, preached before the Legislature of His Majesty's province of Nova Scotia in the Parish Church of St. Paul at Halifax, on Sunday, April 7, 1793*. Halifax, 1793.

Raymond, William O., ed. *Winslow Papers*. 1901. Facsimile reprint. Boston: Gregg Press, 1972.

Robertson, Douglas S., ed. *An Englishman in America, 1785: Being the Diary of Joseph Hadfield*. Toronto: Hunter-Rose, 1933.

Talman, J.J., ed. *Loyalist Narratives from Upper Canada.*. Toronto: Champlain Society, 1946.

Temperley, Howard. *Gubbins' New Brunswick Journals 1811 and 1813*. Fredericton: New Brunswick Heritage Publications, 1980.

Weld, Isaac. *Travels through the States of North America and the Provinces of Upper and Lower Canada during the Years 1795, 1976 and 1797*. 2nd ed. London, 1799.

Wright, Louis B. and Marion Tingling, eds. *Quebec to Carolina in 1785–1786; Being the Travel Diary and Observations of Robert Hunter, Jr., A Young Merchant of London*. San Marino, California: The Huntington Library, 1943.


*Secondary Sources*

Arthur, Elizabeth. "The French Canadian Participation in the Government of Canada 1778–1785." *Canadian Historical Review* 32 (1951).

Barkley, Murray. "The Loyalist Tradition in New Brunswick: The Growth and Evolution of an Historical Myth, 1825–1914." *Acadiensis* 4 (Spring 1975).

Bell, David G. *Early Loyalist Saint John: The Origin of New Brunswick Politics, 1783–1786*. Fredericton: New Ireland Press, 1983.

Berger, Carl. *The Sense of Power: Studies in the Ideas of Canadian Imperialism 1867–1914*. Toronto: University of Toronto Press, 1970.

Brebner, John Bartlett. *The Neutral Yankees of Nova Scotia: A Marginal Colony During the Revolutionary Years.* New York: Russell & Russell, 1937.

Brown, Wallace. *The Good Americans.* New York: William Morrow & Co., 1969.

_____. "'Victorious in Defeat': The American Loyalists in Canada." *History Today* 27 (February 1977).

Burt, A.L. *The Old Province of Quebec.* 2 vols. Toronto: Ryerson Press, 1933.

Canniff, William. *History of the Settlement of Upper Canada, with Special References to the Bay of Quinte.* Toronto, 1869.

Condon, Ann Gorman. "Hope Restored: The Revitalization of the Loyalist Politics in New Brunswick." Paper presented to the Canadian Historical Association, Ottawa, June 1977.

_____. "The Beast at the Banquet: Revolutionary and Loyalist Approaches to Democracy in North America." Paper presented to the Joint Conference Atlantic Canada Studies, Saint John, N.B., May 1983.

_____. "'The Envy of the American States': The Settlement of the Loyalists in New Brunswick: Goals and Achievements." Ph.D. thesis, Harvard University, 1975.

Cruikshank, E.A. *The Settlement of the United Empire Loyalists on the Upper St. Lawrence and the Bay of Quinte in 1784.* Toronto, 1934.

Cuthbertson, Brian C. *The Loyalist Governor: Biography of Sir John Wentworth.* Halifax: Pethorie Press, 1983.

Ennals, Peter and Deryck Holdsworth. "Vernacular Architecture and the Cultural Landscape of the Maritime Provinces—a Reconnaissance." *Acadiensis* 10 (Spring 1981).

Fingard, Judith. *The Anglican Design in Loyalist Nova Scotia 1783–1816.* London: SPCK, 1972.

Forbes, Ernest R. "Nova Scotia's Loyalist Myth: The 18th and 19th Century Background." Unpublished paper, Queen's University, Kingston, n.d.

Fryer, Mary Beacock. *King's Men: The Solider Founders of Ontario.* Toronto and Charlottetown: Dundurn Press, 1980.

Graymont, Barbara. *The Iroquois in the American Revolution.* Syracuse: Syracuse University Press, 1972.

Haliburton, T.C. *An Historical and Statistical Account of Nova Scotia.* 2 vols. 1829. Reprint. Belleville: Mika Publishing Co., 1973.

Hall, Benjamin. *The History of Vermont from its discovery to its admission into the Union 1791.* Albany: J. Munsell, 1868.

Hartz, Louis. *The Founding of New Societies*, with contributions by Kenneth D. McRae, Richard M. Morse, Richard N. Rosecrance, Leonard M. Thompson. New York: Harcourt Brace Jovanovich, 1964.

Herrington, M.E. "Captain John Deserontyou and the Mohawk settlement at Deseronto." *Queen's Quarterly* 29 (1911).

Hosie, R.C. *Native Trees of Canada*. Don Mills, Ont.: Fitzhenry & Whiteside, 1979.

Horsman, Reginald. *Matthew Elliott, British Indian Agent*. Detroit: Wayne State University Press, 1964.

Humber, Charles and Mary Beacock Fryer, eds. *Loyal She Remains: A Pictorial history of Ontario*. Toronto: United Empire Loyalists' Association of Canada, 1984.

Johnston, C.M. *The Valley of the Six Nations*. Toronto: Champlain Society, 1964.

Lajeunesse, Ernest J., ed. *The Windsor Border Region*. Toronto: University of Toronto Press, 1960.

Lydekker, John. *The Life and Letters of Charles Inglis*. London: SPCK, 1936.

MacKinnon, Neil. "The Loyalist Experience in Nova Scotia 1783-1791." Ph.D. Thesis, Queen's University, Kingston, 1974.

MacNutt, W.S. *New Brunswick, A History: 1784-1867*. Toronto: Macmillan of Canada, 1963.

McCalla, Douglas. "The Loyalist Economy of Upper Canada 1784-1806." Paper presented to the Joint Conference Atlantic Canada Studies, Saint John, N.B., May 1983.

Morgan, Robert J. "Orphan Outpost: Cape Breton Colony 1784-1820." Ph.D. thesis, University of Ottawa, 1973.

Morton, H.A. "The American Revolution: A View from the North." *Journal of Canadian Studies* 7 (May 1972).

Neatby, Hilda. *Quebec: The Revolutionary Age*. Toronto: McClelland & Stewart, 1965.

Nelson, William H. *The American Tory*. Oxford: Oxford University Press, 1961.

Ouellet, Fernand. *Lower Canada: Social Change and Nationalism*. Translated and adapted by Patricia Claxton. Toronto: McClelland & Stewart, 1980.

Potter, Janice. *The Liberty We Seek: Loyalist Ideology in Colonial New York and Massachusetts*. Cambridge: Harvard University Press, 1983.

Rawlyk, George. "The Federalist-Loyalist Alliance in New Brunswick 1784-1815." *Humanities Association Review* 27 (Spring 1976).

Senior, Elinor Kyte. *From Royal Township to Industrial City: Cornwall 1784–1984.* Belleville: Mika Publishing Co., 1983.

Senior, Hereward. "The Loyalists in Quebec, a Study in Adversity." Paper presented to the Canadian Historical Association, Halifax, June 1982.

Siebert, Wilbur. "The American Loyalists in the Eastern Seigniories and Townships of the Province of Quebec." *Transactions of the Royal Society of Canada* ser. 3, sect. 2 (1913).

_____. "The Temporary Settlements of the Loyalists at Machiche, P.Q." *Transactions of the Royal Society of Canada* sect. 2 (1914).

_____. "The Loyalists and the Six Nations in the Niagara Peninsula." *Transactions of the Royal Society of Canada* sect. 2 (1915).

_____. "The Loyalist Settlements on the Gaspé Peninsula." *Transactions of the Royal Society of Canada* sect. 2 (1915).

Smith, Stuart A. "Loyalist Architecture of British North America." *Canada's Visual History* (Ottawa) 43 (1981).

Temperley, Howard. "Frontierism, Capital and the American Loyalists in Canada." *Journal of American Studies* 13 (1979).

Upton, L.F.S. *The Loyal Whig: William Smith of New York and Quebec.* Toronto: University of Toronto Press, 1974.

_____. *The United Empire Loyalists: Men and Myths.* Toronto: Copp Clark, 1967.

_____. "The Idea of Confederation 1754–1858." In *The Shield of Achilles*, edited by W.L. Morton. Toronto: MacClelland & Stewart, 1968.

Wade, Mason. "Quebec and the French Revolution." *Canadian Historical Review* 13 (1932).

Walker, James W. St. G. *The Black Loyalists: The Search for the Promised Land in Nova Scotia & Sierra Leone.* New York: Africana Publishing Co./Dalhousie University Press, 1976.

Webster, Donald Blake. *English-Canadian Furniture of the Georgian Period.* Toronto, 1979.

White, Walter S. "The Loyalists at Sorel." Unpublished paper March, 1974. (Montreal Military and Maritime Museum).

Wilson, Bruce. *As She Began.* Toronto and Charlottetown: Dundurn Press, 1981.

Wilson, Ellen Gibson. *The Black Loyalists.* Toronto: Longman Green, 1976.

Winks, Robin W. *The Blacks in Canada: A History.* Montreal: McGill-Queen's University Press, 1971.

Wise, S.F. "The American Revolution and Indian History." In *Character and Circumstance*, edited by J.S. Moir. Toronto: Macmillan of Canada, 1970.

Wright, Esther Clark. *The Loyalists of New Brunswick*. Windsor, N.S.: Lancelot Press, 1977.

Wynn, Graeme. "The Assault on the New Brunswick Forest, 1780–1850." Ph.D. thesis, University of Toronto, 1974.

# index

Ackerman, Sgt. Cornelius  104
Adams, John  7, 11, 28, 121, 135
Adams, Samuel  4, 7
Adolphustown, Ont.  66, 104
Albany, N.Y.  41, 76, 142, 159, 198
Albright family  45
Allan, Lieut. Adam  97
Allen, Andrew  5
Allen, Ethan  116
Allen, Isaac  67
Allen, James  5, 13
Allen, William  5
Allen family  5
Alline, Henry  146, 180
Alsop, John  7
Amherstburg, Ont.  46
Anderson, Samuel  14
Anderson family  165
André, Major  30
Annapolis, N.S.  11, 29, 34, 35, 36, 39,
   50, 73, 97, 103, 175, 183
Anne, Queen  152, 200
Antigonish, N.S.  39
Ardois Hill, N.S.  82
Armstrong, Zimrie  177
Arnold, Benedict  10, 19, 20, 30, 102
Ash, William  184
Auburn, N.S.  103
Australia  28, 126

Bacon, Francis  127

Bagnall, James Douglas  96
Bahamas  19, 28, 31, 51, 173, 195
Bailey, the Reverend Jacob  9, 13, 52, 97,
   98, 99
Baldwin, Robert  126
Baltimore  11, 179
Barclay, Maj. Thomas  155
Bartlett, William S.  99
Bates, Walter  36, 66, 98
Baxter, Simon  88
Bay of Fundy  34, 37, 39, 40, 52
Bay of Quinte  46, 49, 67, 102, 199, 200
Bean, Thomas  104
Bear Island, N.B.  102
Beauharnois, Que.  45
Bedell, Paul  104
Belgium  122
Bell, Richard  184
Belleville, Ont.  82, 105
Benedict, Jabex  103
Benedict, Michael  103
Bentham, Jeremy  127
Bermuda  19, 31
Bethune, the Reverend John  108
Bethune, Dr. Norman  210
Betts, Dr. Azor  89
Bidwell, Barnabas  117–18
Bidwell, Marshall Spring  118
Birch, Col. Samuel  175
Birchtown, N.S.  175, 178, 180, 182,
   184, 185, 186

Black, William   179–80

Bolman, Dr. John D.   177

Bliss, Jonathan   148

Blucke, Stephen   180, 185

Bonnie Prince Charlie   10

Booth, Capt.   110

Boston   4, 7, 11, 20, 35, 50, 196, 208

Boswell, James   10, 197

Botsford, Amos   36

Boucher, Jonathan   11, 127

Boudinot, Elias   29

Boulton family   123, 165

Brant, John   202

Brant, Joseph   14, 43, 96, 116, 188, 192,
    194–201

Brant, Molly   194, 203

Brantford, Ont.   200

Brass, David   105

Bray, Dr. Thomas   180

Breynton, John   179

Brindley Town, N.S.   175, 179, 184

Britain see England

British North America   26, 31, 32, 34,
    59, 61, 73, 97, 119, 135, 158, 174, 207

Brock, Gen. Isaac   118, 165, 201–2

Brockville, Ont.   49, 96, 119, 165–67

Brown, Capt.   38

Brown, George   128, 129

Brown, Thomas Storrow   162

Browne, Col. Thomas   18

Bruff, Charles Oliver   101

Brundage, Jeremiah   101

Brunswick, Gen. George   18

Buell, William Jr.   96, 119, 166

Buell family   166, 167, 208

Burgoyne, Gen. John   17, 18, 44, 198

Butler, Col. John   19, 29, 43, 46, 195–98

Butler family   134, 148

Byles, the Reverend Mather   28, 208

Byrd, William III   10

Caldwell, Col. Henry   142

Camden, S.C.   18

Cameron, Nancy   37

Campbell, Maj. John   196, 198

Campbell, Patrick   79, 80, 84–88, 105

Canada   18, 24, 34, 119, 128–29, 196; see
    also British North America;
    individual colonies and provinces

Cape Breton   33, 38, 40, 77, 158, 159–60

Cape Sable Island   37

Cap Pelee, N.B.   66

Carleton, Sir Guy   24, 29, 33, 34, 44, 58,
    59, 61, 62, 71, 85, 136, 146, 147, 151,
    196

Carleton, Gov. Thomas   65, 66, 67, 104,
    106, 148, 151, 153, 175, 176, 183

Carman, Bliss   100, 210

Carolinas   14, 19, 29, 128; see also North
    Carolina; South Carolina

Cartier, George-Étienne   127, 128, 129

Cartwright, Sir Richard   22, 41, 82, 94,
    96, 110, 112, 124, 163

Cartwright family   165

Cataraqui, N.B.   47, 49, 56

Cataraqui, Ont.   33, 58–60, 67; see also
    Kingston

Caughnawaga   196, 197, 199

Central America   31

Chambly, Que.   45

Chandler, the Reverend Thomas
    Bradbury   20

Charles, Prince   211

Charles II   26

Charleston, S.C.   10, 18, 30, 33, 171,
    174, 179, 180

Charlottetown, P.E.I.   33

Chedabucto, N.S.   39, 175, 184

Cherry Hill, N.J.   198

Chesapeake Bay   15, 171, 189

Chew, William   86

Chillas, Robert   101

Chipman, Ward   27, 109, 110, 116, 148,
    149, 153, 189

Christ Church, Fredericton  179
Christ Church, Shelburne  104
Clarenceville, Que.  143
Clark, George Rodgers  199
Clark, Robert  105
Clarkson, Lieut. John  105, 177, 183–87
Clarkson, Thomas  176–77, 182
Claus, Col. Christian Daniel  43, 195–97
Clinton, George  25
Clinton, Sir Henry  17, 24, 172
Cobbett, Sgt. Maj.  86,111
Cochran, the Reverend William  107
Connecticut  10, 12, 16, 17, 30, 36, 89
Cook, Capt.  79, 104
Copley, John Singleton  10
Cormier brothers  65
Cornwall, Ont.  33, 41, 80, 82, 106, 109, 165, 188
Cornwallis, Gen. Charles  18, 23, 24
Cornwallis, N.S.  110
Cossitt, Rana  159
Coteau-de-Lac  49
Coxe, Tench  13
Craig, Sir James  162
Cummings, Samuel  36
Cushing family  45
Custer, Gen. George  203
Cuthbertson, Brian  104
Cuyler, Abraham  159

Dalton, Thomas  96
Dartmouth, Lord  60
Dartmouth, N.S.  39, 104, 175
Darwin, Charles  123
Davidson, John  209
de Grasse, Admiral  18, 23
De Lancey, James  19, 29
De Lancey, Oliver  10
De Lancey, Stephen  28
De Lancey family  133
Delaware  8, 11, 198
Denison, Col.  125

Des Barres, Gov. J.F.W.  159, 160
Desbrisay, Stewart  160
Deseronto, Capt. John  67, 199, 200
Detroit  27, 41, 44, 46, 48, 49, 50, 59, 72, 118, 119, 199, 201
Dibblee, Filer  16–17
Dibblee, the Reverend Frederick  89
Dickinson, John  7
Digby, Admiral  34, 72
Digby, N.S.  39, 97, 175, 176, 179, 180, 183, 185
Dorchester, Lord  63, 67, 116, 136, 137, 142, 145, 162
Dundas, Henry  106, 183
Dundas, Col. Thomas  72, 85
Dunmore, Lord  172
Dunn, Thomas  142
Dyott, Lieut. William  178

Eddy, Col. Jonathan  20
Edison, Samuel  208
Edison, Thomas  208
Elizabeth I  60
Ellice, Edward  161
Elliot, Matthew  119, 188
England  3–7, 9, 10, 15–20, 23–28, 30, 34, 152, 163, 166, 173–74, 182, 189
Essex, Earl of  60
Eve, Joseph  55

Faneuil, Benjamin  15
Faneuil, Peter  15
Fanning, Col. David  11, 18
Fanning, Edward  159
Farrand family  165
Ferguson, Maj. Patrick  19
Finucane, Bryan  63
Fisher, Mrs. Lewis  66
Fisher, Peter  99
Fitzgerald, Lord Edward  111
Fitzpatrick, Peter  142
Floquet, Father Pierre-René  196

Floridas   19, 30, 31, 33, 41, 173, 174, 187
Fort Cumberland   34
Fort Frontenac   65, 72
Fort George   41
Fort Howe   38, 65, 72, 73
Fort Niagara   65
Fort Oswego   41
Fort Pontchartrain   65
Fort Saint Jean   197
Fort Stanwix   198
Fort Ticonderoga   42
Foster, Benjamin   103
Fox, Charles James   146, 147
Fox, Brig. Henry   146, 147
France   10, 23, 26, 33, 51, 75, 125, 126,
    135, 193, 198, 207, 211
Franklin, Benjamin   10, 15, 23, 24, 26,
    135
Franklin, William   15, 24
Fredericton, N.B.   32, 40, 55, 56, 67, 75,
    76, 80, 81, 89, 95, 97, 100, 153, 176,
    180, 181
Frost, Hannah   38
Frost, Sarah   36, 38
Furmage, William   179

Galloway, Joseph   8, 11, 135
Garden, Dr. Alexander   11
Garrettson, the Reverend Freeborn   179
Gaspé   33, 45, 143
George, David   10, 180, 184, 187
George III   3, 5, 12, 24, 27, 28, 126, 154,
    172, 203, 207, 208
Georgia   11, 14, 180
Germain, Lord George   197
Germany   20, 24, 173
Gibbons, Richard Jr.   159
Gilmour, the Reverend George   108
Glenie, James   151, 152–53
Goddard family   101, 102
Goldsmith, Oliver   99
Grass, Capt. Michael   40, 49, 143, 203

Gray, Alexander   188
Gray, Maj. James   188
Gray, John Hamilton   159
Gray, Robert   159
Great Britain *see* England
Greene, Gen.   75
Gubbins, Gen. Joseph   88, 109, 110, 111
Gugu, Augustus   167
Gunter, Dr. Charles   110
Gurnett, George   96
Guy, Louis   167

Hadfield, Joseph   92
Hagerman, Christopher   119, 165
Haldimand, Sir Frederick   44, 45, 46,
    56, 61, 63, 65, 71, 140, 142, 143, 199
Haliburton, Thomas Chandler   99–100,
    208
Halifax, N.S.   19, 29, 32, 33, 34, 39, 42,
    43, 72, 83, 100–1, 103–4, 146, 157,
    175, 176, 178, 180, 183, 184
Hallett, Capt. Samuel   81
Hamilton, Alexander   8, 15, 16, 127,
135
Hamilton, Robert   163
Hammond, Sir Andrew Snape   34, 36,
    38
Hancock, John   7, 9
Hardy, Elias   151
Harrison, Peter   10, 104
Hartshorne, Laurence   183, 185
Hartz, Louis   125–26, 127, 128
Haszard, William   160
Hauser, Frederick   36
Hawley family   44
Hazen, William   151
Head, Sir Francis Bond   166, 190
Hedley, Henry   177
Hempstead, L.I.   17
Hennesy, John   10
Hesse, N.S.   63
Hiawatha   198

Hildrith, Isaac 104
Hill, Aaron 199
Hill, Isaac 199
Holland, Maj. Samuel 44, 56, 140
Honduras 31
Hopkinson, Francis 11
Horowitz, Gad 128
Howard, Martin 124
Howe, John 95–96, 107
Howe, Joseph 96, 99, 208
Howe, Gen. Sir William 12, 17
Hoyt, Israel 89
Hughes, Mrs. 178
Hunter, James 101
Hunter, Lady 80, 86, 88, 109
Hunter, Robert 86
Hutchison, Thomas 20
Hutchison, Thomas Jr. 23
Hyde family 45

Ile aux Noix. Que 40
Inglis, Bishop Charles 79, 103, 106,
    134–37, 144, 156–57, 163, 179, 181–2
Ingraham, Benjamin 27, 76
Ingraham, Hannah 76
Ingraham, John 76
Ireland 122, 135
Island of St. John 159

Jamaica 31, 51, 173
James I 158
Japan 29
Jarvis, Hannah 110
Jarvis, Samuel 177
Jay, John 7, 9
Jefferson, Thomas 4, 104, 120, 127, 129,
    135, 144, 183
Jeffries, Dr. John 55
Jenkins, Capt. John 119
Jessup, Maj. Edward 44, 49
Johnson, Chief G.H.G. 203
Johnson, Col. Guy 43, 195

Johnson, Sir John 14, 18, 41, 44, 49, 61,
    82, 119, 144, 188, 192, 197, 198, 200
Johnson, Pauline 203
Johnson, Thomas 12
Johnson, Sir William 43, 44, 194, 195,
    203
Johnson family 45, 133, 148, 195, 196
Johnstown, N.B. 56
Jones, John Paul 10
Jones, Stephen 86
Jones family 45, 165
Jouet, Cavalier 25

Kennebec 13
King, Boston 178, 180, 184
King's Landing, N.B. 102
Kingston, N.B. 36, 89
Kingston, Ont. 30, 33, 47, 48, 49, 72,
    80, 96, 102, 104, 106, 119, 163, 165,
    188, 195; *see also* Cataraqui, Ont.
Kirkland, Samuel 195
Knapp, Moses 70, 85
Knox, William 147, 156

Lachine, Que. 40, 46, 196, 199
Lachute, Que. 45
Lafayette, Marquis de 23
LaFontaine, Sir Louis 126, 127
Laird, Joseph 58
La Prairie, Que. 42
Laurens, Henry 25, 28
Laurier, Sir Wilfrid 127
Lavender, Jenny 105
Leake, Robert 44
Lecky, W.H. 26
Leeward Islands 19
Legge, Francis 146
Le Nègre, Louis 196
Leonard, Daniel 7
Leonard, George Jr. 101
Leonard, Joseph 179, 184
LeRoy family 45

Lewis, William   45
Liberia   183
Lincoln, Abraham   126, 172, 173, 183
Little Big Horn   203
Little Tricadie, N.S.   175, 184
Liverpool, N.S.   65, 175
Livingston family   156
Livius, Peter   138
Lloyd's Neck, L.I.   36
Locke, John   8, 127
Logan family   45
London   7, 33, 173
Long Island   12, 17, 19, 36
Long Point   49
Long Sault   46
Louis XVI   126
Low, Isaac   7
Lower Canada   162, 167, 178, 188, 202;
     *see also* Quebec
Ludlow, Gabriel   148, 153
Ludlow, George Duncan   73, 86, 103
Ludlow family   153
Lunenburg, N.S.   63, 177
Lymburner, Matthew   12
Lynch, Judge   16

Mabane, Adam   160
Machiche   40, 143
MacDonald, Flora   10
Macdonald, John A.   126, 128, 166
Macdonnell, Bishop Alexander   150, 166
Mackenzie, William Lyon   96, 119, 150, 156, 167, 190, 209
MacNab, Allan   165, 166–67, 208
MacNutt, W.S.   13
MacNutt's Island   105
Madawaska, N.B.   66, 67
Maine   26, 28, 33
Maitland, Ont.   102
Manchester, N.S.   177, 184
Mansfield, Chief Justice   189

Marblehead, Mass.   56
Marrant, the Reverend John   179
Marston, Benjamin   39, 56, 57, 58, 59, 60, 62, 63, 79, 98, 101, 132, 177
Maryland   11
Massachusetts   3, 4–5, 7, 10, 11, 13, 20, 25, 28, 29, 30, 31, 47, 56, 208
Massey family   210
Mathews, David   159
Matthews, William   103
Maugerville, N.B.   20, 65, 76, 86, 90
McGee, D'Arcy   129
McGillivray family   14
McGregor, Henry   177
McKee, Alexander   116
McLean, Capt.   62
McLean family   165
McNiff, Patrick   57, 63, 140–42, 147, 163
McRae, Kenneth   126–27, 128
Mecklenberg, N.S.   63
Memramcook, N.B.   66
Mercure, Louis   65
Merkley, Christianne   85
Merritt, David Daniel   102
Merritt, William, Hamilton   119, 166
Meyers, Capt. John Walden   82, 105
Miles, Samuel   12
Miles, Stephen   96
Milledge, Stephen   89
Missisquoi Bay   45, 142, 143
Mitchell, Lewis   65
Mohawk Valley   18, 28, 37, 43, 45, 161, 194, 195, 197, 200
Monk, James   28
Montgomery, Gen. Richard   10
Montreal   20, 41, 42, 43, 45, 47, 72, 161, 188, 196, 197, 209
Morden, Col. James   103, 104
Morin, Augustin   167
Morris, Charles   56, 57, 58, 62
Morris, Gouverneur   15
Morris, Isabella   15

Morris, Lewis 15
Morris, Robert 7
Morris, Staats 15

Napanee, Ont. 105
Nase, Henry 89–92
Nassau, Bahamas 195
Nassau, N.S. 63
Navy Island 190
Nelles family 167
Nelson, Admiral 208
Nelson, Dr. Robert 162, 208
Nelson, William H. 14, 45
Nelson, Wolfred 162, 208
Netherlands 122
New Brunswick 10, 11, 17, 19, 27,
    29–32, 35–37, 38, 50–52, 56–58, 61,
    82, 88–89, 96–97, 145–54, 160, 162,
    165, 166, 174, 175, 180, 181, 182,
    184, 185, 187, 189, 194, 206, 208, 210
New Carlisle, Que. 45, 143
New England 14, 17, 30, 32, 35, 50, 55,
    56, 75, 122, 146, 148, 163, 194, 196;
    *see also* individual colonies and states
New Hampshire 11, 31, 138
New Haven, Conn. 99
New Jersey 11, 14, 17, 30, 31, 86, 89,
    105, 148, 183
New Johnstown 33
New Orleans 189
New Oswegatchie, N.B. 56
New Providence, Bahamas 31
New Rochelle, N.Y. 14, 157
New York 8, 11, 13, 14, 17, 18, 19, 25,
    27, 28, 29, 31, 40, 44, 55, 105, 136,
    148, 156, 197, 200
New York City 7, 11, 13, 17, 18, 19, 20,
    30, 33, 34, 35, 89, 90, 136, 144, 159,
    174, 180
New Zealand 126
Newfoundland 43, 50, 95, 118, 210
Newport, R.I. 11, 15, 101, 124

Niagara 27, 41, 44, 49, 50, 66, 67, 72,
    79, 80, 96, 105, 110, 165, 166, 167,
    197, 201
Norfolk, Va. 104
North, Lord 24, 60, 147
North Carolina 10, 11, 18
Nova Scotia 10, 13, 19, 28, 29, 31–35,
    38–40, 50, 51, 56, 61, 74, 80, 83, 95,
    145–46, 157, 173, 174–75, 176–88,
    189, 194, 208, 210

Odell, Jonathan 5, 20, 58, 59, 97, 148,
    185
Ogden, Charles Richard 162
Ogdensburg, N.Y. 41
Ontario 5, 32, 51, 206; *see also* Upper
    Canada
Oriskany 18, 198
Oromocto, N.B. 36, 65
Oswald, Richard 24, 28
Oswego, N.Y. 22, 196, 198
Otis, James 3, 124
Oyster Bay, L.I. 17, 36

Paddock, Dr. Adino 90
Paine, Thomas 10, 126, 135
Paine, Dr. William 106
Palmer, Alphea 177
Palmer, James B. 160
Papineau, Louis-Joseph 208, 209
Parkin, George 123, 125
Parr, Col. John 36, 39, 61, 62, 63, 65,
    73, 74, 104, 146, 147, 151, 154, 155,
    176, 177, 183
Parrsboro, N.S. 39
Passamaquoddy Bay 33, 40
Patterson, Lieut.-Gov. Walter 51,
    159–60
Peachey, Lieut. James 48
Peekskill 12
Pemart, Francis 12
Pemberton, Jeremy 72

Pennsylvania   5, 7, 11, 12, 19, 24, 31, 97, 128, 134, 155, 198

Penobscot, Me.   12, 33

Perkins, Cato   184

Peters, Hector   184

Peters, Thomas   175, 182–83, 184, 185

Philadelphia   5, 11, 12, 13, 18

Pictou, N.S.   39

Pitt, Sir William   64, 147

Platt family   45

Plattsburg, N.Y.   41

Point l'Hébert   105

Poland   129

Pointe Claire, Que.   40

Port Roseway, N.S.   34, 35, 39

Portsmouth, N.H.   11

Poughkeepsie, N.Y.   208

Powell, Anne   47, 87–88

Powell, William Dummer   47, 63, 142

Pownalborough, Mass.   13

Preston, Capt.   15

Preston, N.S.   175, 179, 182, 184, 188

Preston, Richard   189

Prevost, Sir George   162

Prince Edward Island   11, 33, 38, 40, 58, 64, 80, 88, 96, 159, 160, 175

Prophet, the   117

Providence, R.I.   15

Pynchon, Joseph   35

Quebec   11, 19, 26, 28, 31, 32, 33, 34, 35, 40, 43, 44, 50, 51, 60, 64, 138, 153, 159, 160–62, 174, 210

Quebec City   32, 43, 45, 72, 161, 188

Queenston Heights   118, 119, 189, 202

Quincey, Samuel   15

Ramsheg, N.S.   39

Rawdon, N.B.   108

Raymond, W.O.   98

Rhode Island   10, 14, 15, 101, 160

Richardson, John   161

Roberts, Charles G.D.   100, 210

Robertson, Gen. James   2

Robin, Charles   143

Robinson, John Beverley   96, 118, 119, 127, 165, 208

Robinson, Joseph   159

Robinson, Thomas   11

Rochambeau, Gen.   23

Rockingham, Lord   24

Roger, Maj. James   49

Rogers, Robert   20

Romney, George   197

Ross, Alexander   101

Ross, Jacob   85

Ross, Maj. John   72

Rousseau, Jean-Jacques   127

Ruiter, Capt. Henry   142

Rumford, Count   10

Russell, Peter   62, 201

Ryan, John   95

Ryan, Michael   95

Ryerse, Capt. Samuel   50

Ryerson, Egerton   5, 96, 128, 150, 156, 166, 208

Ryland, Herman W.   161

Sacket's Harbor   22, 40, 119

St. Andrews, N.B.   33, 61, 99, 102

St. Andrews, Ont.   80

St. Andrews East, Ont.   45

St. Armand, Que.   142

St. Anne's   56

St. George's Bay   175, 187

St. Jean (St. Johns) Que.   40, 42, 45

St. John, N.B.   17, 30, 32, 41, 55, 56, 60, 72, 73, 77, 79, 84, 95, 101, 104, 149, 175, 176, 177, 178, 180

St. Leger, Lieut.-Col. Barry   198

St. Lucia   173

St. Ours, Que.   40

St. Paul's, Halifax   179

Sandwich, N.S.   46